T0301452

Europe and the Challenge of the Asia Pacific

In memory of my father

Europe and the Challenge of the Asia Pacific

Change, Continuity and Crisis

Brian Bridges

Associate Professor, Department of Politics and Sociology, Lingnan College, Hong Kong, PRC

Edward Elgar
Cheltenham, UK • Northampton, MA, USA

Published by
Edward Elgar Publishing Limited
Glensanda House
Montpellier Parade
Cheltenham
Glos GL50 1UA
UK

Edward Elgar Publishing, Inc.
6 Market Street
Northampton
Massachusetts 01060
USA

A catalogue record for this book
is available from the British Library

Library of Congress Cataloguing in Publication Data
Bridges, Brian, 1948–
    Europe and the challenge of the Asia Pacific: change, continuity
and crisis / Brian Bridges.
    Includes bibliographical references.
    1. European Union countries—Foreign economic relations—East
Asia.   2. East Asia—Foreign economic relations—European Union
countries.   3. European Union countries—Foreign economic relations—
Asia, Southeastern.   4. Asia, Southeastern—Foreign economic
relations—European Union countries.   5. East Asia—Economic
conditions.   6. Asia, Southeastern—Economic conditions.   I. Title.
HF1531.Z4E183   1999
337.4054—dc21   98–45785
                                                                                               CIP

ISBN 1 85898 497 1

Typeset by Manton Typesetters, 5–7 Eastfield Road, Louth, Lincs. LN11 7AJ, UK.
Printed and bound in Great Britain by Biddles Ltd, Guildford and King's Lynn

Contents

List of Tables

Abbreviations

ACP	African, Caribbean and Pacific
AFTA	ASEAN Free Trade Area
APEC	Asia Pacific Economic Cooperation
ARF	ASEAN Regional Forum
ASEAN	Association of Southeast Asian Nations
ASEAN-PMC	Post-Ministerial Conference of ASEAN
ASEM	Asia–Europe Meeting
ATP	Aid and Trade Provision
CEIBS	China–Europe International Business School
CFSP	Common Foreign and Security Policy
CGI	Consultative Group on Indonesia
CSCE	Conference for Security Cooperation in Europe
CTBT	Comprehensive Test Ban Treaty
EAEC	East Asian Economic Caucus
EAEG	East Asian Economic Grouping
EC	European Community
EEC	European Economic Community
EMU	Economic and Monetary Union
EU	European Union
FDI	Foreign direct investment
FPDA	Five Power Defence Arrangement
FY	Fiscal year
G-5	Group of Five
G-7	Group of Seven
GATT	General Agreement on Tariffs and Trade
GNP	Gross national product
GSP	Generalized System of Preferences
HKSAR	Hong Kong Special Administrative Region
IAEA	International Atomic Energy Agency
IMF	International Monetary Fund
INF	Intermediate-range nuclear forces
IPRs	Intellectual property rights
JETRO	Japan External Trade Organization
KEDO	Korean Energy Development Organization

MFA	Multi-Fibre Arrangement
MITI	Ministry of International Trade and Industry
NAFTA	North American Free Trade Area
NATO	North Atlantic Treaty Organization
NEP	New Economic Policy
NGO	Non-governmental organization
NIE	Newly industrializing economy
NPT	Non-proliferation Treaty
OCSE	Organization for Cooperation and Security in Europe
OECD	Organization for Economic Cooperation and Development
PRC	People's Republic of China
QR	Quantitative restriction
SEATO	Southeast Asia Treaty Organization
SLORC	State Law and Order Restoration Council
TSE	Tokyo Stock Exchange
UN	United Nations
UNCTAD	United Nations Conference on Trade and Development
UNHRC	United Nations Human Rights Commission
UNTAC	United Nations Transitional Authority in Cambodia
US	United States
VCR	Video cassette recorder
VER	Voluntary export restraint
WTO	World Trade Organization

Preface

This book derives from a long-standing interest in the Asia Pacific region, frequent visits to the region and two comparatively long periods of residence there during the past two decades and more. My first arrival in Asia coincided with the first 'oil shock', which at least temporarily threatened to destroy the Japanese economic miracle and certainly sent shock waves of panic through a society which was seemingly set on an ever-upward path of economic growth. As I finish writing this book, not just Japan but much of the rest of Asia is gripped in economic uncertainty and, in some instances (most notably in Indonesia) in socio-political instability, thereby threatening the wider Asian economic miracle, which, in the popular mind, has succeeded the earlier Japanese miracle. Japan bounced back from the mid 1970s post-oil shock reconstruction a tougher and more efficient economy; for most of Asia the same is likely to be true this time round too. But the painful process of reconstructing Asian Pacific economic dynamism at the end of the 1990s raises a new, more complex set of challenges for Europe to replace those raised by earlier untramelled Asian economic growth.

I first started studying aspects of the subject of this book seriously while a member of the research staff of the Royal Institute of International Affairs in London, and I have benefited immensely over the years from the helpful inputs and ideas of many former Chatham House colleagues, European, Asian, Australasian and North American.

My various writings about particular sub-sets of Western Europe's relationships with individual countries or sub-regional organizations gradually convinced me that there was a need to try to draw together the broader strands of the Euro-Asian relationship. This has not been an easy task. In part that is a consequence of the vagaries of defining both Europe and Asia; entities for which there are not agreed boundaries and which have taken on as much emotional and political as geographic characteristics. In part it also derives from the multitude of levels and policy differences, especially between the European Commission and related bodies in Brussels, Strasbourg, and so on, individual member states of the European Community, or European Union as it has now become, and companies, non-governmental organizations and individuals in both European and Asian Pacific countries.

Numerous scholars, officials, journalists, politicians and businessmen based both in Europe and in Asia have spent time talking to me about various aspects of this complex subject. I cannot list them all, but I do want to record my thanks for their willingness to share their views with me. Nonetheless, I would like to give special thanks to Zakaria Haji Ahmad, Michele Calcaterra, Reinhard Drifte, Peter Ferdinand, James Hoare, the late Ishikawa Kenjiro, Martin Jacques, Jean-Pierre Lehmann, Jos Loeff, Wolf Mendl, Warrick Morris, Miguel Santos Neves, Odano Nobutake, Simon Nuttall, Oh Jay Hee, Park Jin, Etienne Reuter, Mary Seet-Cheng, Gerald Segal and Shibusawa Masahide. My appreciation is also due to Robert Taylor for his helpful comments on the first draft of this volume. Any mistakes and misrepresentations are, of course, my own responsibility.

I would also like to thank the staff of the libraries of the Royal Institute of International Affairs and Lingnan College for their patience with my requests and also all those European and Asian government departments (including the European Commission) which kindly tried to find me the data or documentation for which I was searching. I wish also to thank Phoebe Cheng Sim-chi and Barbara Chan Shui-wan of Lingnan College for their help in compiling some of the trade and investment data used in this book. I am also grateful to Dymphna Evans, Francine O'Sullivan and Ian Garbutt for their patience and encouragement with this volume.

Hong Kong has proved a fascinating base from which to contemplate not just the end of one particular phase in Britain's own relations with its last major overseas territory, but also the overall changes in Europe's relations with the broader Asia Pacific region. I would like to thank both colleagues and former students at Lingnan College for helping me to understand the dynamics of the local and regional transition a little better.

A debt, as always, is due to my family, who have had to put up with me rambling on about this project from time to time, but I would like to dedicate this book to my father, who sadly could not see it completed but who long before me found himself in Asia and whose occasional recollections of that experience in my younger days had more impact than either he or I realized at the time.

Brian Bridges
Hong Kong

1. Introduction

1998 – the 'Year of the Tiger' in the Chinese calendar – opened with the Asian 'tigers', the dynamic Asian economies, in a sickly state of health. The Asia Pacific region had been the world's fastest-growing region in the 1980s. Until the financial crises in several Asian Pacific states in 1997, which had a dramatic impact on the growth rates of the most-affected countries in the second half of that year, and will certainly cut growth rates across the region in 1998 and 1999, the region nonetheless looked certain to repeat that record again during the decade of the 1990s. However, the bloom has gone from many of the Asian economies, at least for the short term. Faced with a disturbing series of financial crises, Asian governments and economists have resorted to stressing that the fundamentals of these economies are sound. While this is generally true and while also clearly not all the regional countries have been hit with the same degree of disruption, several of the countries are nonetheless being forced to bite the bullet of economic retrenchment and reform, with its attendant bitter social and political costs.

The rise of the Asia Pacific region has been accompanied, at least since the mid 1980s and certainly during the 1990s, with a growing belief across the region that a distinct 'Asian way' or special 'Asian values' underpin the evolution of their economic and political systems. The presumption of a core set of civilizational values, common to the Asian region, acts as a counterweight and as a challenge to the Western model of economic, political and social development. The financial crises since the middle of 1997 are, however, certain to bring about some reassessment of these values, even though some of the strongest advocates of those values have been quick to reaffirm their validity despite the financial crises.

Europe, by contrast, went through its most difficult economic times more than a decade and a half earlier, in the 1980s, which in turn led to efforts through the single market project to revitalize the Western European economies through greater economic, and ultimately political, integration. While this project has been wrought with controversy, not least over the pace and extent to which such integration should occur, it has changed the nature of the economic and political debate within Western Europe. This process has undoubtedly restored some economic vitality to Western Europe and at the same time made it the focus of attention for the newly democratized economies of Eastern Europe. Now, at a time when the European Union (EU), as the European Community (EC) became in 1993, comes to face the next, and probably most difficult, stage of its economic integration process, monetary union, and the Asia Pacific countries are being forced to reassess their own potentialities and priorities after a turbulent period, undoubtedly the inter-relationships between the two regions deserve to be reconsidered.

A few words are necessary about the title and scope of this book. The intention is to examine the contemporary state of relations between Europe and the Asia Pacific region. While the postwar relationship, particularly over the last couple of decades, has been characterized by a preponderance of economic and commercial considerations, the aim is to examine also the less commonly noted political and strategic dimensions of the relationship. However, trying to draw together the broader strands of the Euro-Asian relationship has not been an easy task. In part that is a consequence of the vagaries of defining both Europe and Asia; entities which have graduated from being simply geographical terms to metaphors with political, cultural and even racial meanings (Korhonen 1997, p. 351). For the purposes of this book, Europe is generally taken as the current 15 members of the EU, although on occasion non-members or aspiring members will be mentioned. From time to time the terms 'Western Europe' and 'Europe' will be used to denote wider geopolitical concerns. The Asian focus has similarly had to be limited. In settling on the term 'Asia Pacific', I have taken it to refer to the countries which border the western rim of the Pacific Ocean – namely Japan, North and South Korea, China, Taiwan and Hong Kong – through to the present member states of the Association of Southeast Asian Nations (ASEAN), that is, Brunei, Burma (Myanmar), Indonesia, Laos, Malaysia, the Philippines, Singapore, Thailand and Vietnam, as well as the aspiring member, Cambodia, which has had its entry approved but temporarily suspended. The activities of the sole remaining superpower, the United States, and its former rival, the Soviet Union (now Russia), as well as other countries such as Australia which are either close to, or frequently involved in, the region, will be discussed as and when their actions and policies touch on the themes of this study.

But difficulties also arise from the fact that the EU-level relationship with either individual countries or sub-regional organizations such as ASEAN is closely entangled with relationships between individual EU member states and those same Asia Pacific partners. This complexity is compounded by the EU's strong influence over economic policy matters but its restricted, though admittedly slowly expanding, competence over foreign and even security policy issues. The EU is not a full-fledged actor in the international arena and on certain issues individual member states can play key promotional or blocking roles. Despite the EU's attempts in recent years to construct a comprehensive 'Asia policy', and the welcome region-to-region initiative of the 1996 Euro-Asia summit meeting (known as ASEM, after the formal title of Asia–Europe Meeting), the cross-cutting tendencies add to the complexity of charting this overall relationship.

The Asia Pacific is clearly a region of great diversity, with a multitude of different languages, all the world's major religions represented and significant differences in political systems and levels of economic development, despite the image which was portrayed in the 1980s and 1990s by many inside and outside the region of sustained and region-wide economic dynamism. In the economic numbers game, particularly as it relates to per capita income, many of the Asia Pacific countries have indeed, as shown in Table 1.1, caught up or even overtaken their European counterparts (though the drastic exchange rate fluctuations against the US dollar in 1997–98 are certain to make the Asian figures look less impressive in dollar terms now). Yet, regardless of the numerical impact of the financial crises, sizeable disparities within the region or within individual countries have existed and continue to exist. To a lesser degree, although more than is often suspected, the Europeans have also shown diversity, not least in their economic record over recent decades. Social and cultural differences of course continue to play their part in inhibiting the dream of European unity.

The earliest European travellers to Asia came back with a mixture of feelings: a sense of wonder and incomprehension at this vast continent and an impulse to try to profit from Asian commerce. Although today, seven centuries later, more Europeans than ever are eating Thai food, driving Korean cars, reading Japanese comics and following Asian religions, both those traditional responses still persist. The physical and psychological barriers of geographical distance and differing cultural and linguistic heritages have been reduced. Asia is no longer '*terra incognita*' – the home of legendary peoples and wealthy characters such as the fabled but non-existent Prester John. But, for the Europeans, the apparently 'exotic' characteristics of Asian societies and cultures – and their ways of doing business – still act both as a source of fascination and as an obstacle to understanding. The prism of Rudyard Kipling and Somerset Maugham, through which the British, for example, viewed Asia, has never been completely laid aside. But the British are by no means unique in this respect, for, broadly speaking, other Europeans share the same perceptional problems. Chapter 2 charts the historical patterns of European involvement in the Asia Pacific region and examines how memories and legacies of the period of colonization and the process of de-colonization have an impact on contemporary Euro-Asian relations.

To many Europeans over the past decade or two, the Asia Pacific's economic dynamism, at least as represented through exported manufacturing goods, seemed part of the problem rather than part of the solution to Europe's economic difficulties. The success of the Asia Pacific economies in producing

Table 1.1   Comparative indicators of European and Asian Pacific countries

	Population 1995 (millions)	Surface area (thous. sq. km)	GDP per capita 1995 (US$)	Average annual GDP growth (%) 1980–90	1990–95
Austria	8.1	84	26,890	2.1	1.9
Belgium	10.1	31	24,710	1.9	1.1
Denmark	5.2	43	29,890	2.4	2.0
Finland	5.1	338	20,580	3.3	−0.5
France	58.1	552	24,990	2.4	1.1
Germany	81.9	357	27,510	2.4	1.0
Greece	10.5	132	8,210	1.4	1.1
Ireland	3.6	70	14,710	3.1	4.7
Italy	57.2	301	19,020	2.4	1.0
Luxembourg	4.1	3	41,210	–	–
Netherlands	15.5	37	24,210	2.3	1.8
Portugal	9.9	92	9,740	2.9	0.8
Spain	39.2	505	13,580	3.2	1.1
Sweden	8.8	450	23,750	2.3	−0.1
United Kingdom	58.5	245	18,700	3.2	1.4
Brunei	0.3	6	20,400	–	–
Burma (Myanmar)	45.1	677	300	–	–
Cambodia	10.0	181	270	–	6.4
China	1200.2	9,561	620	10.2	12.8
Hong Kong	6.2	1	22,990	6.9	5.6
Indonesia	193.3	1,905	980	6.1	7.6
Japan	125.2	378	39,640	4.0	1.0
Korea, North	23.9	120	900	–	−4.5
Korea, South	44.9	99	9,700	9.4	7.2
Laos	4.9	237	350	–	6.5
Malaysia	20.1	330	3,890	5.2	8.7
Philippines	68.6	300	1,050	1.0	2.3
Singapore	3.0	1	26,730	6.4	8.7
Taiwan	21.0	36	11,600	8.1	6.6
Thailand	58.2	513	2,740	7.6	8.4
Vietnam	73.5	332	240	–	8.3

Sources: World Bank, *World Development Report 1997* (Oxford: Oxford University Press, 1997); *Asia Yearbook 1997* (Hong Kong: Far Eastern Economic Review, 1997); *Korea Focus*, Nov.–Dec. 1997, pp. 70–72 (for Bank of Korea estimates of North Korean per capita GDP and GDP growth rates); Council for Economic Planning and Development, *Taiwan Statistical Data Book 1997* (Taipei, 1997), Republic of China.

goods more competitively therefore seemed to provide a real challenge to companies, unions and governments in Europe. But at the same time, these fast-growing economies with their burgeoning needs for technology, consumer goods and financial services offer challenging opportunities for European companies to tap into this Asian Pacific market. The economic problems of the Asia Pacific region since mid 1997 are subtly altering the nature of the challenge but have not diminished its significance. Chapters 3, 4, 5 and 6 look primarily at the nature of these commercial challenges, in particular from Japan, the newly industrializing economies (NIEs), the new wave of proto-NIEs and the newest challengers, such as China.

Asian perceptions have also been as problematic as the European views of Asia. Those countries which were colonies of the Europeans tend to have an ambivalent attitude both towards that experience and towards the changing political, economic and military weight of the European powers. To the Asians, the Europeans were an alien and foreboding, rather than an exotic, presence, but nonetheless one from which something could be learnt. Postwar Europe, however, has suffered from a general perception across the Asia Pacific region of being in gentle decline, politically, socially and economically. Europe has seemed far away and out of touch with the fast-changing realities of the Asia Pacific region. Asian perceptions of Europe may appear to be more pragmatic and realistic than the European views of Asia, but this does not mean that they are that much closer to reality. Chapter 7 looks at the European process of regional economic integration, whose reception, at least initially, by the Asians was strongly coloured by past perceptions of that supposed socio-economic decline. The chapter also examines how the Europeans have responded in turn to embryonic Asian Pacific attempts at regional integration.

However, the Euro-Asian relationship is not simply about economics. Although admittedly often played in a much lower key, the political and security side of the relationship cannot be overlooked, especially in the post-Cold War era where it is becoming increasingly difficult to separate economics from politics. Chapter 8 examines the range of political and strategic issues between the Europeans and the Asians, and suggests ways in which the new agenda of international relations is providing reason for greater dialogue and interaction. The following chapter examines the three new elements emerging in the Euro-Asian relationship: the region-to-region interactional process through ASEM now that two such meetings have been held, the fall-out from the series of financial crises in the Asia Pacific region, and the imminent arrival of the European single currency. The concluding chapter draws together the elements of change and continuity in the relationship and suggests ways in which the relationship should develop as the next century beckons.

2. Legacies of history

Wipe out the gang of imperialists, mandarins, capitalists and big landlords.
(Early 20th century Vietnamese nationalist slogan; Mackerras 1995, p. 129)

With the reversion of Hong Kong to China in July 1997, effectively only one European 'colony' remains in the Asia Pacific region – the tiny enclave of Macau. Set to revert to China on 20 December 1999, Macau's return to the motherland has special symbolic significance for China in enabling it to end its direct experience – and, in the eyes of the Chinese, humiliation and suffering – at the hands of European colonialism and imperialism before the end of the millennium. Yet Macau's return will also have special symbolism for Portugal and the other European states. Just as the Portuguese were the first of the Europeans to arrive in Asia as colonists – Macau was established as a Portuguese colony in 1557 – so it is no doubt appropriate that Portugal should be the last to leave.

But, apart from the particular cases of the last colonies – Hong Kong and Macau – it is undoubtedly true that for both Europeans and Asians the legacies of their historical experiences during the centuries of European colonial involvement and, not least, the way in which these experiences have been interpreted and re-interpreted in recent decades, are an important element underpinning the contemporary relationship between Western Europe and the Asia Pacific region. This chapter therefore endeavours to examine the broad trends of early Europe–Asian interactions in order to illustrate how memories and perceptions (and misperceptions) of the past can influence, although admittedly sometimes in a rather nebulous fashion, contemporary policies and exchanges.

COLONIALISM ARRIVES

Until the 16th century the direct European experience of the Asia Pacific region was basically confined to one country, China – though admittedly a vast country, perhaps better described as a civilization, which was undoubtedly technologically in advance of Europe. Although there is now an active debate about whether Marco Polo, usually heralded as the first European to go to China, in the late 13th century, actually did reach Beijing and see everything he wrote about (Spence 1996, pp. 36–45), there is reason enough to believe, from what is known from contemporary Chinese accounts of their own society, that China had developed products and processes such as gunpowder, printing, paper money, silk production and navigation skills which put it well ahead of contemporary Europe. Although the West was to take up many of these inventions and ideas – and on occasion use them against the East – there were, as Robert Lloyd George has argued, often considerable time lags, over 1000 years in some cases, between the basic invention of the Chinese and either its arrival in Europe or occasionally its independent discovery in Europe (Lloyd George 1992, pp. 7–9).

Europe had had some exposure to Chinese – and other Asian – products and inventions in the Middle Ages, as silks, textiles, spices and metalware found their way to Western Europe through Middle Eastern landroutes. However, in the 14th century a combination of Black Death in Europe and the disintegration of the Mongol empire in China disrupted land-based patterns of exchange with China (Howe 1996, pp. 4–6).

It was the 'geographical revolution' led by the Portuguese, who provided Vasco da Gama and his successors with the maritime technology to enable them to reach the Indian Ocean by a sea route round the southern tip of Africa, the Cape of Good Hope, that really brought the Europeans into contact with other parts of Asia. Da Gama reached India in 1497; in 1509 Portuguese warships sailed into the port of Malacca, then the centre of a vast Southeast Asian commercial empire. The Portuguese were the first into the Asia Pacific region, but they were by no means the last (Segal 1990, pp. 35–54; Borthwick 1992, pp. 77–100). In the early 16th century, the explorer Ferdinand Magellan reached Asia by the opposite route, round the tip of South America, and claimed the islands that were to become the Philippines for Spain.

However, the Spanish and Portuguese desire to divide up the known world, including the Asia Pacific region, between themselves soon came under serious threat from other European powers. In turn, the British, Dutch and French moved in to challenge the Portuguese and the Spanish for trade and later for colonies in Southeast Asia. The struggle for control of global long-distance trade between the Portuguese, the Dutch and the British in particular did not have the same result everywhere in the world, but in Asia the Dutch initially came out on top against the Portuguese, only to be superseded in turn by the British (Subrahmanyam 1993, p. 273). Undoubtedly an amalgam of political, religious, strategic and economic motives underlay this European push into Asia. The three most commonly asserted motives have been pithily summarized as 'Gold, Glory and God': to acquire wealth, to win prestige and to gain converts (Mackerras 1995, p. 131). But the relative importance of these motives differed between the European powers and over time as well.

For example, the Portuguese and Spanish in their early endeavours in the Asia Pacific were clearly driven by religious missionary incentives. This inevitably caused an anti-Christian backlash in some parts of the region (most notably in Japan, which expelled almost all foreigners from the mid 17th century).

The Dutch, by contrast, were able to succeed in their later ventures into the region in part precisely because they were not closely associated with any missionary activity (Mackerras 1995, p. 145). Their strength was the Dutch East India Company, an innovative and well-structured commercial operation (backed by Dutch military power), which extended its trading networks throughout the region in the 17th century. The British, too, were initially motivated by commercial needs, which brought them into conflict first with the Dutch and later with the French during the 18th century. Although the French made a great play of their civilizing mission, it was their desire for prestige – and therefore rivalry with the British – which undoubtedly precipitated the struggle for India, where victory for the British brought immense resources ('the jewel of the empire') but also new responsibilities which were to shape British involvement in Southeast Asia thereafter. Indeed, the strategic factor became so important that a British Foreign Office memorandum drawn up immediately after the end of World War I described the defence of India as the 'impulse' of British imperial policy in Asia in the 19th century (Nicolson 1920).

The European colonial involvement in the Asia Pacific region can be broadly divided into two phases. The first, dating from approximately the beginning of the 16th century through to the middle of the 19th century, can be characterized as 'informal imperialism' or 'mercantile colonialism', when commercial imperatives – the desire for profits from trade – predominated. The second phase, which reached its peak at the end of the 19th century but which in practice survived until post-World War II independence, has been called 'formal imperialism' or 'industrial colonialism', when the Europeans sought to acquire tracts of territory in order to exploit their resources (Drakakis-Smith 1992, pp. 18–20).

China was the key trading target of the Europeans in the first phase, but the Chinese, self-confident and self-sufficient, seemed unexcited about the prospects of trade with Europe; as one Emperor made clear to a distinguished British envoy, Lord Macartney, at the end of the 18th century, his empire possessed 'all things in prolific abundance', so there was no need to 'import the manufactures of outside barbarians' (Segal 1990, p. 53). The Europeans were interested in Chinese products, however, and so the Chinese allowed them to squabble among themselves for access to this market. The problem was that the Europeans wanted to exchange goods with the Chinese rather than pay for Chinese goods such as tea, silk and porcelain with valuable metals. In particular, the British taste for Chinese tea, which had to be paid for by silver shipped from India, became a major drain on the British empire's financial resources. By the late 18th century, the British had decided that selling opium to the Chinese was the only answer (Borthwick 1992, pp. 89–99); the resulting trade had disastrous consequences for China's socio-political stability. The British fought the Opium War, 1839–42, in order to ensure that China allowed this lucrative trade in drugs to continue. Their victory ensured that the British were able to impose the first of a series of 'unequal treaties', gaining Hong Kong island in the process and regulating trade on British terms.

The remainder of the 19th century therefore saw other European states following the British approach. The weakened Chinese empire could offer little serious resistance to modern European military power. Under successive 'unequal treaties' Britain enlarged its Hong Kong colony and the French and the Germans carved out small areas of territory, surrounding the so-called 'treaty ports', under their control. Ironically, it was squabbling among the European powers over their respective territorial ambitions that probably ensured that China was not completely carved up. Nonetheless, the Europeans did gain a significant presence in the coastal regions of China. China was therefore never colonized in the orthodox sense; it might better be described as a 'semi-colony' of the Europeans. But the manner of the European expansion into China was to have a lasting impact on Chinese psychology and was to motivate first Chinese nationalists in the early decades of the 20th century and then subsequently Chinese communists to try to overturn 'the century of national humiliation'.

Japan, by contrast with China, had less appeal for the European traders. Smaller, further away and apparently lacking the riches of the vast Chinese empire, Japan was able effectively to lock itself away from European interest from the early 17th century until the mid 19th century. The extensive measures to create a closed country (*sakoku*) after 1639 allowed an extremely limited European (in this case only Dutch) presence in only a single port, Nagasaki (Howe 1996, pp. 16–32). Even though Japan was unable to resist the power of the Americans and the Europeans when they returned in force in the 1850s to open up the country, the series of unequal treaties concluded by Japan were never as wide-ranging as those that China had to suffer. Indeed, Japan proved much more adept than China in learning industrialization and modernization from the Europeans and in asserting itself against the Europeans. As Howe has argued, 'without entirely destroying traditional structures and values, [Japan's] people learned how to devise new economic institutions and to mobilise resources for the acquisition of new skills and technologies' (Howe 1996, p. 426). So not only did Japan not sink into the semi-colonial status of China, but by the end of the first decade of the 20th century it had already defeated one European power (Russia) in war and removed the last of the treaties granting other Europeans extra-territorial rights. In the process it was beginning to show that it had learnt something else from the Europeans – a desire to establish its own spheres of imperialist influence.

Sandwiched between its two larger neighbours, Korea largely escaped European interest. Apart from a handful of European missionaries, the Europeans had barely any contact with Korea until the late 19th century. The first Briton to reach Korea, for example, did not do so until 1797, and not until the 1880s, after the Japanese and the Americans had shown interest in Korea, did Britain and other European powers conclude trade treaties with Korea (Hoare 1997, pp. 1–17). Situated off the main sea-lanes and apparently rather poor, Korea remained outside the European sphere of colonial interest and, despite the interest of the Chinese and the Russians, it was Japanese colonialism to which it soon fell prey.

The picture in Southeast Asia, however, was vastly different from that in China and Northeast Asia. In Southeast Asia the presence of the Europeans was increasingly felt as they turned from simple trading to trying to control the supply of the most valuable products. This in turn meant establishing greater control over local populations and kingdoms and, on occasion, fighting with other European rivals to secure that control.

British interest in Southeast Asia can be traced back to the East India Company's involvement in the China trade and what was seen as the importance of securing trading posts along the Malayan peninsula to help support that trade. Between 1786 and 1824 Penang, Singapore and Malacca were acquired, despite competition from the Dutch, and became jointly administered under the 'Straits Settlements' system. But the foothold in Malaya inevitably involved the British in conflict with neighbouring Thailand, or Siam as it was often called (Lowe 1981, pp. 18–23, 41–48). As the British tried to tap the resources (especially tin in the mid 19th century) and extend their control over other parts of the Malayan peninsula, the Thais stressed their interest in the northern Malayan states. Four Malayan states were brought under a degree of British control as the Federated Malay States in 1896, and in 1909 the Thais were forced to give up their rights in four other states, which with the addition of Johore became the Unfederated Malay States, under loose British influence. This rather untidy division of the Malayan peninsula into three forms of British control continued until the Japanese invasion in 1941 (Esterline and Esterline 1990, pp. 147–157).

The consolidation of British rule in India brought the British to the borders of the kingdom of Burma. Border disputes led to armed clashes and, by treaties imposed by force in 1826 and 1852, the British seized the lower half of Burma. Fearful of French ambitions, the British then went one step further in 1885 and annexed the remaining areas of Burma (Tarling 1992, pp. 34–

41). Rivalry with the Dutch, the Spanish and the Germans accounted for the British interest in the northern part of the island of Borneo. Originally taken over by James Brooke, a British adventurer and businessman, in 1839 the area now known as Sarawak gradually expanded under the Brooke family, backed by the British government, until the whole northern part of Borneo was effectively British territory (Wright 1970).

France established its empire in the Indochinese region. Whereas the British justified some of their acquisitions as being necessary to prevent French takeovers, the French in turn argued for expansion as a way to thwart British colonial advances into Indochina. France invaded Vietnam in 1859 and, shortly after capturing Saigon, established a colony of Cochin China, together with a protectorate over Cambodia. With the Mekong route proving unsatisfactory as a way into China, the French moved north along the coast, adding Annam, Tonkin and Laos by 1893 (Duncanson 1968, pp. 72–117). Attracted by the greater populations and mineral resources of the northern part of Vietnam, the French moved the capital to Hanoi, which was virtually rebuilt as a French city. Thailand was left in the middle between the British and French spheres of influence. Shrewd diplomacy by the Thai kings, coupled with a gradual appreciation by both Britain and France that there was some advantage to there being a buffer state between them, led to a tacit agreement by the end of the 19th century to leave Thailand alone.

From the early 17th century the Dutch had ruled parts of the Indonesian archipelago indirectly through the Dutch East India Company, which established an extensive trading network based around Malacca (on the Malay peninsula) and Batavia (modern Jakarta) on the island of Java. But by the early 19th century the Dutch had decided to institute direct rule to replace the financially troubled Dutch East India Company. However, it took the Dutch nearly a century to consolidate their control over the outer islands of Indonesia, with the pacification of Bali only being completed in 1908.

By the beginning of the 20th century, therefore, the Europeans had carved up most of the Asia Pacific region. The British had consolidated their control in the western part, with Malaya, Singapore, Burma and Hong Kong under their control; under the so-called 'White Rajahs' north Borneo was ruled as an 'independent' but basically British-backed family empire. The French were in control of the Indochinese states of Vietnam, Laos and Cambodia, as well as, to all intents and purposes, China's Yunnan province. The Dutch retained their extended East Indies. Portugal was left only with Macau and Timor. Germany had achieved a late and short-lived incursion into New Guinea. One exception was the Philippines, where Spain had just handed over control to the United States. Russia had tried to extend its power in the Far East, especially into Korea, but was in the process of losing out to the new aggressive colonizing state, Japan. The other European colonial power,

Belgium, which was to gain territory in Africa, found itself cut out of the Asia Pacific scene (despite some half-hearted attempts to get into Thailand). Consequently, Thailand was never to be colonized, ending up as a buffer state between the British and French empires in Southeast Asia.

DECOLONIZATION

The European colonizing process had been protracted and at times disjointed. Decolonization came about much faster, but again not in a uniform manner across the region. Ironically, it was Japan, which itself avoided colonization by the Europeans but learnt from them all too well the ambition to secure its own colonial empire, which helped to precipitate the end of the European colonial era.

Imperial Japan first established colonial control over Taiwan in 1895 and Korea in 1910 before expanding its military control into Manchuria, northern China and then southern China during the 1930s. The Japanese saw colonialism as 'a matter of prestige' but their colonialism lacked the romanticism of the Europeans and, unlike the British example, it was 'overwhelmingly military in character' (Gann 1984, pp. 502–503). Military expansion, however, helped to create new economic interests and needs. In 1941 Japan embarked on what its leaders considered to be a necessary expansionist war to ensure the natural resources needed for its survival (Coox 1988, pp. 315–349, 376–382). In addition to the notorious attack on the US base in Pearl Harbor, Hawaii, in December 1941, the Japanese attacked European possessions in Southeast Asia. With the Europeans laggardly in appreciating the full extent of Japanese ambitions and distracted by the war in Europe (which had anyway by 1941 overwhelmed both France and Holland), the colonial administrations were poorly equipped to face up to the ferocious and well-planned Japanese attacks. The initial Japanese attacks were immensely successful and Western colonial rulers in Malaya, Singapore, Borneo, the Dutch East Indies, Hong Kong, Macau, Vietnam and the Philippines were replaced by Japanese and puppet native administrations (Tarling 1992, pp. 329–341). Although the Japanese were to control most of this new Asian empire until their final defeat in August 1945, within barely one year of their initial victories they found themselves on the defensive as the Americans won the battle of Midway and began the gruelling and bloody process of expelling the Japanese from their new Pacific territories. The military burden in the Pacific War was borne almost alone by the United States; the European contributions were extremely limited (Thorne 1978, pp. 288–302, 401–416, 520–542).

War touched all parts of the region. The Japanese talked much about freeing 'Asia for the Asians', but for many Asians the much-vaunted 'Greater

East Asia Co-prosperity Sphere' just meant substituting Japanese domination for European or American control. The brutality of the Japanese actions, their inability and unwillingness to grant independence for the former colonies, and their subsequent postwar failure to apologise adequately for their actions have left a legacy which still colours Japanese interactions with the region.

But the Japanese occupation of much of the Asia Pacific region also played a crucial triple role in altering the nature of Europe's relations with the region. First, the Japanese destroyed the myth of the invincibility of the European powers during their rapid initial military defeat of the European forces during 1941–42. The Dutch forces in the East Indies surrendered within a week; the British lost Malaya and Singapore within two months. These military disasters were 'profoundly humiliating as well as materially damaging' (Tarling 1992, p. 340). The Japanese showed that the Europeans, for all their past coercive military power, could indeed be defeated militarily – this lesson was not lost on the Indonesian nationalists, for example. Moreover, the element of prestige, even bluff, which had also been necessary to underpin European colonial rule, given the comparatively limited number of Europeans which had been in control of much larger local populations, was shattered for ever.

Second, the Japanese served as a catalyst to ensure that in 1945, after their own defeat, the returning Europeans were confronted by new and ultimately uncontrollable political forces which were reluctant to allow them to slip easily back into old patterns of control. Few Europeans were able to grasp the extent to which the countries of Southeast Asia, in particular, had changed as a result of the Japanese occupation experience. Nationalism and anti-Europeanism had not been unknown in the region in the 1920s and 1930s, but the Japanese had helped to stimulate it both directly and indirectly. In some countries the Japanese actually encouraged local forces to collaborate with them in their administration, such as in the former Dutch East Indies and Burma. In others, guerrilla operations fought in the jungles against the Japanese led to armed groups being active and committed to a radically new order after 1945.

Third, the Americans came to have a much greater say in Asian Pacific affairs. Militarily, they had shown that they were a powerful force in the region and that they were prepared to prevent the domination of the region by any one power. In due course, the Americans were to show, especially in the Vietnam War, that they were prepared again to take over from the Europeans in the struggle against any hegemonic threat. The heightened involvement of the Americans, who had already been timetabling independence for the Philippines even before the war, also meant additional pressures on the Europeans to follow suit and end colonialism. Having declared in their wartime propaganda and in pacts with the Americans that they were fighting against tyranny,

the European Allies were on weak ground in facing US opposition to reim-
posing any form of 'tyranny' on the liberated Asian peoples (Thorne 1978,
pp. 676–696; Copland 1990, pp. 162–164).

The volatile mix of nationalism, communism and the returning European
colonial governments' misguided expectations produced different results across
the region after 1945 (Tarling 1992, pp. 341–385). But none of the former
European colonies were to find decolonization as peaceful and as easy as in
the Philippines, where the Americans granted independence as early as 1946
(Fifield 1958, pp. 60–63). The British, especially under the postwar Labour
government, were the most receptive of the Europeans to the idea of moving
towards independence for their colonies. They were comparatively quickly
pushed out of Burma, with only limited violence, by 1948 (Fifield 1958,
pp. 167–194). The British took longer to go from Malaya, because of the
perceived need to combat the communist insurgency first. With that threat
under control, Malaya became independent in 1957 and was joined in 1963
by Singapore and the north Borneo states of Sabah and Sarawak (although
Singapore separated from the newly created Malaysia two years later). Brunei did not achieve independence, and then only after some pushing from
Britain, until 1984. The British Commonwealth served to maintain some
British institutional links with the newly independent Southeast Asia, but
these ties were not as pervasive as some British hoped or as some continental
leaders, such as France's Charles de Gaulle, feared.

It was the Dutch and the French who were involved in the bloodiest
transitions. The Dutch fought a long rear-guard political and military action
against Indonesian republican forces, until finally in the last days of 1949 the
Dutch government, with its forces bogged down and suffering under strong
US pressure, grudgingly agreed to Indonesian independence (Fifield 1958,
pp. 108–130). But even then the Dutch retained control of part of one island,
Irian Jaya; this was to be a source of Dutch–Indonesian contention throughout the 1950s (Fifield 1958, pp. 130–137). The Indonesians nationalized
Dutch assets in the country and expelled most Dutch citizens, until finally, in
1963, the two sides agreed, under the auspices of the United Nations (UN)
that Indonesia could take over control of the province. The bitterness engendered by the military struggle in the 1940s, together with the lingering Irian
Jaya problem, coloured Indonesian views of Holland in the post-independence years. Ironically, the almost complete breakdown in relations at the end
of the 1950s – and the consequent break in psychological dependence –
actually helped the two sides to work out a new, more equal, relationship in
the 1970s and 1980s, which was in many ways better than that between the
British and Malaysians until they went through a similarly cathartic experience in the early 1980s. Nonetheless, the Indonesians still remain not only
proud of their record of seizing their own independence (rather than having it

handed to them on a plate), but are also, as will be discussed in Chapter 4, sensitive to signs of the Dutch lecturing them.

The French attempts to return to Indochina were even bloodier than the Dutch efforts in Indonesia, especially with Vietnam at the centre of an emerging nationalism which increasingly took on a socialist hue. In 1945 France recovered control of Cambodia and Laos relatively easily, but found that the veteran communist Ho Chi Minh, who had emerged as an important anti-Japanese figure, had considerable popular support, especially in the north of Vietnam. After the communists took control in China in 1949, external support for Ho's Vietminh forces increased. The French effectively gave independence to Laos and Cambodia in 1953 but refused to give up the main prize, so they carried on fighting in Vietnam until the humiliating defeat of French forces at Dien Ben Phu in 1954 (Duncanson 1968, pp. 140–203). The subsequent withdrawal of French power left an ideologically divided Vietnam, which needed another 21 years of debilitating warfare before reunification could be achieved, and disarray and instability in Laos and Cambodia. There was not much exaggeration in Mao Zedong's later dry remark to France's first ambassador to the People's Republic of China that 'France's role in Asia ended with Dien Ben Phu' (Domenach 1990, p. 187). France has continued to maintain a nostalgia for Indochina, recalled evocatively in the award-winning film *Indochine*, but not until the mid 1980s, when France started to play an increasingly active role in trying to broker a settlement of the Cambodian crisis, was it again taken seriously among its former colonies.

Hong Kong and Macau remained as anomalies long after the wave of decolonization had broken over the European colonies. Not only did these two remain under European administration throughout the postwar period, but they were destined not for independence, as other Asian Pacific colonies had been, but for return to mainland China. The Portuguese, indeed, for political reasons after their own internal political revolution, did actually try to hand back Macau to China in the mid 1970s, but the Chinese preferred to leave it nominally with the Portuguese while gradually extending their influence over all sectors of the economy and administration. The negotiations from 1984 to 1987 to set up Macau's formal reversion to China in 1999 drew heavily on the model of the earlier Sino-British agreement over Hong Kong but were a much more problem-free process. Since the late 1980s, too, the process of implementing the Sino-Portuguese declaration has been low key and uncontroversial, in large part due to the lack of enthusiasm by the Portuguese for raising contoversial issues such as democracy. In return, the Chinese have rewarded Macau's 'docility' with an easier path over issues such as major infrastructure projects, passports and localization of the civil service (Leung 1997). The problem for the Portuguese is how to avoid any knock-on effects from the earlier Hong Kong handover (and Portuguese officials have been disturbed by signs of Chinese heavy-handedness towards Hong Kong during 1996–97) and how to retain a distinctively Portuguese flavour to the culture, economy and society of Macau after reversion (Ngai 1996).

Hong Kong's path back to China has been much more contentious than Macau's. Although it was a British initiative which precipitated the Sino-British negotiations in 1982, China had already made public statements declaring that it would resume control of Hong Kong. It was clear from the beginning of the negotiations that China had no intention of conceding sovereignty; it soon also became obvious that there was to be no administrative role for Britain after 1997 either, despite Prime Minister Mrs Margaret Thatcher's own hopes. With a poor hand to deal, British negotiators found themselves forced to agree to a treaty which promised Hong Kong a 'high degree of autonomy' for 50 years under the rubric enunciated by Deng Xiaoping of 'one country, two systems' (Roberti 1994, pp. 36–126). The deal brought neither particular gratitude from the people of Hong Kong nor any especially notable commercial benefit for Britain in China. The process of implementing the agreement was altered irrevocably by the June 1989 massacre in Tiananmen Square and the emotional reactions within Hong Kong, where more than 1 million people took to the streets in an unprecedented show of support for democracy in China. Subsequent efforts to restore confidence within Hong Kong and ultimately, under Governor Chris Patten, to embed democracy more firmly in the territory did not go down well with the Chinese, who were anyway predisposed to be suspicious of the British (Yahuda 1996, pp. 69–108). The final years of British rule were therefore marked by persistent clashes between the British and the Chinese over a wide range of issues which reflected underlying differences of political culture. Hong Kong finally returned to China on 1 July 1997, but with question marks over its political and economic future, and the likelihood, as will be discussed in more detail in Chapter 5, that its importance in European relations with China and with Asia as a whole is set to grow.

Apart from Macau, Portugal has been involved in one more colonial experience in the Asia Pacific region, in East Timor. But here the impact of the domestic political changes within Portugal in the mid 1970s was very different from the Macau case. A Timorese independence movement, the Fretelin, decided to make a clear bid for independence while the Portuguese were distracted by events back home. With a pro-Indonesian party losing out in the conflict with the Fretelin, the Indonesians launched an invasion in late 1975 and in 1976 formally incorporated East Timor into Indonesia. The Portuguese, left as bystanders, were thrown out and the territory, despite persistent attempts at armed rebellion by the remaining Fretelin forces, has been under Indonesian control ever since (Taylor 1991, pp. 16–74, 171–174). The Portuguese acquiesced and their protests appeared little more than formalities. Ironically, more than a decade was to pass before Portugal began to take a more vigorous attitude both in the UN, which continues to regard Portugal as the legitimate authority in the territory, and in European forums against the Indonesian actions. East Timor has, therefore, become – and remains – an evocative issue in Portuguese relations with the Asia Pacific region as well as acting as a focal point of broader European concerns about human rights and democracy in the region.

COLONIAL LEGACIES

Post-colonial relationships invariably tend to be a mix of contradictory emotions and unrealistic expectations. The relations of Britain, France, Holland and Portugal with their former colonies have been no exception to this rule. Although the Asians do see the Europeans as much less dominant or potentially threatening than the Americans, or for that matter the Japanese, the Europeans have not found it easy to exorcise the ghosts of the past.

In part, the ambivalence among the Asians about the Europeans derives from their perceptions about the European record of colonialism. Arguably, the European influence until the 19th century was 'more destructive than constructive', but after that 'the record becomes better' (Copland 1990, p. 170). Certainly, the European states did try to exploit their colonies economically, and this in turn brought social dislocation. But the Europeans also brought modernization through infrastructure development, rule of law, and scientific and medical knowledge, although some scholars argue that in terms of gross national product (GNP) per capita, the overall standard of living of the Asian populations did not noticeably improve under colonialism (Copland 1990, p. 179).

Although the era of European colonialism is all but dead and buried in the Asia Pacific region, its legacies are still apparent in surviving – and occasionally disputed – administrative and national boundaries, transport networks, parliamentary institutions, language and literature, science and technology, and even sports and popular culture (Copland 1990, pp. 196–198). In a final paradox, the formerly colonized have often found themselves having to communicate among themselves in the languages of the colonizers. The meetings of officials of ASEAN are usually conducted in English because that is the best-understood language among the nine member countries. The colonial influences have not been entirely one way, however, since the European powers took back home, though admittedly often in modified form, foods, phrases and fashions which have become accepted parts of European life.

'Special relationships' derived from colonial links and which work substantially in favour of European interests may have long since gone, whatever the French may think to the contrary, but in much more nebulous forms the knowledge and perceptions (and misperceptions) derived from the colonial period, or from the manner in which knowledge about it is received, still influence the relationships between Europe and the region. As the Asians have developed economically and demanded that the Europeans treat them as equals – or even, on occasion, as betters – they have found it difficult to resist the temptation to remind the Europeans about their past politically incorrect transgressions. The Asian concern with past dependency and exploitation helped to account, for example, for the phraseology adopted in the Chairman's concluding statement at the end of the first ever ASEM summit in March 1996 about strengthening 'dialogue on an equal basis between Asia and Europe' (Chairman's statement, 1996). Echoes have also been found in the rhetoric of some Asian Pacific leaders in ascribing the series of financial crises hitting the region in 1997–98 to the machinations of jealous former colonial powers, although often the United States and its supposed surrogate, the International Monetary Fund (IMF), have loomed larger as a scapegoat than the Europeans.

In the three decades after World War II, the European withdrawal from the Asia Pacific region, involving the removal of colonial administrations and the reduction of military commitments, was accompanied by a loosening of economic and commercial ties. In the 1950s most Asian countries appeared poor, devastated or unstable. Their resources seemed less accessible than African ones, their markets less able to absorb European exports than Latin American ones. The British refusal to join the European common market at its creation, ironically, further held back general European contacts with several of the newly independent nations of the region which were conceived of by other European states as being within the British 'domain' (Grilli 1993, pp. 271–273).

The net effect of this loosening of contacts between Europe and the Asia Pacific region was that the Europeans were shielded longer than the Americans from the export expansion first of Japan and then of the NIEs. However, at the same time, they also missed out on significant business opportunities in the region. The commercial initiative passed first to the Americans and then, in the 1970s, to the Japanese. When the Asian exporters did start to penetrate the European markets, therefore, they appeared all the more threatening because of the suddenness with which these unfamiliar companies and trading states arose. The commercial challenge from the Asia Pacific is the main theme of the next four chapters.

3. Japan: beyond competition

The wind blows hard among the pines
Toward the beginning
Of an endless past.
Listen: you've heard everything.

('Wind among the Pines' by Takahashi Shinkichi
(Stryk and Ikemoto 1973, p. xlvi))

In 1991 Bastille Day, 14 July, was celebrated not just by the French as usual, but also by a group of Japanese ultra-nationalists in Tokyo who publicly beheaded an effigy of the then new French Prime Minister, Edith Cresson. Their anger had been provoked by a series of disparaging remarks about the Japanese – including describing them as 'ants' and 'outcasts' – which she had made after asssuming office a few weeks earlier (Takeuchi 1991, p. 76; Bridges 1992, p. 231). Arguably, her comments reflected not just her own personal prejudices but also a long-standing French political tradition which, at the very least, can be dated back to President Charles de Gaulle, who in 1962 disparagingly dismissed the then visiting Japanese Prime Minister as a 'transistor radio salesman' (Saito 1990, p. 30).

While few occasions have been as dramatic as the above, it is undoubtedly true that Mrs Cresson's remarks struck a chord with industrialists, and associated politicians, across Europe, who have looked askance at the success of Japanese industry in producing quality goods that European consumers want to buy. But this has not been the only reaction, for, as will be discussed below, some Europeans have actually seen opportunities to work with the Japanese to bring about industrial revitalization.

Japan, of course, was the first of the Asia Pacific economies to emerge as a serious competitor of the European economies after World War II. From an economy devastated by war in the 1940s, Japan has become, by the late 1990s, one of the world's top three trading nations, a major overseas investor, the largest provider of economic assistance to the developing world, and the world's largest creditor nation. The spectacular economic growth of Japan since the early 1960s has obscured the strong element of continuity in Japanese economic growth throughout this century, interrupted only by the war years, the oil shocks of the 1970s and the post-'bubble' recession of the 1990s. The postwar interruptions in turn have been almost blessings in disguise for the Japanese, forcing them to restructure their industrial activity in ways which in the medium term have only served to enhance competitiveness. In the prolonged recession of the 1990s, with Japanese growth bumping along at around the 0 to 1 per cent mark for most of the decade, the silver lining has so far been notable by its absence. As the recession reached its nadir in 1997, with a series of major corporate bankruptcies, especially in the financial industry, and massive stimulation packages in early 1998 proving uninspiring, Japan has finally been pushed into a new stage of financial restructuring which holds out the promise of eventual recovery.

Scholars and practitioners remain divided over the explanation for Japan's economic success. Undoubtedly it owed something to the land, labour and corporate structure reforms introduced during the Allied Occupation period (1945–52), but much also depended on certain socio-political features which survived from the prewar period and earlier. Primary among them was a tolerance, cultivated since the 19th century Meiji period, of the government's flexible involvement in promoting economic growth. This feature has led some scholars, such as Chalmers Johnson, to describe Japan as a 'corporate developmental state' with the government manipulating economic activity and nurturing industry through long-term planning (Johnson 1982; van Wolferen 1989). Other scholars feel that the role of government, particularly the much-vaunted Ministry of International Trade and Industry (MITI), has been over-stated. Scott Callon suggests that it has been companies, not government bureaucrats, which have been at the heart of Japan's postwar success (Callon 1995), while Penny Francks looks even further back to the agricultural and small-scale company sectors of 19th century and prewar days (Francks 1992). Above all, industrialization by learning, by both the government and companies, seems to have been crucial (Mathews 1996, pp. 8–9).

As a resource-poor state, the need to import natural resources and gain access to foreign export markets and technology has spurred Japan's integration into the global economy. Consequently, Japan's economic activities are an important underpinning to its foreign policy and are often vital in defining its relationships with its neighbours and partners. This has clearly been the case in Japan's relations with Europe. Economic issues, above all trade issues, have indeed been the mainspring of postwar Euro-Japanese relations. The competitive element of the bilateral economic relationship has tended to have three specific characteristics: large imbalances in comparison to a relatively constrained trade relationship; sectorally concentrated and rapidly expanding imports from Japan; and a Japanese market difficult to penetrate. This chapter looks at the origins and evolution of the Japanese economic challenge to Europe, how it has been changing since the mid 1980s, and how far the predominant (and often contentious) economic relationship is slowly being broadened and softened by the development of political dialogue.

JAPAN'S EXPORT SURGE

Several European states, most notably Holland and Portugal, have had long historical links with Japan, but in this century Japan has been closely associated with Europe through two alliances: first, with the British from 1902 to 1922, perhaps the first real sign that Japan had arrived as a power in international relations, and second with Germany (and subsequently Italy) through the Axis Pact from 1936 until defeat in 1945. Although many Western European states resumed diplomatic relations with Japan after it regained its international identity at the end of the postwar Allied Occupation (to which several European countries provided troops), links were minimal during the 1950s. Europeans remembered not only Japan's wartime aggression but also its prewar dumping of cheap textiles; so they initially opposed granting most favoured nation status to Japan when it joined the General Agreement on Tariffs and Trade (GATT) in 1955 (Rothacher 1983, pp. 85–92). Symbolically, GATT membership came at the time that Japan was just beginning its economic take-off, although its fast economic growth path was not confirmed until the early 1960s, when the ruling Liberal Democratic Party deliberately switched the Japanese people's attention away from domestic political confrontation to growth targets such as the 'income-doubling plan' (Sheridan 1993, pp. 143–157).

In the 1960s, as Japan became the first, and until 1996 the only, Asian state to join the Organization for Economic Cooperation and Development (OECD) and then it overtook successively Italy, Britain, France and West Germany in size of economy, trade links with Europe began to develop quite rapidly. Japanese producers became interested in the growing European markets; at the same time, the Japanese government worked away steadily at whittling down the various European quotas and restrictions on Japanese products. 1969 proved a turning point, when Japan for the first time ran a trade surplus with the EC. After that, Japanese exports to the EC began to accelerate substantially and certain European industrial sectors, notably steel, ships, cars, televisions/radios and tape-recorders, began to feel under pressure.

The Japanese drive into Europe was prompted both by changes in Japanese industrial structure and by new factors in the international trading environment. Japan was probably the hardest hit of all the industrial economies by the first oil shock, but in the mid 1970s it made 'a rapid shift away from energy-intensive heavy industries toward higher-value-added, more knowledge-intensive industries' (Callon 1995, p. 149). Semiconductors, cars and sophisticated consumer electronics became the force behind the market leaders within Japan and, ultimately, on the global market when the Japanese began to export them too. Externally, Japan's trading patterns were affected by the emergence of trade tensions in the late 1960s with the United States which led on to the 1971 'Nixon shock' (the new economic policies of the Nixon administration in the United States), coupled with the 1973 oil shock, which exposed Japanese vulnerability in terms of relying on one source of energy supply (Akao 1983, pp. 15–44). These events encouraged the Japanese to think much more about diversification, not just of import sources of food, energy and raw materials, but also of export markets. Western Europe emerged as the new prime target.

The European Commission had seemed rather a by-stander in the earlier years of Euro-Japanese trade, and its limited attempts to bring about some commonality in approach to Japan had been sabotaged by individual EC member countries' reluctance to risk losing their own tough restrictions on Japanese products and by clever Japanese divide-and-rule tactics (Nester 1993, pp. 207–209). But after its common commercial policy came into effect in 1970, the European Commission began negotiations with the Japanese over a comprehensive trade treaty. However, the Commission was in a difficult position because EC member states differed widely over how to deal with the rising tide of Japanese goods (Ishikawa 1990, pp. 19–21) and the Japanese preferred concluding bilateral 'voluntary export restraints' (VERs) with individual governments and even industrial organizations (Rothacher 1983, pp. 146–167).

These bilateral agreements were not very effective. They provoked stiff confrontations between the European Commission, which was endeavouring to ensure its competence over all external trade matters, and individual member states, during the period 1972–74 in particular (Ishikawa 1990, pp. 18–20). They also showed European industry to be on the defensive. The European logic was that these 'temporary' VERs would give European companies in the sectors concerned a 'breathing space', during which they could carry out internal restructuring so as to be better able to meet the Japanese challenge. Unfortunately, too often, in the opinion of one European bureaucrat (and he was far from being alone in this view), the 'breathing space' was not used properly to improve productivity (Wilkinson 1990, pp. 174–175).

A second turning point was reached in October 1976, when members of a mission of Japan's premier business organization, the Keidanren (the Federation of Economic Organizations), were surprised by the degree of European resentment against Japanese exports and by the extent to which the European leaders they met spoke in unison (Rothacher 1983, pp. 218–224). This shock can in some ways be compared with the shock that the Japanese had received two years earlier in Southeast Asia, when a visiting Japanese Prime Minister had learnt first hand how Japanese economic activities in that region of the world were resented.

The Japanese government moved rapidly to strengthen VERs in the five major problem sectors, especially cars, as well as introducing tariff cuts on

European goods being imported into Japan at a rate faster than had been agreed in the Tokyo round of GATT talks. Nonetheless, Japanese exports to the EC continued to increase unremittingly. Unmatched by equivalent increases in European exports to Japan, the trade surplus for Japan rose from just under $6 billion in 1977 to close to $12 billion in 1981.

EURO-PROTECTIONISTS FIGHT BACK

Pressures for action were growing within Europe, particularly as most EC member countries were faced with rising unemployment and sluggish economic growth at home. Politicians increasingly came to depict Japan as one of the major causes of Europe's socio-economic problems. Fears, for example, that the automobile and other key industrial sectors might also suffer from the 'motorbike syndrome' – a reference to the destruction during the 1960s of the European motor-cycle industry by its Japanese competitors – typified the politicization of commercial competition.

Even the European Commission became more critical, allowing its notorious internal report, which described Japan as 'a country of workaholics who live in what Westerners would regard as little better than rabbit-hutches', to be leaked in 1979 (Ishikawa 1990, p. 24). Although the report did also pay tribute to the 'hard work, discipline, corporate loyalties and management skills' of the Japanese, it was the more critical comments which were picked up by the European media and public.

The heightened tensions which emerged in the economic relationship in the early 1980s were nowhere more clearly exhibited than in the conflicts over the two key industrial sectors of that era: cars and consumer electronics.

In many countries the automotive industry has a prized place in their national industrial pantheon; for several European countries, which pride themselves on being car producers, the issue of imports from Japan therefore has become especially sensitive. From the mid 1950s onwards, even while Japanese car exports were still only a trickle, piecemeal restrictions or quotas had begun to be imposed on Japanese car imports; these became more restrictive in the mid 1970s (Wilkinson 1990, p. 185; Lehmann 1992, pp. 37–53; McLaughlin 1994, pp. 149–165).

In the 1970s, while European car makers began to suffer from over-capacity, rising costs and declining productivity, the Japanese were to harness their investment in advanced technology and production efficiency into effective export campaigns. Japanese car exports to Europe rose by 15 times during the 1970–80 decade, primarily through Japanese exporting to the more open European markets such as West Germany. Pressures from European car manufacturers and certain governments for Community-wide controls on imports gathered force. In July 1980 France actually began a new informal system of restrictions by holding up Japanese cars at French ports until new licensing arrangements had been completed (Ishikawa 1990, p. 26); the Japanese had to threaten to take France to the GATT to get these regulations dropped. Even the Germans pushed the Japanese into an 'understanding' that exports to West Germany in 1981 would be no more than 10 per cent higher than in 1980 (Wilkinson 1990, p. 186).

The most worrying development for the Europeans was the 1981 US–Japanese VER agreement over cars. Fearing that the net effect of this agreement would be to divert Japanese car exports from the United States to Europe (in fact, the main impact was that it encouraged Japanese car companies to set up manufacturing plants inside the United States (Lehmann 1992, pp. 45–46)), the European Commission demanded a similar agreement from Japan. The Japanese balked at any kind of general agreement, but in 1986, as the pressure built up, the major Japanese car companies came to an informal export restraint agreement, which had the effect of actually reducing the registration of new Japanese cars in the main European markets the following year (Wilkinson 1990, p. 186), though this was to be a temporary phenomenon. The European pressures, as in the US case, did, however, also help to push the major Japanese car companies into building manufacturing plants within the EC. As will be seen below and as will be discussed in more detail in Chapter 7, the car sector was wracked by new controversy in the late 1980s over the role of these transplants in Europe. In part, this new controversy was caused by the fact that the European car industry had done little during the decade to take advantage of the 'breathing space' for industrial restructuring which had been one of the rationales for proposing such restraints to the Japanese (Jackson 1993, p. 95).

The other sector which came to the forefront in Euro-Japanese trade friction was the consumer electronics industry. Once again it was French industry which was to the fore, though this time joined by Dutch industry or, to be more specific, the influential Philips company. As early as 1972 Philips had argued for a VER with Japan on electronics exports to Europe (Ishikawa 1990, p. 51), but pressure for action from Philips and from French consumer electronics producer, Thomson increased towards the end of the 1970s, especially as Japanese colour television exporters targeted Europe. However, the friction was to reach its highest point over the next example of consumer technology, video cassette recorders (VCRs). In October 1982 the French government announced that all Japanese VCRs being imported would have to come through the small and inconvenient port of Poitiers, over 200 miles from Paris. Imports slowed dramatically. Not only the Japanese protested but so did the European Commission and several other member states, which argued that the French move set a dangerous protectionist precedent. Threatened with legal action from the Commission, France backed down. But the

EC then went into negotiations with the Japanese which resulted in early 1983 in a VER on exports of VCRs and television tubes for a three-year period (Ishikawa 1990, pp. 28–30). It was a short-term gain for European producers – though a loss for European consumers, who faced higher prices – which, as in the case of cars, was not used as effectively by European industry as the advocates of restructuring for competitiveness argued.

The growth in Japan's trade surplus with Europe did indeed level off during the early years of the 1980s, but by 1984 it was rising again to reach $14.6 billion in 1985 and nearly $23 billion by 1988. This was to lead to a rethinking on the European side and another change in European tactics, by focusing next on opening up Japan's 'closed market' and by joining in multi-lateral attempts to use exchange rate manipulation to modify Japanese surpluses. The intention, as one European official stationed in Tokyo at that period has admitted, was 'to persuade Japan to consume more and to produce less for export' (Wilkinson 1990, p. 197).

OPENING THE JAPANESE MARKET

The degree to which Japan's market is genuinely open to foreign products, especially foreign manufactured goods, has been a subject of continuing debate and controversy among Europeans and between Europeans and the Japanese. Critics contended that 'Japan's markets are protected by a series of concentric walls of which the outermost are tariffs and quotas, while the dozen or so inner walls are a succession of increasingly subtle nontariff barriers' (Nester 1993, pp. 137–138). Japanese officials counter-argued that 'Japan is probably less protectionist than the Community' and that it was up to the Europeans 'to produce equally attractive products and make more efforts to sell to the Japanese market' (Hanabusa 1982, p. 120).

Most Japanese would have accepted the Europeans' argument that in the early years of Japan's postwar economic take-off the government, mainly through MITI, had kept a close regulatory eye on emerging industrial sectors, usually described as 'infant industries', and worked to protect them from competing imports where necessary. But formal barriers, such as tariffs, have indeed, as the Japanese correctly claim, been progressively reduced so that they are in most cases below those maintained by the Europeans and the Americans, and this has been acknowledged by outside governments. Where the Japanese and the Europeans parted company was over how far non-tariff barriers, including the practice of 'administrative guidance' or administrative protection, still continued to operate in the 1980s.

The European Commission did admit in 1985 that visible import barriers, such as tariffs and quantitative restrictions, had been significantly reduced by

Japan and that they no longer constituted a real barrier to imports from Europe (Ishikawa 1990, p. 32). The EC instead saw the fundamental problem as being Japan's 'low import propensity' or, to be more precise, a low propensity to import manufactured goods which was seen as being derived from a range of informal barriers or non-tariff barriers (Meynell 1982, p. 109). Early European attempts to focus on opening up the Japanese market to European manufactured goods, in the second half of the 1970s and the first half of the 1980s, had been, in the words of one EC official, 'clumsy', 'unfocused' and 'unproductive' (Richardson 1989, pp. 7–8, 11). Lengthy lists of identified obstacles were handed over to the Japanese without any serious attempt to categorize them or arrange them in order of priority. Appreciation of the failure of this approach made it politically possible to go for more focused sectoral negotiations. From the mid 1980s, therefore, the Europeans, either in tandem with the Americans or more often following one step behind, picked up on a number of socio-cultural and commercial practices which were identified as hindering trade and discouraging the Japanese from 'buying European' in specific sectors.

Negotiations during the second half of the 1980s did result in the opening up of a number of sectoral markets, notably automobiles, pharmaceuticals, cosmetics, medical equipment, alcoholic beverages and leather goods. To take one example: alcoholic beverages, which are of particular importance to the British whisky industry and the French wine and brandy industry. The Tokyo delegation of the EC spent over a year researching the Japanese liqueur industry, producing a two-volume report on protectionist policies which was translated into Japanese and distributed to Japanese ministries, politicians and media. After initial Japanese responses were unsatisfactory, the EC took the Japanese to a GATT panel which ruled in the Europeans' favour (Richardson 1989, pp. 12–13). The Commission felt that these kinds of sectoral negotiation had been largely, though not wholly, successful (Commission Communication to the Council of Ministers 1992). However, some sectors of importance to the Europeans, notably the agricultural and financial services markets, were only marginally affected and became intricately involved in the multilateral negotiations associated with the Uruguay Round of the GATT negotiations from 1986 onwards. Indeed, by the early 1990s the Japanese government was adopting the position that outstanding issues of market access should be left to be dealt with during the GATT negotiations (Japanese Foreign Ministry 1992).

The Europeans identified a number of non-tariff barriers which they saw as being caused either directly or indirectly by governmental policies. One was the complex list of Japanese technical product standards, especially testing and certification procedures and safety standards, which were seen as being unnecessarily convoluted and working to the benefit of domestic Japanese producers (Meynell 1982, p. 109). Attempts were made during the 1980s by the Japanese to simplify some of these, but European exporters continued to claim that many still acted to make exporting to Japan a time-consuming and complicated task.

Another, and even more regularly cited, target for the Europeans was the complex and costly distribution system within Japan. In 1982 the EC took Japan to the GATT under Article 23 procedures, citing the restrictive practices of the Japanese *keiretsu*, the integrated corporate groups of suppliers, distributors and subcontractors linked to one dominant manufacturing company, as a key element of the Japanese distribution and retail system. These acted, to use the words of one French prime minister complaining to Japanese businessmen, as a 'screen' against foreign companies setting up sales and after-sales networks (Wilkinson 1990, p. 205). The GATT panel ruled in the Europeans' favour, but the follow-up bilateral procedures, which included a cumbersome EC–Japan trade expansion committee, faded out over the following year or two. The lack of a serious response from the Japanese side to what one scholar has described as the 'homework' that it had been asked to undertake (Tanaka 1992, p. 8) meant that nearly a decade later the Americans had to go back to the same issue through the Structural Impediments Initiative talks.

Japanese claims that their market was already open were undercut by some of their own actions, in particular the series of market-opening packages introduced during the 1980s and the recommendations of the 1986 Maekawa Report, drawn up by an *ad hoc* committee of experts, on transforming the Japanese economy by reducing its export orientation and stimulating imports and domestic demand (Saito 1990, pp. 86–87). But the law of diminishing returns seemed to be operating. Although each package did contain some helpful measures, the fact that the Japanese government had to produce yet another package time and time again, apparently grudgingly under pressure from the Europeans and the Americans, only reinforced the arguments of the critics that the market was still not truly open.

The market-opening approach of the Europeans ran parallel to similar American steps. But even more closely coordinated were the attempts of the Europeans and the Americans to use exchange rate manipulation as a way to reduce Japanese trade surpluses. However, these international efforts in the mid 1980s did not provide more than a short-term answer to the Europeans' trade problems. The United States took the lead in pushing the finance ministers of the G-5 countries (Japan, Britain, France and West Germany together with the United States) into the infamous Plaza Accord in September 1985 (Saito 1990, p. 87). The plan was to cut the value of the dollar; by 1988 the yen's value had almost doubled against the 1985 dollar. Japanese global trade and current account surpluses did decline slightly and temporarily, but Japa-

nese companies proved adept at restructuring to beat the *endaka* (high yen).
The impact on Euro-Japanese trade was marginal.

NEW EUROPEAN EFFORTS

The EC–Japanese trade balance did stabilize and Japan's surplus even declined
modestly in the late 1980s, but that was primarily due to the 'Heisei boom' –
later to be cursed as the 'bubble economy' – in Japan, which encouraged a
much faster growth in imports, particularly of manufactured goods. Between
1987 and 1990 EC exports to Japan grew by around 25 per cent per annum,
with exports of luxury goods, especially motor vehicles, clothes, paintings and
alcoholic beverages, accounting for nearly half this growth (Commission Communication to the Council of Ministers 1992). However, ominously for the
Europeans, Japan's domestic growth began to falter in 1991; luxury imports
collapsed and EC exports declined by 4 per cent during the year. Japanese
companies returned to exporting with a vengeance, and the newly unified
German market in particular sucked in Japanese goods. So, as shown in Table
3.1, in 1991 Japan's trade surplus with the EC grew once again – to $43 billion.
The following year it rose to $46 billion, and by early 1993 the EC's ambassa-
dor to Japan was moved to warn that the 'ballooning Japan–EC imbalance' was
'a kind of time bomb' which could explode into 'a protectionist backlash 'in
Europe (Foreign Broadcast Information Service, 1993).

The Japanese responded to European frustrations and complaints by point-
ing out that manufactured goods accounted for more than half of total Japanese

Table 3.1   EC/EU trade with Japan (US $million)

	EC imports from Japan	As % of total EC imports	EC exports to Japan	As % of total EC exports
1980	19680	2.55	6694	0.97
1985	22689	3.42	8049	1.24
1990	67506	4.37	30911	2.07
1991	72603	4.56	29464	1.98
1992	74936	4.55	28723	1.82
1993	66564	4.77	28790	2.00
1994	68982	4.35	34465	2.09
1995	76908	4.03	43040	2.14
1996	72022	3.69	44978	2.20

Source: IMF, *Direction of Trade Statistics Yearbook*, 1987 and 1997 editions.

exports for the first time in 1989. The blame therefore lay with insufficient efforts by European companies to penetrate the Japanese market. This was of course a criticism levied at American and other foreign companies too.

In the 1980s the European governments tended to agree that European companies should try harder but still put the larger onus on to the Japanese to make their market more open. The European propensity to blame the Japanese carried through into the 1990s. The European Commission analysis in 1992 was that 'structural obstacles ... are currently the main barriers to do business in Japan, whether by exporting or by investing there' (Commission Communication to the Council of Ministers 1992). However, at the same time, the early 1990s did see a greater appreciation on the part of the Europeans that there might actually be some justification to the Japanese criticisms of weak European corporate expertise and commitment. Several European governments undertook campaigns to increase corporate awareness of the commercial opportunities available in Japan.

The first to take the initiative were the British, who emerged from a period of bruising bilateral trade disputes and headline-catching sabre-rattling with a belief that one way to boost trade with Japan was to persuade British company boards of directors that Japan was actually changing. The Opportunity Japan campaign, launched in 1988, was considered by British trade officials to have been successful in raising awareness of Japan and also boosting British exports by 75 per cent over three years (Whitehead 1992). A follow-up campaign, Priority Japan, designed to encourage British firms to take the next step from arms'-length trading and actually to invest inside Japan was less successful as it coincided with recession in both Britain and Japan, but the British government felt it important to keep the momentum going with a further campaign, launched in 1994, called Action Japan, which focuses on ten priority sectors which present 'new or untapped potential for business where British firms have a competitive advantage' (*Japan News*, April 1994).

The comparative success of the British approach certainly inspired other European states. After a particularly frosty two-year period in relations, in large part due to the role of Mrs Cresson first as Trade Minister and then as Prime Minister, the French in 1992 launched a '*Le Japon: c'est possible*' campaign, modelled very closely on the British Opportunity Japan campaign. The Dutch also instituted a similar campaign.

Of course, these various national campaigns to boost awareness and in turn exports tended to be competitive with each other. Commission officials, while welcoming these kinds of national initiative, were therefore concerned about building synergies between national programmes and Community-level approaches. As an attempt to do that, in the spring of 1994 the Commission itself followed up with a Community-wide campaign called 'Gateway to Japan'. Over the medium and longer term, these kinds of campaign will have the effect of widening the base of EC exports to Japan but in the short term the characteristics of duplication seem pronounced.

Nonetheless the various campaigns did have some initial impact, for EU exports to Japan showed signs of slow but steady growth during the mid 1990s, to reach nearly $45 billion in 1996, although Japan's share of total EU exports remained low. On the other hand, Japanese exports to the EU suffered a hiccup in 1993, but continued at a high level in the mid 1990s. As shown in Table 3.1, the trade imbalance was thus slowly narrowing – down to $27 billion in 1996 – but still remained at a level which generated political tension.

At the same time, by the early 1990s the EC–Japan trade conflicts were becoming increasingly entangled with the effects of the EC's own moves towards a single market under the '1992 process' and the long-standing, but stumbling, multilateral negotiations for the Uruguay Round of GATT, both of which will be examined in more detail in Chapter 7. It is necessary here, however, to examine two other aspects of EC–Japanese economic interaction: the invisible trade balance and the investment gap.

EUROPE'S COMPARATIVE ADVANTAGE: INVISIBLE TRADE

Even though the Europeans have been on the defensive for a long time over visible trade issues, in the invisible trade area, especially in the services and financial markets, they feel that they have a comparative advantage. The growing visible trade surpluses for Japan during the 1980s were indeed partially redressed by a European surplus in invisible trade with Japan.

The Japanese financial system was born in the late 19th century, with external forces acting as the midwife. The result is a mixture of foreign structures and indigenous practices, operating in a particularly Japanese mode. In the postwar period the system has been very rigid and highly segmented, with each generic type of financial institution having control over strictly demarcated areas of business. Although since the mid 1980s slow but progressive liberalization and deregulation of the financial system has worked to break down some of this segmentation and open up more areas to foreign enterprise, the speculative 'bubble economy' of highly inflated asset values served only to postpone much-needed reform. It was only in 1997 – as the vain efforts by companies and the government to whitewash the severity of the economic problems deriving from the bursting of that bubble finally caught up with them and set off a chain reaction of corporate bankruptcies – that the Japanese government began seriously to consider implementing financial system reforms of sufficient breadth for them to be characterized as a 'Big Bang' reform equivalent to that carried by the City of London in 1986. Japan's 'Big Bang' therefore started in April 1998 under the slogan of 'free, fair and global', implying that Japan's financial markets had been none of these in the past.

British banks and securities houses represent the largest European financial sector presence in Tokyo. They and their European counterparts – backed by their respective governments – undertook protracted campaigns in the 1980s to open up the Japanese financial system to European financial institutions. In due course in the late 1980s the negotiations for greater openness and transparency of financial services in Japan became entangled with the EC's own internal debates (and discussions with external partners) over the concept of 'reciprocity' in the newly integrated service and investment markets envisaged within the EC under the 1992 process. This particular issue will be covered in more detail in Chapter 7.

Gaining admission to the Tokyo Stock Exchange (TSE) became one of the symbolic issues of the early 1980s, with considerable political clout being wielded, most notably by British Prime Minister Margaret Thatcher, until in 1985 Warburgs, Jardine Fleming and Vickers da Costa became the first British (and therefore European) stock-broking companies to gain a seat on the TSE (Newall 1996, pp 46–47). However, the costs of doing business on the TSE are heavy and one former European Commission official has drily described the European experience of doing financial business in Japan as 'not exactly a bonanza' (House of Lords Select Committee on the European Communities 1989, p. 52). One British diplomat explained more laconically that the British government had 'fought hard to allow British financial companies to have the right to lose money' (interview, Tokyo, September 1994). The combination of the high costs and a relatively depressed stock market in the early 1990s (at least compared with the dizzy heights of 1989) ironically led several European financial houses to reduce their exposure in Tokyo. For example, in 1993 one British brokerage house, County Natwest, actually sold off its previously prized TSE seat.

The flow is far from all one way and Japanese financial institutions are now heavily represented in London, Frankfurt, Paris and other European financial centres. Indeed, since the European markets deregulated earlier than Japan, the Japanese presence there emerged earlier than the European stake in Tokyo. Once the wartime disruption in both Europe and Japan had passed and emotions caused by that war had begun to cool, financial links grew in tandem with the development of Euro-Japanese trading links, notably from the mid 1960s onwards (Newall 1996, pp. 20–41). The expansion of Japanese involvement in the financial centres of Europe became increasingly visible. The first phase of Japanese foreign direct investment (FDI) was indeed service sector-oriented (Sekiguchi 1982, p. 167). Up until 1985 over 90 per cent of cumulative Japanese FDI into Britain was still in the non-manufacturing sector. Up to 1986 Japanese investment in the manufacturing sector in the whole of the EC was little more than that invested in Luxembourg banking alone (Richardson 1989, p. 5). In large part this was because the Japanese initially saw their investments in financing (and in distribution and after-sales servicing) as a back-up for their exporting activities.

That picture began to change in the mid 1980s, as the Japanese began to put considerably more emphasis on the manufacturing sector, especially with the approach of the single market. Nonetheless, Japanese FDI in the non-manufacturing sector continued to increase as commercial banks and the 'big four' securities houses expanded rapidly on the back of huge capital flows. Britain was the favoured location for Japanese financial institutions, followed by Switzerland, Germany, France and Luxembourg. In contrast to their less profitable operations in the United States, in London and other European financial centres the Japanese securities companies did not try to compete with domestic business but concentrated on activities such as issuing Eurobonds, which were then sold mostly to Japanese institutional investors (Emmott 1992, pp. 147–153). In 1989 the top four issuers of Eurobonds were all Japanese, with close to 40 per cent of the market share between them. The banks too tried to widen their international operations through a base in London; their share of all non-sterling loans booked in London rose from 24 per cent in 1982 to a peak of 37 per cent in 1988, making the Japanese banks, as a group, the largest of any nationality (Emmott 1992, pp. 155–156).

There was a time in the late 1980s when it looked as if Japanese financial companies, like their manufacturing counterparts earlier, were about to sweep all before them in conquering the European market. However, in the 1990s the bursting of the Japanese 'bubble economy', which meant a marked reduction in the supply of capital to support loans, and a succession of scandals involving different parts of the financial system and even the seemingly all-powerful Finance Ministry itself, have exposed the structural shortcomings of the Japanese financial empire. This has led one financial journalist to comment that Japan's financial sector, 'far from posing a competitive threat to Europe ... is actually far behind' (Jackson 1994, p. 53). Already by 1991 the Japanese banks' share of non-sterling loans had decreased to 32 per cent. This did not mean the end of Japanese financial involvement. Japanese banks contributed more to the loan finance of the Eurotunnel consortium, which built the under-the-sea rail tunnel between France and Britain, than banks from any other country, and Japan's Export–Import Bank in 1993 made its first ever untied loan for a European infrastructure development, for a railway link between Heathrow airport and London (Drifte 1996, p. 99). However, overall it is fair to say that, from the perspective of the late 1990s, the

Japanese have not become quite as overpowering in the financial sector in Europe as was often feared in the late 1980s.

THE INVESTMENT GAP

Although the early postwar decades of Euro-Japanese economic relations were dominated by trade issues, over the past two decades investment has become an increasingly important facet of the relationship. Indeed, Thomas Bourke has argued that the growth of Japanese FDI in Europe has 'radically transformed' EC–Japan relations since 1985 (Bourke 1996, p. 48). Japanese FDI in Europe remained at a fairly low level until the early 1980s, but rapid increases in flows in the second half of the 1980s provoked both positive and negative responses among the Europeans and raised the spectre that, as in trade, imbalances were building up. European FDI into Japan continues to lag well behind the flows out of Japan into Europe, and some European officials claim this gap could be considered to be the major bilateral issue of the 1990s (interview, EU official, November 1994).

Globally, the 1980s can anyway be characterized as an era of FDI outflows from all the major economic powers in the world, and growth in FDI far outstripped that of world trade (Julius 1990, pp. 14–24). However, Japanese FDI grew particularly fast, by seven-fold during the decade, with the high yen of the mid 1980s undoubtedly helping to spur this massive global outflow of Japanese FDI. Total Japanese FDI rose from US $4.7 billion in fiscal year (FY) 1980 to $12.2 billion in 1985 and $67.5 billion in 1989. Since 1991 annual flows have fluctuated around the $35–40 billion mark, although 1996 did see a recovery to $54 billion. FDI flows into the EC rose steadily from annual levels of around $2 billion in FY 1985 to a peak of nearly $15 billion in 1989. As can be seen from Table 3.2, the level then dropped slightly the next year and more markedly in FY 1991 to $8.8 billion. For the next few years, annual Japanese FDI flows into the EC fluctuated around the $6–7 billion mark, but rose again in line with the general rise in outward FDI to around $8 billion in 1996. This compares with EC FDI into Japan of around $260 million in FY 1987 to $1.1 billion in FY 1991. Although EC FDI into Japan grew by around 20 per cent per annum in the late 1980s, growth levelled off in the early 1990s and even declined in FY 1993 (to only $870 million) before beginning slowly to build up to reach $1.9 billion in 1996. There was therefore still a considerable investment gap.

Before considering the reasons for the comparatively poor performance of the Europeans in investing in Japan, it is important to consider in more detail the Japanese record in Europe. In terms of geographical distribution, the EC's share of Japan's total world-wide FDI grew from less than 5 per cent at the

Table 3.2   Japanese FDI in Europe

Fiscal year	FDI in EU (US$millions)	Total Japanese FDI world-wide (US$millions)	FDI in EU as % of total Japanese FDI
1990	13336	56911	23.43
1991	8858	41584	21.30
1992	6665	34138	19.52
1993	7111	36025	19.74
1994	6022	41051	14.67
1995	7930	49583	15.99
1996	8045	54094	14.87

Note: On approval basis.

Source: Ministry of Finance, Japan, statistics.

end of the 1960s to around 12 per cent at the beginning of the 1980s; thereafter its share grew slowly but steadily until in FY 1990 it had reached 23 per cent, with Britain alone receiving more Japanese FDI that year than the whole of the Asia Pacific region. However, the following year FDI flows into Britain dropped by around half, a slack that was not entirely taken up by European rivals, so that since the early 1990s the EU has taken around 15 per cent of total Japanese FDI. Although Britain is still the largest recipient, it is no longer quite so far ahead of its closest rivals. Contrary to expectations that the newly unified Germany would prove an attractive base for Japanese companies hoping to enter both the Western and Eastern European markets, Japanese FDI growth there has remained unspectacular. It is Holland which continues to act as Britain's closest rival, with Luxembourg having a special attraction as a financial centre. According to Japanese statistics, in cumulative terms from 1951 to 1994, Britain still outranked the rest with a 34 per cent share of Japanese FDI to the EC, followed by Holland with 19 per cent and Germany, France and Luxembourg in the 6–8 per cent range (Bourke 1996, p. 111–118). In both FY 1995 and FY 1996 Britain still remained the largest recipient of Japanese FDI in the EU, with more than twice as much as its nearest rival, Holland.

As discussed above, in the first phase of Japanese FDI distribution, agents and financial institutions led the inflow into Europe in the 1960s and remained dominant until the early 1980s, when the second phase, in which manufacturing operations became steadily more important, began. As a result, the share of manufacturing has grown from less than 10 per cent of all

Japanese FDI in the EC in 1985 to more than 22 per cent by 1991; in FY 1996 as much as 38 per cent of all Japanese FDI flowing into the EU was in the manufacturing sector.

As with FDI around the world, both push and pull factors operate to determine the timing, direction and character of Japanese companies' decisions to set up operations in Europe. Pushing companies outwards were macro-economic influences, most notably Japan's swing from a current account deficit to a surplus in 1982–83 and the rise of the yen from 1985. To Japanese companies, the costs of producing goods at home increased compared with making them abroad and, at the same time, domestic interest rates were cut, causing cheaper capital to become available to invest elsewhere (Emmott 1992, pp. 9–11). The Japanese bought into property, set up offices and established manufacturing plants overseas. A desire to make the most of opportunities for globalizing their business activities has consequently featured among stated reasons for undertaking FDI (Japan External Trade Organization (JETRO 1990)).

But why did Japanese companies choose the EC or, to be more accurate, certain countries within the EC? One important factor was existing – and anticipated – obstacles to trading, straight selling, in the large European consumer market. Psychologically, according to one Japanese analysis, the 'Poitiers affair' in 1982 was a 'milestone' in affecting Japanese corporate attitudes (Ishikawa 1990, pp. 99, 103). The Community-wide restraints which followed from the resolution of this problem apparently convinced many Japanese that this was the thin end of the wedge; better to be inside than out. Later in the 1980s, as the EC began its move towards the single market, this factor of trying to circumvent a rise in European protectionism gained added importance in Japanese eyes.

A second significant factor was the encouragement of the European governments. Although occasionally Japanese companies have invested in order to appease individual governments, such as the investment in compact-disc player manufacture in France in the mid 1980s, the Japanese generally have been more responsive to investment incentives and, more importantly, to positive attitudes from individual national or even sub-national (regional/ state) governments. Often the incentives offered by national or regional governments have been designed to promote FDI in depressed areas with high or rising unemployment (Sekiguchi 1982, pp. 171–173). However, early efforts to invest in the manufacturing sector around Europe received a mixed reception. European manufacturers were critical of any sign that the Japanese were looking for mere assembly sites fed on imported components, while European trade unions were suspicious of the different approach the Japanese took to industrial relations within companies (Sekiguchi 1982, pp. 176–177). In 1977 Hitachi tried to open a wholly owned colour television factory in

Northern Ireland, but was forced to abandon its plans because of opposition from local industries and trade unions (Ishikawa 1990, p. 96). The Labour government of the time kept out of the dispute. By the early 1980s, however, the British government, now under Mrs Thatcher, had changed tack and decided to adopt a positive attitude to attracting Japanese FDI; regional administrations and, eventually, even trade unions followed in turn. Although some observers do pick up on the long-standing Japanese interest in British tea, golf and, above all, language as explanations for the Japanese preference for investing in Britain, Japanese trade officials and businessmen themselves put more emphasis on the investment climate (Ishikawa 1990, p. 99).

The Thatcher government's tough campaign to rid Britain of an image of inflation and strikes in order to create a disciplined but still relatively low-wage workforce undoubtedly played a part, but so too did the particular efforts, right up to the highest political level, to court Japanese companies with positive incentives. A key decision, which did much to encourage other Japanese companies to follow suit, was that made by the Nissan car company to establish a car plant in the north-east of England (it had first been mooted in 1981, but the first cars did not come off the production line until 1986). The negotiations were 'tortuous and long drawn out' and Mrs Thatcher herself had to use considerable political and financial capital to secure the decision (Cortazzi 1992, pp. 176–177; Emmott 1992, pp. 46–63), but the result was to have tremendous importance in British industrial relations and manufacturing history. As more Japanese companies followed, more British industrialists – and even trade unions – became convinced of the benefits of cooperation with the Japanese. Thanks to Japanese manufacturing plants, Britain in 1991 became once again a net exporter of colour televisions (*Financial Times*, 13 November 1992) and it achieved the same turn-around with cars the following year. In return, the Japanese have often secured, most notably in the case of Britain, sympathetic governments which have been prepared to stand up for them in intra-EC debates. This has meant, for example, to take the case of other Europeans disputing the 'Britishness' of cars made in Japanese plants in Britain, that Britain 'is not only on the side of the Japanese, but indeed championing the cause' (Lehmann 1992, p. 45).

The British example undoubtedly affected other European governments and industrialists. In some cases the response was emotional and negative. Jacques Calvet, the head of the French car company Peugeot-Citroen, accused Britain of becoming 'an offshore aircraft-carrier' from which Japanese firms could launch attacks on the rest of Europe (Emmott 1992, p. 17). The 'Trojan horse' criticism found echoes in other parts of Europe too, especially in Italy. The implication was that this kind of FDI was only aimed at getting inside market barriers and that it was detrimental to rival European companies.

Other European countries, however, were either already more positive about encouraging inward FDI anyway or saw advantages in keeping up with British moves. Holland has long had a positive disposition to inward and outward foreign investment, and financial deregulation in 1986 encouraged subsidiary finance companies. Japanese FDI in Luxembourg has had an even stronger financial sectoral interest, because of the government's especially liberal attitude towards such investment (Bourke 1996, pp. 120–121). Significantly, though too late to catch the great outflow of Japanese investment in the late 1980s, France and Italy, which for long proved the coolest towards Japanese foreign investment, have begun to change their attitudes in the 1990s. France has traditionally adopted 'inconsistent and inconstant policies' towards inward FDI from anywhere, not just Japan (Turner 1987, p. 27), but it has shown some ability to increase its share of inward FDI from Japan by comparison with its European rivals in recent years, even though it has much ground to make up (Bourke 1996, pp. 124–125). Germany is perhaps the most unusual case, with its great economic strength and powerful companies but rather 'neutral' attitude to inward FDI, if anything discouraging Japanese companies from moving there, although there have been a few important technological tie-ups (Bourke 1996, p. 123).

At the Union level, the main concern is that Japanese FDI should be fully integrated into the European economy – and should bring real benefit, not just become 'screwdriver' operations in the manufacturing sector – and that member governments should not endeavour to 'outbid' each other to obtain Japanese FDI. Indeed, in 1986 the Commission specifically warned member states against a 'beggar-my-neighbour policy to attract new investments' (Ishikawa 1990, p. 103). While these admonitions may have had some impact temporarily, the overall decline in the supply of Japanese FDI in the early 1990s tended only to encourage competition among the potential host countries. Undoubtedly, the implementation of the 1992 process, to be discussed further in Chapter 7, has also subtly affected the nature and distribution of Japanese FDI. The European Commission no doubt would prefer that Japanese FDI is more evenly distributed across the EU, but there is little that it can do to influence Japanese investors away from or towards any particular country.

The European Commission has also become much more concerned in the 1990s about the poor record of EU FDI going into Japan, which is lagging well behind both Japanese FDI flows into Europe and the growth in EU trade with Japan. Of course, the EU is not alone in this concern as Japan, by comparison with the other major economies, is still host to a comparatively small amount of foreign FDI. Discouraging government regulations and a business culture which abhors hostile takeovers undoubtedly contributed to this situation (Julius 1990, pp. 57–58). The Europeans have therefore echoed the calls of the Americans and others for the Japanese to make their investment climate more attractive. MITI has responded with a series of measures, such as the Global Business Partnership programme launched in 1992, and regional and prefectural governments across Japan have been encouraged to offer more incentives. Although many European companies accept the logic of the argument that to prove they are a serious globally competitive company they do need to have a presence in the Japanese market, the distance, the costs (particularly of land, labour and office rents) and cultural differences appear daunting to many European companies. The US precedent, whereby approximately 15 years elapsed between the United States starting as a major outward investor and becoming an important recipient of inward FDI (Julius 1990, p. 59), seems unlikely to be repeated in the Japanese case.

INDUSTRIAL COLLABORATION

Associated with FDI, in whichever direction it flows, is industrial collaboration or cooperation. Joint ventures have often seemed an easy way both of accessing the other's market and of sharing the risks and costs of developing new products for both markets. There have been some successful examples of Euro-Japanese joint ventures dating back to the 1970s, but the dangers of the partners going into such ventures with mismatched expectations have also been shown to be very real. The collapse of two of the earliest joint ventures, the television production collaborations by Hitachi–GEC and Rank–Toshiba (Turner 1987, pp. 41–43), made the Japanese more inclined to invest in single-ownership greenfield sites and the Europeans more suspicious of being 'used' by actual or potential Japanese partners. The case of the British Leyland (later renamed Rover) link-up with Honda in 1980, which continued until Honda reacted acrimoniously to Rover's sale in 1994 to the German BMW group, demonstrated also that both sides should ensure that they learn something substantial from the joint venture process. Rover, which went into the joint venture in a state close to desperation, became overly dependent on Honda manufacturing and design capabilities, while Honda gained more by adopting longer-term strategies; it acquired a growing presence in the European market which it has now consolidated through direct manufacture at a separate plant in Britain (Pilkington 1996, pp. 90–114).

In the second half of the 1980s, as Japanese manufacturing FDI into the EC increased, a new form of industrial collaboration began to emerge. The impetus for this change was the need of the major Japanese manufacturing companies to secure supplies of high-quality locally made components to put into their products. The EC's evolving and often *ad hoc* rules on local content encouraged – or, more correctly, forced – many Japanese companies to purchase a high proportion of their components locally. The EC's 1987 regulation against so-called 'screwdriver plants', which set a maximum for 60 per cent of parts coming from the country of origin of any firm establishing new assembly plants inside the EC after the imposition of anti-dumping duties (Ishikawa 1990, pp. 82–94), played an important role in this respect. In part this need was met by the tendency of the larger Japanese companies to bring in their wake the smaller and medium-sized companies which in Japan had supplied components. One study has shown, for example, that recent Japanese FDI in Wales, in Britain, can be largely explained as component suppliers being linked to earlier FDI by major Japanese manufacturers, especially the electronics giants Sony and Matsushita (Han 1994, pp. 130–131). But the need for locally made parts also opened up new opportunities for European suppliers to form business relationships based on meeting the invariably strict Japanese requirements on quality, price and reliability.

As a result, some Japanese companies, such as Sony which first invested in Europe back in 1973, now use almost exclusively local components on their mature product lines. In addition, Sony has set up technical centres in three EU countries to enable its engineers to work with local suppliers to refine, design or develop components for its newer products entering the European market (Jackson 1994, p. 148). Valeo, a major French parts producer, by 1993 had 5 per cent of its total sales going to Japanese manufacturing plants in Europe; by 1996 this was expected to have reached 10 per cent (*Fortune*, 18 October 1993).

Individual European governments have tried to facilitate industrial cooperation. Several EC member states have signed science and technology agreements with Japan which act as a framework for exchanges of researchers and information. An EC–Japan Centre for Industrial Cooperation was set up in 1987. This is a non-profit organization funded by the European Commission, MITI and private firms to run management training programmes and promote business opportunities, and has offices in Tokyo and Brussels.

There is also a growing number of collaborative links between Japanese companies and European universities in scientific and technological fields, although the corresponding links between European companies and Japanese universities and scientific research centres are far fewer. Japanese companies claim to have over 250 research and development facilities in Europe, although probably only about a quarter of those are actually independent or non-factory-based. Examples from Britain, which along with Germany has the largest number of such centres, include Hitachi and Toshiba working with Cambridge University on quantum physics, drugs company Eisai working with University College London on neuro-sciences and Canon working with Surrey University on software (*Financial Times*, 17 October 1994). However, the general European perception that, for a range of reasons including the tendency of the Japanese education system to inhibit creative thinking, the Europeans are stronger at creative basic research while the Japanese are more adept at production engineering has led some industrialists within Europe to question whether these research ventures actually lead to the Japanese being put into an advantageous position to exploit European inventiveness. The European Commission was trying to make the same point when its 1992 policy guidelines called for scientific and technological cooperation with Japan to be arranged in such a way that 'benefits flow in both directions to an adequate extent' (Commission Communication to the Council of Ministers 1992).

Such suspicions also made themselves felt in the European reaction to the purchase of the major share of Britain's last office mainframe computer company, ICL, by the Japanese computer company Fujitsu in 1990. In 1986 Fujitsu had had to pull out of a similar kind of deal to buy up US computer manufacturer Fairchild because of a storm of protest within the United States. But the ICL deal was allowed to go through by the British government. Under pressure from other European computer-makers, notably the French state-supported computer company Groupe Bull, fearful of leaking research secrets to the Japanese, the EC barred ICL from participation in some EC-wide joint research projects (Jackson 1994, pp. 108–109).

But the ICL case, despite the brief burst of controversy within Europe, did serve to demonstrate that Japanese FDI in European high technology has not attracted quite the same degree of 'psychological sensitivity' as Japanese FDI going into the United States. Indeed, in 1993 the now French–Italian company SGS-Thomson announced plans to collaborate with Sanyo Electric to develop large-scale integrated chips for audio-visual processing (*South China Morning Post*, 15 June 1993). Early in 1997 it was announced that the EU wanted to involve Hitachi, through its research links with Cambridge University, in a new EU-wide research project to develop new semiconductor memories under the ESPRIT programme (*Nihon Keizai Shimbun*, 18 January 1997).

One final aspect of Japanese FDI should be noted: the demonstration effect. In some EU countries, local competitors of the newly incoming Japanese producers have taken this Japanese advance as a challenge that requires them to improve their own product quality and productivity and to rethink the management of their own workforces (Turner 1987, p. 91).

EMERGING POLITICAL DIALOGUE

When Mrs Thatcher made her first prime ministerial visit to Japan in 1982 she observed that 'economic success brings power, and this in turn brings political obligations' (Japan Information Centre 1983, p. 3). However, Japan – and for that matter the EC/EU too – has had difficulty in becoming a 'normal' political actor in the international arena. Indeed, one of the paradoxes of Japan has been that this massive economic power has been such a faltering, and at times even immobile, force in international political and security affairs. Certainly the political dimensions of the Euro-Japanese relationship have always remained secondary to the commercial issues. Broader aspects of the political and security relations between Europe and the Asia Pacific region will be discussed in Chapter 8, but here a few specific points relating to the Euro-Japanese relationship need to be explored.

Undoubtedly, for both sides their own respective political and security relationships with the United States have been far more important and central than those with each other (Mendl 1984, pp. 140–142). Most Western Europeans nations are involved in the multilateral framework of the North Atlantic Treaty Organization (NATO), which closely tied the United States to the political and strategic survival of Western Europe during the Cold War confrontation with the Soviet Union. After defeat, and even after regaining independence, Japan was far more isolated, surrounded by hostile neighbours and with little choice but to fall back on the United States. The bilateral alliance has remained in force ever since. For more than 40 years, therefore, Japan's foreign relations have been dominated by its relationship with the United States and the need to manage it effectively. The net result of both the EC and Japan concentrating on the United States has been a skewed triangle, with the Euro-Japanese side by far the weakest.

In fact, until the early 1980s Japan was of little political importance to European policy-makers. Seen as too much of a surrogate or a 'protectorate' of the United States (Mendl 1984, p. 25), Japan was given marginal attention, even in the 1970s when it had already become a major economic power. Even though Japan had differed from the United States over recognizing China in 1972 and over oil supplies during the 1973–74 oil shock, 'in the main Japan relied upon and followed the US position' on international issues, whether in the Middle East or elsewhere (Saito 1990, p. 63). This apparent conformity with US policies meant that, in the words of British Foreign Secretary, Sir Geoffrey Howe, Japan remained 'pretty much of an after-thought' for the Europeans (Howe 1992, p. 127).

To the Japanese, the EC seemed to lack any cohesion and to be unable to 'address international political issues with a unified voice' (Murata 1987, p. 8). Moreover, the EC appeared uninterested in the regional political and security issues of most concern to Japan.

The G-7 economic summit mechanism after 1975 helped to bring Japanese and Europeans together in some discussion of political and security affairs. In the early years of the annual summit process economic problems had dominated, and both the French and the Japanese, though for slightly different reasons, had been reluctant to become involved in political discussions. The 1980 Venice G-7 summit, which took place against the background of the Soviet invasion of Afghanistan and the seizure of American hostages in Iran, proved a turning point; for the first time Japan took part in the 'formal process of Western political coordination' (Saito 1990, p. 68).

Moreover, there were occasional signs of the European members of the G-7 (West Germany, Britain, France and Italy) and Japan having common perceptions which differed from those of the Americans, such as their opposition to the strict US embargo on supplying strategic materials to the Soviet Union which arose at the 1981 and 1982 summits (Saito 1990, p. 101). The 1983 Williamsburg summit, which included the key concept of the 'indivisibility' of Western security (a phrase apparently suggested by the Japanese Prime Minister Nakasone Yasuhiro himself), marked yet another stage in the opening up of Japanese involvement in Western/European political and security issues. These steps in the early 1980s did show the Japanese becoming more interested in, and committed to, political and security issues of concern to the Western Europeans (and the Americans, of course). But they also show that the Japanese moved closer to the Europeans rather than the other way round; when the Japanese tried to raise the issue of the Vietnamese invasion of Kampuchea at the Venice summit none of the Europeans showed any real interest (Saito 1990, p. 68). Even the Williamsburg initiative was poorly followed up by the Japanese and poorly reciprocated by the Europeans. By the end of the decade, in 1988, when the Japanese had begun to propose the involvement of Europe in their 'new' pillars of foreign policy concept, an admittedly vaguely articulated concept, the situation had not really improved. Direct Euro-Japanese political discussions were stilted and the G-7 summits provided one of the few opportunities for real, albeit brief, political discussion.

At the EC level, regular foreign ministerial meetings between the *troika* of European foreign ministers and their Japanese counterparts began in 1983 but these meetings did not prove very helpful in strengthening the political relationship as they were, as one EC official later admitted, 'devoid of genuine dialogue' (Nuttall 1996, p. 107). A senior Japanese diplomat agreed, describing political consultations with the Europeans as tending 'to be nothing more than *tours d'horizon* of the political situation in the Soviet Union and the Third World' (Murata 1987, p. 9). Neither side was guiltless. The EC side was more concerned with discussing economic issues at these meetings, while the Japanese failed to take the EC seriously as a political force. Moreover, primarily as a result of domestic political problems within Japan, the annual EC–Japanese ministerial meetings were in suspension from 1986 to 1990. EC President Jacques Delors was correct when he complained to visiting Japanese Prime Minister Kaifu Toshiki about the lack of 'political visibility' in the relationship (*Agence Europe*, 29 March 1990). When he himself visited Tokyo in May 1991 he was the first Commission President to visit for five years.

But Delors did visit at a crucial time, because the final negotiations were being conducted for a joint declaration which was intended to enhance the whole range of Euro-Japanese relations, but in particular the political dimension. The July 1991 EC–Japan Declaration was derived from an initiative in late 1990 by the Japanese Foreign Ministry, whose senior officials noted the EC–US Declaration which had been signed that same autumn. The transatlantic declaration had been designed to renew that relationship in the light of the changes being wrought to international affairs by the transformation of Eastern Europe and the end of the Cold War. The Japanese, as some within the EC predicted, felt that it would also be opportune to redefine the Euro-Japanese relationship. In Japanese calculations, emphasizing potential areas of cooperation, particularly in political dialogue, would not only enhance the Japan–EC relationship but would also restore some of Japan's prestige, which had been battered in European as well as in American eyes by its failure to contribute other than financially to the 1990–91 Gulf crisis.

The negotiations for the Declaration were not easy because both sides suspected the other of having a hidden agenda. Some European politicians and officials felt that Japan, by stressing the need for political cooperation, was trying to divert attention from core economic issues. The Japanese, on the other hand, felt that some European member governments, most notably the French, were trying to impose managed trade as the price for political dialogue.

The result was, in the words of one EC official closely involved in the negotiations, a final text which was 'largely composed of verbal compromises' (Nuttall, 1996, p. 110). But it did at least set out new mechanisms of dialogue, primarily the annual meeting at the heads-of-government level (actually the Japanese Prime Minister with the Presidents of the European Council and the Commission), which would include within its remit political and 'international security' questions. Reviewing the situation one year later, the EC Council of Ministers concluded that there had been a 'qualitative leap' in the political dialogue as a result of the July 1991 Declaration (Council of Ministers Conclusions 1992, para. 3). This is clearly an exaggeration, although understandable in the atmosphere of the time, as the second heads-of-government summit, held less than a month later, proved to be 'lengthy, well-prepared and substantial' (Nuttall 1996, p. 110). The following year's meeting was less useful, the 1994 meeting was never held and the 1995 summit was prepared in a rush. A summit was held in Tokyo in September 1996 but, judging by one senior Japanese diplomat's assessment of its results, it was more concerned with microeconomic issues such as pig meat exports than substantial political dialogue (Tokinoya 1997, p. 1). The January 1998 summit was inevitably dominated by discussion of the financial crises sweeping Asia and so had little time for political issues (*Nihon Keizai Shimbun*, 13 January 1998).

While the summit-level meetings have not fulfilled their initial promise, officials on both sides feel that there has been a slow improvement in the political dialogue at lower levels. This is seen by the Japanese side as being due to a greater propensity on the EC side, since the 1991 Maastricht Treaty, to take coordinated foreign policy stances, although the Japanese remain sceptical about how far the EC/EU can really move towards a common foreign and security policy (CFSP) and the Europeans themselves continue to demonstrate how divergent their ideas and policies can be. But at least the Japanese now accept the European Commission as an institution with which it is important to have a dialogue. The EC, for its part, has noted Japan's emerging debate about its international role – symbolized by the passing of legislation in June 1992 to allow Japanese Self-Defence Forces to participate in UN peace-keeping operations and by Japan's push for a permanent seat on the UN Security Council – although the policy confusion and hesitancy associated with a series of coalition governments in Japan since 1993 have not helped push this debate to a real conclusion.

If the political dimension of Euro-Japanese relations can be described as weak, then the formal security linkages have been close to non-existent. But the end of the Cold War has altered the nature of the security debate both in Europe and in Asia. Apart from the new dialogue allowed for under the rubric of the EC–Japan Declaration, the Japanese began edging towards a relationship with both NATO and the Conference for Security and Cooperation in Europe (CSCE), which has now been transformed into the Organization for Security and Cooperation in Europe (OSCE).

Since 1990 Japanese diplomats have attended occasional NATO seminars and NATO officials have intermittently visited Japan (Drifte 1996, p. 83). More substantial, however, has been Japanese involvement with the CSCE. Japan had some difficulty with 'Basket I' of the CSCE, since accession could be interpreted as a recognition of the 'final settlement' of postwar borders between Japan and the Soviet Union/Russia. It was also cautious over Basket III, covering human rights, but clearly had an important role to play in Basket II, dealing with the economic and environmental aspects of Europe's renewal. Japan first floated the idea of observer status in 1990 (Freudenstein 1991, pp. 13–16). Even though it received a mixed reaction initially (Italy headed those European countries in favour and France led those opposing), Japan was able to attend the July 1992 CSCE conference in Helsinki as a 'guest' observer, after which arrangements were made for the Japanese to participate in CSCE meetings at which subjects of specific relevance to non-members were discussed. This was a result of the Japanese reassessment of the CSCE's worth – seeing it as a way of obtaining greater transparency of security, particularly as one of its members, Russia, stretched right to Japan's borders (Drifte 1996, p. 83) – coupled with a belated realization by some Western European governments that if Japan were to provide financial aid to Eastern Europe, as it had done through the G-24 mechanism and through aid efforts coordinated by the EC after the 1990 G-7 Summit, then it would also expect to be involved in political discussions.

Japan also attended the 1996 OSCE conference, but with the nature of Eastern European needs changing now that the first post-democratization and liberalization traumas have passed, the first flush of enthusiasm shown by the Japanese for involvement has disappeared and European expectations of Japanese (and, for that matter, South Korean) aid and assistance, too, have been tempered.

SPECIAL RELATIONSHIPS

The ability of EC/EU member governments to act alone in economic – and political – policy matters towards Japan in areas outside the EU's formal competence has allowed the development of 'friends' and, for that matter, 'foes' of Japan within the EU membership. Only a minority of EU member states have a rounded relationship with Japan.

Britain is undoubtedly the European country which has by far the most active and wide-ranging bilateral relationship with Japan. Although both the British and the Japanese (though more often the latter, surprisingly) tend to wax poetically about the long history of relations between the two countries, the alliance in the first two decades of this century and the alleged similarities in national character and geographical situation, the postwar period was by no means an easy one in Anglo-Japanese relations, especially when trade issues became complicated or memories of Japanese attrocities during the Pacific War were resuscitated. Indeed, one EC official commented that the British 'had historically been among the most anti-Japanese' of the European states (Nuttall 1996, p. 108). However, that attitude, at least at the governmental level, seemed to shift significantly during 1987–88, when after a particularly severe bout of trade friction and sabre-rattling, the Thatcher administration took a conscious decision to change tack. With several of the trade issues of most specific concern to Britain (such as whisky and TSE seats) reaching a degree of resolution, the British began to look more positively at Japan. Foreign Secretary Howe returned from a trip to Japan in early 1988 convinced, as he told his officials, that Japan should be drawn into a much wider range of consultations (interview, Foreign Office, January 1989).

In the name of industrial regeneration at home, therefore, Britain has become a stout defender of Japanese inward investors, as well as becoming the European country most active in trying to involve Japan in international affairs. In the process, the British move helped to shift the weight of opinion within the EC towards dialogue rather than confontation with Japan (Nuttall 1996, p. 108). However, that 'special relationship' has not always endeared either country to other EC members. Moreover, some British officials have come to feel that Britain had become by the mid 1990s too much of a 'soft touch' for the Japanese – that Britain was rarely receiving the commercial benefits to balance its efforts in the political sphere (interview, British Embassy, Tokyo, November 1994).

Despite being at the core of European reconstruction, France and Germany do not have such mature relationships with Japan. For four decades, because of historical associations (the wartime alliance from 1936 to 1945), the West German government tried hard to give the impression that there was not a special relationship with Japan. Although it has been argued that some industrial links, such as the tie-up between Fujitsu and Siemens, were motivated by loyalties dating back to the prewar period (Turner 1987, p. 101), this aspect has tended to be played down by both sides. This meant that, by and large, the Germans have not strived in the way that the British very consciously have done since the late 1980s to improve the relationship. The Japanese tended to see the Germans as harder-working and more efficient than the British, at least during Britain's strike-prone 1970s (Nester 1993, p. 200), but that did not imply any really close links. Nonetheless, the effect of German reunification, the gradual shift in the 'centre' of the enlarging EC/EU to Germany and the key voice of the Germans in European single currency negotiations have certainly raised the importance of Germany in Japanese eyes. Also, as Japan has begun searching for its role in the international community in the 1990s, Germany, a country which like Japan is burdened with constitutional and emotional sensitivities about overseas military action, has become an important point of reference (Bridges 1992, p. 239).

The French relationship with Japan is the closest to a love–hate relationship of any EU country. The Japanese 'have long been attracted to France as a treasure house of European culture' (Takeuchi 1991, p. 76); in the 19th century at least the French reciprocated with a fascination for the aesthetic aspects of Japanese culture which brought the word *japonaiserie* into wide European usage (Wilkinson 1990, pp. 110–118). In the postwar world, the emphasis has been much more conflictual, though tempered intermittently by the appeal to cultural interest. As shown above, the French have had a suspicion of Japanese industrial might which has tended to lead to a disparaging tone at times. Mrs Cresson's career as cabinet minister and then Prime Minister in 1989–91 was the epitome of this approach, but her successor, Pierre

Beregovoy, appreciated the counter-productive nature of such vehemence. The launch of the 1992 export promotion programme was the first sign of a change in attitude, although the conversion was never as profound as that undergone by the British. The emotional ups and downs have continued during the 1990s. When the French resumed nuclear testing in the Pacific in 1995, the Japanese Finance Minister, Takemura Masayoshi, described their actions as 'crazy', which in turn earned him a rebuke from the French Foreign Minister (*South China Morning Post*,13 September 1995). Although French President Jacques Chirac visited Japan in November 1996 with the intention of moving France closer to Japan – the two sides announced a package of cooperative measures called '20 actions for 2000' (*Asahi Evening News*, 21 November 1996) – the Japanese remain wary of France as the European country which could most easily turn 'anti-Japanese'.

For the other European countries, the intensity of relations is not sufficient to justify any thought of a special relationship. History plays a role in Portuguese and Dutch relations with Japan, although in the case of the Dutch this is a double-edged legacy as memories of traditional 'Dutch learning' and the special privileged access through Nagasaki during the closed centuries of Japanese history are invariably counter-balanced by more recent memories of Japanese wartime actions in the Dutch East Indies (now Indonesia). However, history by itself has not proved sufficient to sustain a prolonged special relationship for either of these countries.

The past Euro-Japanese relationship has appeared unbalanced in two respects: it has predominantly been based on economic interactions, with little political or cultural interchange, and, even within that economic relationship, the trade and investment surpluses have long been in Japan's favour. Trade friction acted as a catalyst in bringing Japan and Western Europe together, but the tension was not always creative. The EU and Japan can both be seen as economic powers searching for a wider role in the international community. This means that in the post-Cold War world political contacts have been developing and the relationship is markedly broader than in the 1980s but the traditional emphasis on commercial issues has nonetheless remained paramount.

In the second half of the 1990s, indeed, there has been a tendency for the relationship to mark time. The sluggishness of the Japanese economy (and the seemingly inordinate effort necessary for European companies to access it), the weak and preoccupied political leadership of Japan, the attractions of emerging and faster-growing markets elsewhere in Asia and the EU's rethinking of its overall approach to Asia (which almost by default meant a relative down-grading of interest in Japan) have all contributed to the 'by-passing' of

Japan. The phenomenon of 'by-passing', recently noted in relation to American investment attitudes towards Japan (Calder 1996a, pp. 28–29) is well on the way to becoming a European characteristic in a broader sense. By 'by-passing' is meant the feeling that the Japanese market is so hard to crack, and so expensive to operate in, that it would be more profitable either to give up or miss out Japan and move elsewhere in the region. Changing business perceptions have been followed by politicians and policy-makers. Japan's image in the Asia Pacific region and in Europe has suffered further through its perceived failure to 'come out to bat for everyone' during the Asian financial crisis, to use the words of Hong Kong's Chief Executive, Tung Chee-Hwa (1998). By contrast, China survived the early months of the Asian financial crisis with its status enhanced and its stability praised. This means that not just economically but politically, too, there is now greater interest in Europe in interacting with China than before. Efforts to stimulate greater Euro-Japanese contact and convergence, therefore, may well be running out of steam.

4. The Asian tigers

All along the river, skyscrapers
  have ousted the old tenement blocks.
  They rise higher each year,
  an imposing creed of perfection.

('The Old Timers' by Boey Kim Cheng, 1992)

The problem for Europe has been that Japan has not been alone. Following in its wake have been first the NIEs, then those countries such as Malaysia and Thailand which have earned themselves the title of proto-NIEs, and then a third generation which includes not just China and Indonesia but potentially Vietnam and even Burma. The seemingly never-ending conveyor belt of dynamic Asian economies did suffer some severe, though not totally destructive, jolts from mid 1997, but in the process created the beginnings of a new challenge, both for the economies of the region and for the Europeans as well.

As the Japanese economy began to mature and slow down in the second half of the 1970s and particularly in the first half of the 1980s, the baton of the fastest-growing economy in the region was passed to a group of four contenders, the NIEs – Hong Kong, South Korea, Singapore and Taiwan – which jostled with each other to be at the head. From 1965 to 1980 the Asian NIEs averaged GNP growth rates which ranged from 8.6 per cent for Hong Kong to 10 per cent for Singapore. Even with a slight slowing down in the 1980s, the lowest rate of 6.6 per cent, recorded by Singapore in the 1980–91 period, was still more than double the world average growth rate and well ahead of the Japanese rate (Yang 1994, pp. 4–5). From 1986 to 1988 South Korea figured as the world's fastest-growing economy, with a growth rate of around 12 per cent for three consecutive years (Shibusawa, Ahmad and Bridges 1992, p. 66).

The challenge for Europe was that in succession to Japan, which was already a well-developed economy before it began to export significantly to Europe, for the first time there was a sharp increase in manufactured imports from a number of developing countries. Indeed, export-led growth, through making the most of changing comparative advantages in the international system, has been the hallmark of these four 'tigers' or 'little dragons'. Hong Kong had always been outward-oriented, but it was not until the 1960s that the other three countries began to give priority to export-oriented strategies based on manufactured goods. Their share of world trade grew from 2 per cent in the mid 1960s to 11 per cent in 1987, when their share was almost exactly the same as Japan's. Crucially for the purposes of this study, Western Europe became an important market for these four nations in the same way that it had earlier become for Japan.

THE ARRIVAL OF THE NIEs

Industrialization is essential for economic growth in most countries (Riedel 1988, p. 6). In the Asia Pacific region only one country, Brunei, has been able to achieve a high level of per capita income without industrializing in the usual sense of the word, and that is because of its small population and rich oil and gas resources. All the other countries, even those with significant agricultural sectors, have been travelling down the road of industrialization. Some are, of course, further down it than others. Arguably, in terms of income derived from industry, especially manufacturing, the four Asian NIEs 'appear to have nearly completed the journey' (Riedel 1988, p. 6) or, to put it another way, they are close to graduation from the class of NIEs.

There is no doubt that for all four NIEs political survival, at least in the early years, was closely tied to economic development. It is a curious coincidence that all four have been geographically and politically isolated: they could thus count on popular support in their struggle to survive as entities. Singapore is a predominantly Chinese city-state floating in a sea of Malays: it has two large 'Malay' bumiputra-dominated neighbours, Indonesia and Malaysia (Shibusawa, Ahmad and Bridges, 1992 p. 67). Hong Kong, to use one long-term resident's memorable phrase, was a 'borrowed place living on borrowed time' (Hughes 1976, p. 13), always aware of the tremendous weight of China so close at hand. Taiwan, although itself claiming to rule all China, was ever conscious of the threat, military and ideological, from the mainland. South Korea, another part-country, had fought an internecine war with its erratic northern neighbour and remained fearful of a renewed challenge. Whether or not the nearby external 'threat' was as real as perceived, it does seem to have engendered both a sense of competition and a consensus that development was essential to regime, and even state, survival.

The role of government remains a controversial factor, but in at least three of the NIEs concrete economic performance became the touchstone of political legitimacy and national progress. Hong Kong has often been described as a classic *laissez-faire* economy, but in reality there has been a limited degree of governmental involvement following a policy which has aptly been called 'positive non-interventionism'; the government acts as facilitator. In the other three NIEs, however, governmental intervention has been far more overt. Successive governments have endeavoured to pick winners not only through a commitment to developmental planning but also through close relations with industry. Costly mistakes were made in both South Korea and Singapore in the 1970s, but the administrative and technocratic elites had an impressive record in designing economic policies, at least through into the mid 1990s. To take but one example from their high-technology industrialization programmes, by 1995 South Korea and Taiwan had become the third and fourth largest producers of semiconductors, ahead of European producers such as Germany (Mathews 1996, p. 1).

All four NIEs are densely populated and poorly endowed with natural resources. As a result, they have to rely not only on imported raw materials but also on making the best use of their human resources. Education, therefore, has been an important tool in creating efficient and well-equipped labour forces.

Japan has acted as both a model and a mentor to the four NIEs – to a greater extent than nationals of those countries might wish to admit but to a lesser extent than outside observers sometimes believe. Japan is either the first or second largest source of both imports and FDI for all the NIEs. Its economic aid to the NIEs has decreased to its lowest level, but technology transfer has in part helped to compensate. The high degree of inter-linkage with Japan has, however, created a certain amount of ambivalence among the NIEs towards Japan, not least where feelings are coloured by historical memories (most obviously in the South Korean case). The 'Japan factor' has also played a role in the NIEs' relations with Europe, as will be seen below.

Hong Kong adopted an export strategy for light manufactured goods in the early 1950s, once its historical entrepot role for China had been disrupted by the communist takeover of the mainland and the subsequent UN trade embargo (Ho 1992, p. 55). Chinese businessmen and skilled workers, fleeing from Shanghai in particular, combined with the British and Chinese merchant houses of Hong Kong to channel the manufactured products of hundreds of small producers into external markets (Rhee 1994, pp. 54–55). Hong Kong's early export successes were based on textiles and clothing, electrical goods and plastics. But from the late 1970s increased competition in overseas markets, more stringent quota restrictions on textiles and garments, and rising labour costs led to increasing moves up market. Hong Kong has, however, remained one of the world's largest exporters of clothing because it has been able to utilize low-cost labour across the border in southern China for its labour-intensive activities, leaving high-fashion and high value-added operations within Hong Kong (Chen and Li 1994, p. 107). By the late 1980s the number of workers directly employed in manufacturing, much of it 'outward-processing' in south China by Hong Kong companies, was larger than for Hong Kong's own workforce in the manufacturing sector. Undoubtedly, the ability of Hong Kong entrepreneurs to tap into the Chinese market has made 'the China factor ... the single most important factor underlying Hong Kong's robust economic growth in the 1980s' (Ho and Kueh 1993, p. 349). This conclusion is no less valid for the 1990s, not least as the resilience of the Chinese market helped to support Hong Kong while other regional economies suffered in the second half of 1997. By early 1998, however, Hong Kong, too, was beginning to suffer, recording –2 per cent growth in the first quarter.

During its period of British colonial rule, Singapore, like Hong Kong, operated as a centre for entrepot trade and, apart from a brief period of flirtation with an import-substitution strategy in the late 1950s, it has maintained its role as a city-state open to the outside world and as a commercial centre for Southeast Asia. From the mid 1960s Singapore vigorously pursued a policy of attracting foreign capital to promote industrialization, so that by 1985 foreign multinationals accounted for 70 per cent of manufactured output and 82 per cent of exports. Worried about labour shortages, from the 1970s the Singapore government tried to upgrade the country's industrial structure; if anything, it tried to do it too fast, with a resulting hiccup in 1985 when negative growth was recorded (Shibusawa, Ahmad and Bridges 1992, pp. 82–83). Growth and competitiveness were soon restored and Singapore has bloomed into a high-tech and service-oriented economy, but one which seems to be over-regulated and averse to risk-taking. Indeed, creating a real Singaporean entrepreneurial culture remains one of the major challenges for Singapore in the 1990s (Regnier 1993, p. 312). Like Hong Kong, Singapore initially seemed relatively immune to the financial crises afflicting its neighbours in 1997, but its close linkages with Malaysia, and especially with the much-troubled Indonesia, inevitably sent jitters through its stock market from time to time and may well contribute to reduced growth in 1998, though not to the same extent as in Hong Kong.

South Korea and Taiwan had both been 'agricultural appendages' of Japan under Japanese colonial rule in the first half of the 20th century and then involved in military confontations with North Korea and China respectively (Haggard 1988, pp. 266–267). Both initiated outward-oriented development strategies in the early 1960s. In South Korea an authoritarian–bureaucratic style of government was committed to economic growth and development, planning, nurturing and encouraging the huge conglomerates (*chaebols*) to expand their manufacturing capabilities. South Korea emphasized light, labour-intensive industries first, followed by a move into some heavy industries, with mixed results (Clifford 1994, pp. 101–112). But in the 1980s it began to make real inroads into the global consumer electronics goods market: Korean manufacturers did not start exporting microwave ovens until 1980, yet by 1987 they were the world's largest exporters, ahead of even the Japanese

(Bridges 1993, p. 92). In the 1990s the *chaebols* continued to expand globally, so much so that Samsung became one of the world's 20 largest companies, but in the process they sowed the seeds of their own later financial difficulties. In 1996 South Korea was rewarded with entry into the OECD. Yet within a year of becoming only the second Asian country (after Japan three decades earlier) to join this exclusive club of rich countries, it was forced by its mounting short-term debt crisis to go on bended knee to the IMF to receive the largest ever financial bailout ($57 billion) in that organization's history (*Korea Newsworld*, December 1997). 1998 therefore promised to be a year of 'bone-carving' hard times for the Korean economy, with mounting unemployment and negative growth (–3.8 per cent in the first quarter of 1998), but with the prospect that if the country took the bitter medicine properly under its new president it could bounce back renewed and more competitive by the end of the decade.

Taiwan, like Hong Kong, benefited from Chinese entrepreneurs fleeing the mainland, but like South Korea it switched in the mid 1960s from import substitution to an export-oriented industrialization strategy based on light manufactured goods. But Taiwan differed from South Korea in its greater reliance on inward FDI (especially in favoured export-processing zones), more direct government ownership of enterprises and the greater importance of small and medium-sized companies (with almost no large conglomerates). The two oil shocks of the 1970s hit Taiwan hard, but it recovered through a new emphasis in industrial strategy on high-technology and skill-intensive activities which was consolidated in the 1990s with a massive six-year programme aimed at developing key technologies for emerging industries and with efforts to boost the under-developed service sector (Ferdinand 1996, pp. 41–57). As its foreign currency reserves continued to mount steadily during the 1990s, putting it second only to Japan in the world, Taiwan proved able to resist the commercial-confidence-sapping threats of Chinese military manoeuvres in the spring of 1996 and the financial contagion sweeping much of the Asia Pacific region in the second half of 1997.

If, as can be seen from even the brief survey above, the 1980s saw a marked tendency for the NIEs to move into more sophisticated manufactured products for export, then in the 1990s we can also detect that the NIEs' economies have been undergoing further shifts in industrial structure. Indeed, for all four one can say that they are in transition to a service economy, although this process is more advanced in Hong Kong than in any of the other three. One senior UN trade adviser has even argued that rather than concentrating on the newly industrializing aspects of these economies, they would better be described as 'new service economies' (von Kirkbach 1990, p. 276). These structural shifts have clearly impacted on the nature of the Europe–NIE economic relationship.

EUROPE'S ENCOUNTER WITH THE NIEs

The competitive elements of the EC–NIE economic relationship have had close parallels with the EC–Japanese relationship, at least in the early decades of interaction. There have been three common defining characteristics: large imbalances within a relatively small overall trade relationship; sectoral concentration and rapid penetration of imports from the NIEs; and, in the case of Taiwan and South Korea at least, markets difficult to penetrate for European exporters. A fourth characteristic, increasing FDI flows from the NIEs to Europe, has been comparatively recent in evolving to any serious level.

European trade with the four NIEs has grown steadily since the 1960s. The various enlargements of the EC and the absence of Taiwanese data from international statistical sources make rigorous comparison across decades difficult, but certain broad trends can be identified from those figures available from the IMF and the Taiwanese government. As shown in Table 4.1, EC imports from the four NIEs grew from $13.4 billion in 1980 to $40.8 billion in 1990. EC exports to the four NIEs grew from $8.7 billion in 1980 to $31.4 billion in 1990. This means that the EC's overall trade deficit with these four countries grew from $4.7 billion in 1980 to $9.4 billion in 1990.

These overall figures, however, mask some important differences in EC trade with the individual NIEs. At the early stage of trading with Europe, it was Hong Kong which was the most vigorous exporter, particularly of tex-

Table 4.1   EC/EU trade with the NIEs (US $millions)

EC/EU with	Hong Kong		South Korea		Singapore		Taiwan	
	Import	Export	Import	Export	Import	Export	Import	Export
1980	5312	3047	2915	1343	2039	2440	3121	1861
1985	3984	3470	2637	2109	1777	2878	3169	1740
1990	10542	8860	9430	8268	7059	7571	13044	6724
1991	11286	9662	10881	9512	7598	7516	15223	7385
1992	11026	11296	10633	8705	8302	8523	15569	8675
1993	11841	13876	10148	9610	9049	9600	14046	9498
1994	11326	16641	11198	12859	11094	11632	14307	10987
1995	13429	20852	14934	16200	13136	13829	16657	13394
1996	15099	22067	14090	18247	14375	15800	17800	12552

Note: The figures for Taiwan's trade in 1980 are with 'Europe' not with the EC.

Sources: IMF, *Direction of Trade Statistics Yearbook*, 1987 and 1997 editions (Washington: 1987 and 1997); Council for Economic Planning and Development, *Taiwan Statistical Data Book 1997* (Taipei: 1997).

tiles. But during the 1970s the other three NIEs began to catch up, and in the late 1980s Taiwan overtook Hong Kong to become the leading exporter to the EC from within this group. In the early 1990s, as shown in Table 4.1, Hong Kong's exports to the EC levelled off, so that South Korea and Singapore have been either very close to overtaking or have even briefly overtaken it in the mid 1990s.

Although these four economies are often lumped together as one group by European observers, they can better be sub-divided into two pairs: the geographically small, comparatively open 'city-state' economies of Hong Kong and Singapore, and the larger, but traditionally more protected, economies of South Korea and Taiwan. By considering them in this way, a few basic characteristics of their trading and investment interactions with the EC/EU can be highlighted.

Hong Kong and Singapore

The British colonial connection – and associated with it the Commonwealth preference system – meant that when Hong Kong began exporting light manufactures, especially cotton textiles, to Europe in the 1950s, Britain was the obvious target market. Between 1953 and 1958, for example, the Hong Kong share of the British market for grey-cloth rose from 1 per cent to 34 per cent (Lin and Mok 1980, pp. 27–28). The growth in textile exports to Britain, however, was limited as early as 1959 when, under what became called the 'Lancashire pact', Hong Kong's exports of garments and piece goods were restricted to an annual total of 164 million yards (Chen and Li 1994, pp. 108, 130). This bilateral agreement was subsequently widened in coverage and extended three times by 1974, by which time Britain had entered the EC. In 1961 Hong Kong had to agree to a GATT long-term cotton textile agreement, which set quotas for textile exports to the EC (Chen and Li 1994, p. 108). In 1974 the Europeans supported the Americans in replacing this agreement by the wider-ranging Multi-Fibre Arrangement (MFA), which covered both cotton and non-cotton textiles and has survived through several extensions and re-negotiations, with progressive tightening of its controls on each occasion. It was ironic that, since Hong Kong was not at that time a member of GATT, it was Britain that acceded to the MFA on its behalf (Lin and Mok 1980, p. 49). Hong Kong was of course not only the NIE to have its exports to the EC adversely affected by the MFA.

British accession to the EC undoubtedly encouraged Hong Kong exporters to think in broader terms about the European market. Prior to that West Germany had been the only other significant European export market, but even then well behind Britain; figures for the early 1960s show Britain receiving around 20 per cent of Hong Kong's total domestic exports, with

West Germany lagging behind with less than 4 per cent (Ho and Kueh 1993, p. 342). Nonetheless, reflecting the phenomenon that Hong Kong's exports have generally been concentrated in only a few major markets, Britain and West Germany remained key markets for Hong Kong's domestic exports through into the 1980s, although it should be noted that the British share steadily declined as the West German share grew slightly, so that by the early 1980s their market shares were roughly level (Chen and Li 1994, p. 113). However, in 1984 China overtook both Britain and West Germany to become Hong Kong's second largest export market (after the United States). Textiles continued to predominate in the manufactured exports to Europe through the 1970s, followed by transistor radios and toys, but since the 1980s, while textiles and clothing have remained important, electronic products, televisions and computer equipment have become much greater in importance. In May 1998 Hong Kong was phased out of the EU's Generalized System of Preferences (GSP) tariff scheme, but the impact was expected to be limited because, reflecting the changing nature of its exports to the EU, the range of Hong Kong's exports still eligible for GSP was already quite limited (*South China Morning Post*, 3 January 1998).

Hong Kong trade statistics are complicated by the fact that the adoption of open-door economic policies in China in the late 1970s meant a dramatic rise in re-exports; by 1988, indeed, the volume of re-exports had exceeded that of domestic exports (Ho and Kueh 1993, p. 340). Using IMF data, which do not differentiate between exports and re-exports, it can be seen that exports to the EC actually levelled off at around the $4 billion mark in the first half of the 1980s, before beginning to grow steadily again in the second half of the 1980s. Another plateau, this time around the $11 billion level, does seem to have been reached in the early 1990s, until 1995 when exports again began to take off reaching $15.1 billion in 1996.

However, Hong Kong has continued to import European goods steadily, so that its trade surplus with the EC as a whole has fluctuated around the $1 billion level from the early 1980s. Remarkably, however, from 1992 Hong Kong has actually been suffering from a steadily growing deficit situation with the EU. As shown in Table 4.1, this deficit began to widen significantly from 1993, to reach nearly $7 billion by 1996. This sudden growth in the deficit can be accounted for by the sucking-in of European goods eventually destined for re-export to the booming Chinese market, especially after Deng Xiaoping's southern tour in 1992 sparked off a new high-growth surge in China. As with exports, Britain and West Germany have been the two largest sources of imports from Europe and, once again like exports, the British share has been steadily declining so that in the 1990s it is roughly level with the German share. It should be noted that since the second half of the 1980s the Italians have been making inroads into the Hong Kong market, particularly with high-fashion clothing and footwear, so that they are now not far behind the British and Germans in terms of Hong Kong import market share (Ho and Kueh 1993, p. 343). However, all three are small players compared with China, Japan, Taiwan and the United States as suppliers of Hong Kong's imports.

Singapore's highly developed economy, like Hong Kong's, combines elements of an outward-oriented manufacturing sector and an international service sector, although the decline in the contribution of manufacturing to domestic growth so noticeable in Hong Kong since the early 1980s is less pronounced in the case of Singapore. Singapore has indeed continued to welcome European manufacturing investment as part of its overall belief in maintaining manufacturing competitiveness. Despite the strong early trading links with the former colonial power, Britain, EC–Singaporean trade levels, at least from the late 1980s, have consistently lagged behind the levels of EC trade with the other NIEs (see Table 4.1). Singaporean exports to the EC stagnated around the $2 billion level for most of the first half of the 1980s, but performed better in the second half of the decade, to reach $7 billion by 1990, and they continued to show steady growth in the mid 1990s, reaching $14.3 billion in 1996. Although Singapore acts as a conduit for exporting some agricultural products sourced from elsewhere in Southeast Asia through to the European market (and, as a result, has become embroiled in disputes over anti-import campaigns and restrictions from EU member countries (Ng and Yang 1994, p. 185)), electronic products have proved to be the mainstay of Singaporean exports to the EU. Like Hong Kong, Singapore was phased out of the EU's GSP scheme in 1998, but again the impact is expected to be limited.

However, Singapore has persistently run an overall trade deficit and its trade with the EU is no exception. But it has been a narrow trade deficit, for since the early 1980s it has rarely exceeded $1 billion and then has been only marginally above that level (in one year (1991) Singapore actually recorded a minute surplus of $82 million).

Given the extremely open nature of these two economies, the EC/EU has had few problems with market access in general. Disputes have tended to be confined to highly specific product issues, such as French protests in 1994 over Hong Kong's revised alcohol taxes (*South China Morning Post*, 20 April 1994). However, both Hong Kong and Singapore have been involved in disputes with individual EC countries or the EC itself over export surges or concentration. In the early decades, this meant attempts by the EC to limit textiles, clothing and toy export surges. More recently, electronic goods have been the focus of concern of EC industries. Singapore's exports of colour televisions have, for example, been subject to restrictions since the early 1980s (Ng and Yang 1994, p. 185).

South Korea and Taiwan

Neither South Korea nor Taiwan had the same historical links with Europe that Hong Kong and Singapore had, and in part this hindered the early development of trade ties. When South Korea began its industrialization in the early 1960s, it was closely tied to the US and Japanese economies. Trade with Europe was very limited. Indeed, the South Korean export surge to the EC did not really begin until the mid 1980s, after which a considerable increase in exports occurred. 1988's total exports to the EC of $8.8 billion were more than triple those of 1985. But in the early 1990s exports levelled off and hovered around the $9–10 billion mark, before begining to rise again in 1994, reaching $14.1 billion in 1996.

However, contrary to popular perceptions South Korea had not consistently maintained a Japanese-style large surplus with the EC. The South Korean trade surplus hovered around the $1 billion level for most of the first half of the 1980s and rose to $3 billion in 1988, but has subsequently declined significantly and since the early 1990s South Korea has even been in deficit with the EC. Inevitably, as has been the case in EC–Japanese disputes, the exact amounts, and therefore the exact year when this change occurred, are disputed, but according to IMF figures (see Table 4.1), the switch-over to an EC/EU surplus occurred in 1994 and the surplus was as high as $4.1 billion by 1996. Within the EC, (West) Germany, Britain and France have been South Korea's main trading partners, between them accounting for over 60 per cent of the EC's imports from, and exports to, South Korea.

Well into the 1980s over half the EC's imports from South Korea consisted of textiles and footwear, but subsequently significant categories have included ships, steel, consumer electronics, electrical machinery, office machinery and cars. The EU supplies South Korea mainly with machinery and chemical products.

The industrializing Taiwanese economy, like that of South Korea, had developed deep economic links with the US and Japanese economies, although these were tempered to some extent after the diplomatic 'de-recognition' of Taiwan by both countries in the 1970s. Europe was therefore a limited trading partner until the 1980s (Chiu 1993, pp. 195–198). In 1975 total bilateral trade was still under $2 billion and even in the first half of the 1980s it hovered around the $5 billion level. However, in much the same way as South Korean exports to the EC surged in the 1987–88 period, so too did Taiwanese exports. In part this new Taiwanese attention to Europe was a result of increasing difficulties with the United States, as the trade surplus and intellectual property law violations became more politicized than they had been in the past (Ferdinand 1996, pp. 45–46). But in part it was also a response to what was seen as the first break in the previous European attitude of indifference towards Taiwan, when a 1985 European Parliament resolution stressed the advantages of Euro-Taiwanese trade. The Taiwanese responded by dubbing 1986 as the 'year of trade with Europe' (Hsieh 1996, pp. 90–91), although the marked growth in trade did not really begin until the following year.

The difference with South Korea came in the early 1990s, when Taiwanese exports to Europe did not tail off to the same degree as South Korea's. Taiwanese exports to the EC, as shown in Table 4.1, therefore grew from $3 billion in 1985 to $13 billion in 1990 and over $15 billion in 1991 and 1992. After a slight slowdown in the next two years, exports rose again, to reach $17.8 billion in 1996. A four-year working plan to boost commercial ties with Europe seems to have played a role and the Taiwanese government in fact extended this plan twice, in 1993 and 1997 (*China Post*, 19 April 1997). Since 1971, when it first achieved an overall trade surplus, Taiwan has managed to maintain a trade surplus with the EC every year with the exception of 1974–75 (Shih 1990, p. 15). Since EC exports to Taiwan were unable to keep pace with the rapid growth in Taiwanese exports to the EC in the late 1980s, the Taiwanese trade surplus, which had been in the $1–2 billion range in the first half of the 1980s, rose steadily to reach $7.8 billion in 1991. Better EC export performance since then has narrowed the surplus, but in 1996 it was still more than $5 billion.

Manufactured products have been overwhelmingly dominant in trade in both directions between the EC and Taiwan. This has meant that trade relations have been more competitive than complementary (Shih 1990, p. 19). Consequently, although total trade between the EC and both South Korea and Taiwan has increased significantly since the mid 1980s, trade relations have become increasingly politicized. A plethora of sectoral disputes, bilateral export restraints, piecemeal restrictions and anti-dumping actions have emerged. Repeating earlier concerns about Japanese export tendencies, European producers in the 1980s put pressure on their national governments and the EC to impose some degree of control on imports from the NIEs, especially Taiwan and South Korea. For example, over the 1983–87 period the South Korean share of the EC market in small-screen colour televisions rose from 0 to 12 per cent, while the EC producers' share dropped by 15 per cent to 46 per cent; they complained, and the EC Commission agreed, that such rapidly increasing imports 'at dumping prices caused huge harm to the Community industry' (*Agence Europe*, 28 October 1989). The EC has responded by concluding sectoral arrangements to cover certain products, deemed 'sensitive', which face highly competitive South Korean and Taiwanese products. For example, by 1990, 30 different VER agreements were in place for South Korean products (Lee 1990, p. 61). Anti-dumping actions have been taken against Korean colour televisions, VCRs, compact-disc players, microwave ovens, fax machines, and video and audio tapes. In an unprecedented and unlikely to be repeated move in the service sector, in 1988 Hyundai Marine's shipping services on the Europe–Australia container route were accused of being a form of dumping (Bridges 1990, p. 73).

In the case of South Korea a number of export products have regularly come up in negotiations with the EC. Textiles have been governed by the MFA, which has been negotiated at the EC level and then divided into national quotas for sensitive products. From 1978, as part of the EC's general steel policy, VERs have been negotiated with Korean steel producers, with limits becoming more strictly enforced progressively through the 1980s. In footwear, where Italian producers have been vocal, and in ship-building, the EC has consistently pushed for restraint by Korean industry.

Several of the EC actions against South Korean products, especially where anti-dumping suits have been instituted, have been simultaneous with action against Taiwanese products. The Taiwanese always feel themselves to be at a disadvantage when negotiating with the Europeans in that, unlike South Korea, Taiwan since the early 1970s has not had diplomatic relations with any EC member country. In fact, the only European state still recognizing Taiwan is the Vatican. Again unlike South Korea, neither does it have an official delegation to the EU in Brussels nor an EU office on its territory. Taiwan has been allowed to maintain trade offices, with quasi-diplomatic functions, in most of the EU member countries, but only under 'a somewhat bewildering variety of names' (Chiu 1993, p. 203), such as the Dr Sun Yat-Sen Centre in Luxembourg, the Institute of Chinese Culture in Austria and, at least initially, the Free Chinese Centre in Britain, now called Taipei Representative Office. One consequence of this lack of formal diplomatic recognition is that Taiwan has never been eligible for the GSP concessions offered to imports from developing countries (Shih 1990, p. 37). Furthermore, although its application to join the World Trade Organization (WTO) has been pending for many years (entry is tacitly accepted to be contingent on China's entry into the Organization), Taiwan is not a member of international economic organizations such as GATT, the IMF and the World Bank, where it could negotiate over economic issues with the Europeans in a multilateral context.

This lack of diplomatic clout has tended to make Taiwanese exporters feel vulnerable when their exporting practices bring them into conflict with the EC/EU or its member states. The sectors or products where the Taiwanese have come into conflict with the EC, led by textiles, footwear and consumer electronics, have some parallels with the South Korean experience. For example, EC investigations into South Korean and Taiwanese footwear took place at the same time in 1988, as Taiwanese footwear exports to the EC rocketed up from 63 million pairs in 1985 to 106 million pairs in 1987. Taiwanese footwear exports had already peaked and begun to decline by the time the investigation began, so in 1990 the Taiwanese producers agreed to a VER of only 45 million pairs for that year (*Agence Europe*, 28 June 1990). One Taiwanese survey in 1990 picked up a wide range of import quotas on Taiwanese products; some at the EC-wide level, such as on textiles and canned mushrooms, and others by individual countries, such as colour televisions by Britain, France and Greece, umbrellas by Germany and Italy, and cutlery by Denmark (Shih 1990, pp. 37–38). In general, however, Taiwanese products do seem to be spread over a wider range and therefore are less apparently guided by the 'laser beam' approach often associated with South Korean export surges.

Although the maritime transport case noted above specifically singled out South Korea in an unusual manner, in general the actions taken by the EC against imports from the NIEs have been either strongly reminiscent of similar action taken against Japanese imports in the 1970s, such as against textiles, or actually in tandem with actions being taken contemporaneously against Japanese products, such as over VCRs or compact-disc players in the late 1980s and early 1990s. Therefore, at least since the late 1970s, some of the NIEs have been 'sucked into such trade disputes where the primary trading problem was seen to be Japan's export success' (Turner 1982, p. 138). In part, this reflected a tendency among the Europeans to see the NIEs as clones of Japan, with South Korea in particular cast in the image of a 'second Japan'. South Korea and Taiwan were therefore guilty by association. In part, it also represented a feeling that constraints on Japan's export performance would be 'nullified' unless this new wave of NIEs was also brought under restraint (Turner 1982, p. 139). The heightened awareness of NIE imports because of the European experience with Japan, led to some examples of an almost knee-jerk reaction, even before the NIEs had become serious exporters to the EC. For example, in January 1983, less than a year after the Hyundai group started selling cars in Britain, the EC, at British instigation, imposed an import charge on all cars sold after an initial 10,000 a year had been imported, even though this target level was not even reached until 1987 and in 1988 the Korean share of the EC car market was barely 0.2 per cent (Bridges 1990, p. 71). Even after steady growth in Korean car exports to the EC during the 1990s, by 1995 the Korean car companies held only 1.4 per cent of the total EU market (*Korea Herald*, 10 May 1996). Nonetheless, the EU is South Korea's largest export market for cars.

The above discussion has focused on European responses to imports from South Korea and Taiwan, but from the second half of the 1980s there has also been growing emphasis on the other side of the trade equation: opening up the fairly heavily protected South Korean and Taiwanese markets. Typical of European views was British Chancellor of the Exchequer Nigel Lawson's complaint at a May 1988 OECD ministerial meeting about South Korea's 'very controlled

and un-open' economy (*Korea Herald*, 20 May 1988). Progress has been made
by the Koreans in opening up their market, specifically by tariff reduction, in
adhering to international intellectual property regulations, and in reforming and
liberalizing the financial market. However, much as has been the case with
Japan, while the tariff barriers were being progressively though not totally
reduced, the Europeans have found themselves faced with a range of non-tariff
barriers. One example which has continued to upset the Europeans throughout
the 1990s, as the Koreans tried to bring their growing overall trade deficit under
control, has been the covertly government-inspired campaign against 'con-
spicuous consumption'. A visiting British Foreign Office minister, Lord
Caithness, was moved to complain about the 'anti-imports flavour' of this
frugality campaign as early as 1991 (Caithness, 1991, p. 34). In frustration, in
1997 EU delegates raised the frugality campaign at several WTO meetings and
called on the Korean government to express a firm stance against it (*Korea
Herald*, 26 April 1997), but the anti-import mood of the Korean people has, if
anything, been reinforced by the financial collapse of late 1997.

    Not unconnected with this campaign have been European complaints about
access for luxury cars and liquors, especially whisky. German car producers
have been complaining that while South Korea exported 160,000 cars to the
EU in 1995, the EU sold only 7000 inside South Korea (*Korea Herald*, 10
May 1996); the first half of 1997 actually saw a decline of one-third in
European car sales to Korea (*Korea Herald*, 11 October 1997). The Koreans
say this poor performance is due to the excessive cost of European cars. The
Europeans, who in the autumn of 1997 began to consider filing a complaint to
the WTO, argued that the cause was Korea's discriminatory tax and customs
regimes. Whisky and brandy have been subject to a massive 130 per cent
import tax, and after a frustrating series of negotiations over many years, the
EU threatened to take the Koreans to the WTO in early 1997. This prompted
the Koreans to consider raising taxes on its domestic spirit, *soju*, and lower-
ing taxes on imported whisky and brandy (*Korea Herald*, 18 March, 11 April
1997). While the IMF-imposed economic reform package does require South
Korea to make drastic improvements in its market access provisions, the
benefits of new measures in that direction are likely to be more than outweighed in 1998 by the drop in purchasing power and the heightened mood
of austerity among the population.

    Intellectual property rights (IPRs) are one example of an economic issue
which became politicized in the 1980s and which the Europeans took as a test
case of South Korean sincerity about fair market-opening. The Europeans
were upset by the Korean decision in 1987 during bilateral IPR negotiations
with the United States over South Korean accession to international patent
conventions to grant retrospective privileges to US companies only. When the
South Koreans proved unwilling to extend similar provisions to the Europeans,

the EC responded by suspending GSP benefits for South Korea from May 1988. Despite South Korean officials privately admitting the counter-productive nature of the lop-sided concessions to the Americans, domestic political constraints in the newly democratized political climate meant that not until September 1991 did the Koreans finally agree to equalize IPR treatment for pharmaceuticals (a key area for European producers), farm chemicals and several other sectors. South Korea's GSP status was then reinstated (*Korea Times*, 13 November 1992). The Europeans have continued to complain, however, about pirating and forgery of European products, especially fashion goods (*Agence Europe*, 26 May 1993).

However, despite remaining problems such as market access and export surges, by the middle of the 1990s the Europeans were beginning to feel that some progress was being made in commercial relations with South Korea. European Commission Vice-President Sir Leon Brittan spoke about the 'favourable evolution of bilateral trade and economic relations' (*Agence Europe*, 26 May 1993). As a result, when the South Koreans approached the EU with an initiative to conclude a form of framework agreement somewhat similar to the 1991 EC–Japan agreement, the EU was prepared to enter into negotiations in 1995. However, the five rounds of negotiations tended to follow the EC–Japanese process too. The South Koreans attached weight to a political declaration, not least because it was seen as reinforcing the South Korean position *vis-à-vis* North Korea, and preferred a general, rather bland economic and cooperation agreement. The EU, on the other hand, pushed by some member states which felt that the Japanese had been allowed to get away with too many generalities, argued for more specific commitments to be included in the EU–Korean agreement. In the end, the text of the Framework Agreement for Trade and Cooperation, which was signed in Luxembourg in October 1996, called for closer cooperation in fields such as environment, energy, agro-fisheries, shipping, science and technology, but with an absence of specific provisions (*Korea Herald*, 11 June 1996). Nevertheless, it was a sign of the relationship maturing.

The EU approach to Taiwan mirrored to a large extent its approach to South Korean market-opening. However, formal negotiations were less easily instituted, more initiative being left to individual member states with representative offices on the ground in Taipei. Although there has been no Taiwanese equivalent of the frugality campaign, the Europeans have found much to complain about in terms of obstacles to selling in the Taiwanese market. Ironically, with no GSP system in place for Taiwan, the EU's instruments for leverage over Taiwan have actually been more limited. Only Taiwan's desire for WTO membership is available.

There has also been no possibility of any form of cooperation agreement being signed with Taiwan. With Singapore a partner to the long-standing EC–

ASEAN Cooperation Agreement of 1980, with South Korea now linked to the EU by the framework agreement and Hong Kong likely to be linked through a new trade and cooperation agreement if the new Hong Kong Special Administrative Region (SAR) government agrees to the pending EU proposal, then only Taiwan will be left outside the emerging EU network of arrangements with Asian Pacific trading partners.

THE NEW INVESTORS

As with the EC–Japan relationship, so too with the EC–NIE relationship: trade flows have grown, only to be followed by increasing flows of FDI. However, at least one difference in the patterns of FDI can be discerned. European FDI into Japan has always been comparatively low, and since the mid 1980s has been totally outweighed by the flows of Japanese FDI into Europe. However, European FDI into the NIEs has had a much higher profile and still holds its own against the counter-flows from the NIEs, despite the latters' take-off during the 1990s.

The Europeans' enthusiasm in the early postwar period for investing in the NIEs was largely determined by the degree of openness of the various economies. South Korea, for example, maintained tight restrictions on FDI inflows until the mid 1980s, but even since then the Europeans have been unable to catch up with the overwhelmingly dominant Japanese investors. Taiwan welcomed FDI at a much earlier stage, from the 1960s, but the diplomatic disruptions of the 1970s prevented much real expansion until the huge infrastructure projects and expanding consumer market proved attractive to European investors in the late 1980s. Singapore and Hong Kong also welcomed FDI from the early stages of their industrialization process, and through the British colonial presence and legacies European FDI has been more prominent in these two economies than in any other Asian Pacific economy.

The South Korean restrictions on inward FDI were primarily aimed at protecting Korean companies from foreign, above all Japanese, competition. Small and medium-sized Japanese companies did find ways round the restrictions, mostly by going into joint ventures. European companies, which favoured wholly owned investments, were clearly handicapped; they held barely 3 per cent of the stock of FDI in South Korea in 1978 (Parry 1988, p. 120). Even after the South Koreans began to lift the restrictions, from 1984 onwards, the Japanese proved best able to exploit the opportunities. Cumulative totals from 1962 through to the end of 1987 show the Europeans with a mere 9 per cent of South Korea's inward FDI. EC FDI did pick up in the late 1980s, reaching a cumulative total of $945 million by the end of 1990 and $1.74 billion by the end of 1993. While still lagging behind their Japanese and US competitors, the EC companies did slowly and steadily increase their share, so that by cumulative value the EU accounted for as much as 20 per cent of total FDI in South Korea by June 1995.

Even though the Taiwanese took a more open attitude to FDI than the Koreans, the European record has been fairly poor. Up until the late 1970s there were barely five cases a year of European FDI into Taiwan, with total values usually less than $30 million annually (Chiu 1993, p. 199). Not until the mid 1980s was there a significant growth in European FDI, and annual flows reached a peak of $531 million in 1989 (the marked upsurge in that year was probably connected to the concern of many European companies about investing in the mainland, given the Tiananmen Square massacre that year), before dropping back to $348 million in 1990 (Chiu 1993, p. 200). The largest European investor of the 1980s had been the Dutch electronics manufacturing company Philips, which helped to give the Dutch pride of place at the top of the list of European investors (Mengin 1993, p. 105). In the late 1980s the Taiwanese government began a five-year 'little Europe' programme specifically designed to encourage European manufacturers of world-recognized brand names, such as Benetton and Pierre Cardin, to manufacture in Taiwan with the aim of selling into the lucrative Japanese market (Ferdinand 1996, p. 47); some success was achieved in attracting such manufacturers.

Most European FDI has been in the manufacturing sector, but the 1980s, as the service sector component of Taiwan's economy began to grow significantly, saw a total of 19 EC banks open either branches or representative offices in Taiwan (Chiu 1993, p. 199). Another initiative by the Taiwanese to attract foreign, including European, FDI in the early 1990s was to try to create regional operations centres, to provide opportunities for foreign companies to link up with partners in Taiwan that had contacts around the region. Again, a number of European companies, including ICI, Philips, Bayer and Glaxo, have taken advantage of this programme (Ferdinand 1996, p. 54). By the end of 1996, accumulated European FDI in Taiwan was calculated to have reached $2.92 billion in a total of 624 projects (*China Post*, 19 April 1997).

When Singapore severed its constitutional links with Malaysia in 1965, and almost simultaneously began a rapid industrialization programme to guarantee the new state's survival, the government felt it had little option but to call on foreign investors (Regnier 1993, p. 305). The British connection gave the Europeans a head start, so that even by 1977, when Japanese and American companies had made serious inroads into Singapore, the Europeans still had 32 per cent of the stock of FDI (Parry 1988, p. 120). However, by the early 1990s, the Europeans were still averaging around 20–25 per cent of the new flows of FDI into the manufacturing sector (the only sector with regularly available statistics from Singapore) (Regnier 1993, p. 306).

FDI inflows into Hong Kong began even earlier than into Singapore, in the 1950s, but it has to be said that FDI has not been an important factor in Hong Kong capital formation, remaining at a relatively low level until the late 1980s, when the China factor came very actively into play (Leung 1995, p. 217). Nonetheless, like Singapore, the British connection gave a boost to the European presence in the early years. As in all the other NIEs, Japanese and US investors became the EC's serious rivals and, in the 1990s, so too have Chinese enterprises. But as in the case of Singapore, although recent flows of FDI have come from these rivals to a much greater degree than from Europe (according to European Commission figures, in 1990–93, for example, the EC's share of new flows into the Hong Kong manufacturing sector was only 12.8 per cent compared with 17.2 per cent in the years 1985–87), in terms of cumulative total the EC still comes out on top. Indeed, Britain by itself, according to Hong Kong government statistics for the total of net assets in both the manufacturing and non-manufacturing sectors, was the largest foreign investor, with $26 billion or 27 per cent of the total FDI stock in 1995 (Census and Statistics Department, 1997).

The structural changes in Hong Kong's economy have impacted on European investment in Hong Kong. In the dwindling manufacturing sector it is now around $1 billion, but this is dwarfed by the huge European investment in the financial and services sector. By 1995 European assets in the non-manufacturing sector were estimated by the Hong Kong government to have reached $29 billion (Census and Statistics Department, 1997).

The China factor has always been an element behind European investment decisions, but since the beginning of the 1990s many European companies have come to see Hong Kong as an increasingly vital gateway to the vast Chinese market. Hong Kong's expertise in finance, design, marketing and the cultural–linguistic aspects of doing business in China has proved beneficial to the Europeans. Many companies, especially small and medium-sized ones, have used the 'stepping stone' approach of joint ventures with Hong Kong companies as a useful way of entering China (Whitla, Bridges and Davies 1995, p. 2).

The other side of the coin from increasing European FDI in the NIEs is, of course, the reverse flows from the NIEs into the EU. This began seriously in the 1980s, but has become more pronounced in the 1990s, partly reflecting the fact that three of the four NIEs (Singapore being the exception) had become by the mid 1990s net outward investors (United Nations Conference on Trade and Development (UNCTAD) 1996, p. xiii), partly because of the perceived need to respond to the EC's 1992 process, which will be discussed in more detail in Chapter 7.

Of the NIEs, South Korea has had the highest visibility in Europe, although the less visible Hong Kong investors were still, in 1993, slightly ahead of the Koreans in terms of total FDI stock (UNCTAD 1996, p. 23), in part because of the practice of some Hong Kong-based European companies, especially financial ones, re-investing back into Europe. Despite Jindo's path-breaking investment in Britain in 1980, South Korean FDI flows into Europe did not become significant until the mid 1980s. The amounts rose slowly and steadily to reach $228 million invested in the EC by 1992, but this represented only 6 per cent of Korea's total overseas FDI stock at the time. However, by recalculating Bank of Korea figures for Europe as a whole (which include Russia and even the newly independent Central Asian states in the geographical category of 'Europe'), it is clear that Korean FDI inside the EU has grown significantly since then, reaching over $1 billion on a cumulative basis by the end of 1995 and a share of around 10 per cent of total Korean FDI outflows (Dent and Randerson 1996, pp. 539–541).

The existing – and anticipated – system of effective protection for certain EC industries seems to have been an important factor behind Korean FDI in the manufacturing sector since the late 1980s (*Far Eastern Economic Review*, 5 February 1998). In terms of location within the EC, South Korean companies seem to have been less concerned about labour costs and technological factors than about investment incentives, geographical location, market size and infrastructure development. Reflecting West Germany's position as South Korea's largest trading partner within the EC, it tended to be the leading recipient of early Korean FDI, primarily in trade-related investments (Dent and Randerson 1996, p. 540). Although Ireland briefly excited Korean interest and secured a major $22.5 million video tape plant investment from Saehan in 1990, it is Britain which has become the focus of recent FDI flows into the EU. This FDI has been both in the financial sector and, more noticeably, in the manufacturing sector. In the 1994–96 period a total of 30 Korean companies chose Britain as their site for investment, making it, according to British government figures, the top location within the EU for Korean manufacturing FDI (*Korea Herald*, 19 March 1997). All the top four *chaebol* are represented: Daewoo has a VCR and television components plant in Northern Ireland, Hyundai has a $1.4 billion semiconductor plant in Scotland, Lucky Goldstar has a similar plant costing $2.6 billion in Wales, and Samsung has a $600 million microwave oven and computer plant in north-east England. The Lucky Goldstar plant, which will employ over 6000 people if its final extensions are completed (initially targeted for 2002), is said to be the largest single investment ever made by a South Korean company (*South China Morning Post*, 19 October 1996).

South Korean companies have been late-comers in merger and acquisition activity, with Anam's acquisition of a Scottish electronics company in 1990 being a rare early example. However, a heightened awareness of the need to catch up technologically has led to greater emphasis in recent years on 'acquisitional FDI' (Dent and Randerson 1996, p. 547), although the record so far has been rather mixed. Neither Samsung's interest in the bankrupt Dutch aerospace group, Fokker nor Daewoo's bid for the French consumer electronics company, Thomson Multimedia reached fruition. Samsung's negotiations failed for commercial reasons; initially interested after a Sino-Korean aircraft construction consortium collapsed in the summer of 1996, it finally aborted the deal when it became clear that the financial cost of salvaging the Dutch company would be just too great. Daewoo's bid for Thomson, however, undoubtedly failed for political reasons. After initially agreeing to the Daewoo bid of one franc to take over the heavily indebted company, the French government reversed course under pressure from labour unions, opposition parties and the media, which criticized the decision to privatize the 'fallen pride of France' by handing it over to a Korean company (*Korea Herald*, 8 November 1996). Korean business organizations accused France of 'racism and xenophobia' and President Kim Young-sam told an uncomfortable French envoy sent out to explain the fiasco that he felt that France could not be 'trusted' (*Korea Herald*, 18 December 1996; *South China Morning Post*, 15 January 1997). Although France promised that any Korean bid in the future for the reorganized privatization of the company would be welcomed, the damage was already done. It is difficult to avoid the conclusion that French actions against South Korea strongly resemble those against Japan some years earlier.

FDI into Europe by the other three NIEs has not had as high a profile. Taiwanese FDI into Europe did not seriously begin until the late 1980s (according to official Taiwanese statistics, from 1980–86 Taiwan averaged barely one investment project a year in Europe (Chiu 1993, p. 200). Tatung's television factory in the north of England, set up in the early 1970s, was for a long time the only significant Taiwanese investment anywhere in Europe. However, FDI gradually took off in the late 1980s, rising from $10 million in 1987 to $265 million in 1990 and $428 million in 1992. By the end of 1996, the accumulated total had reached $570 million in 188 projects (*China Post*, 19 April 1997). More than half of this FDI is in Britain. Unlike Hong Kong and Singaporean FDI in the EU, more than half of Taiwanese FDI is in the manufacturing sector. Taiwanese trade-related FDI has been closely linked to its electronics-manufacturing FDI, so that, for example, Kunnan markets personal computers through an exclusive dealer network in France (UNCTAD 1996, p. 28). The Taiwanese totals may be due for significant improvement, since Chunghwa has announced plans to build a large factory in Scotland to produce cathode-ray tubes for televisions and computer monitors beginning in 1997; when finally completed this will be the most technically advanced factory of its kind in the world, with a total investment value of $400 million (Invest In Britain Bureau 1996, p. 11). Other Taiwanese companies may well follow where Chunghwa leads, once the financial crisis, admittedly less severe for Taiwan, is over.

Data on Singapore's overseas investment flows are restricted, although it is clear that by far the largest proportion of its FDI has been in Asian countries. The late 1980s, as in the case of South Korea and Taiwan, saw some improvement in Singaporean FDI into Europe, which rose from $190 million in 1989 to $570 million in 1990 (Regnier 1993, p. 310). In the 1990s it has remained fairly constant as a share of total Singaporean FDI, at around 8 per cent of total flows in 1990 and 7.7 per cent in 1994 (Kimura 1997, p. 36). Anecdotal evidence since then suggests that FDI into Europe has continued to be fairly low key, and has almost certainly fallen below that of Taiwan. Investments tend to be small scale, with the few manufacturing plants set up, such as those in Britain by PCI, (for electronic products) and Singapore Food Industries (for ready-made meals), being typical. As of 1994, over 80 per cent of Singaporean FDI in the EU was in the finance sector (UNCTAD 1996, p. 9). Britain takes more than half of Singaporean FDI in the EU, with the Netherlands as the other major recipient. Efforts in the 1990s to make Singaporean businessmen more 'entrepreneurial' and risk-taking overseas have, by in particular encouraging Singaporean companies to invest in the newly emerging markets of China, Vietnam and Burma, done little to reverse the strong emphasis on Asia.

Hong Kong companies have of course emerged as the major investors in China since the early 1980s, but the 1990s have also seen a significant expansion of Hong Kong FDI elsewhere; to Southeast Asia and, in an interesting twist on Hong Kong's colonial history, to Britain and other parts of Europe. Indeed, in the 1993–95 period Hong Kong outward FDI exceeded that of Japan, but it should be remembered that a significant proportion of Hong Kong's FDI, possibly as much as 30 per cent, actually originates from foreign companies based in Hong Kong (UNCTAD 1996, pp. 7–8). Most of Hong Kong FDI in the EU is in the wholesale and retail trade. The city of Hamburg, for example, hosts about 20 representative offices of Hong Kong companies (UNCTAD 1996, p. 28). As of May 1997 there were only 14 Hong Kong companies manufacturing in Britain, producing goods such as knitwear, mobile phones/pagers, toys, semiconductors and bicycles. Hong Kong entrepreneurs have also moved into the property and retail trade in London, with Dickson Concepts buying up the Harvey Nichols department store in 1991 for $90 million and taking over a French shoe company the following year. Great Eagle spent $150 million in 1996 to acquire the Langham Hilton hotel (*Hong Kong Standard*, 4 July 1997). But by far the largest example of FDI was by Hong Kong's premier bank, the Hongkong and Shanghai Bank, which in 1992 acquired the final 85 per cent share of the Midland Bank, one of Britain's top four banks, having already bought 15 per cent of it in 1986.

It should be noted that, from the perspective of the EU, these inflows of FDI from the NIEs are still very small, especially by comparison with Japanese inflows. In 1995, for example, non-Japanese Asian FDI stocks represented less than 1 per cent of the EU's total inward FDI (UNCTAD 1996, p. 23); the Japanese share was around 6 per cent. Although the rise in deals announced during 1996–97 and discussed above will probably increase the NIEs' share of flows in those years, the series of financial crises across the region in late 1997 are almost certain to ensure that FDI flows to the EU, from South Korea in particular but probably from all the NIEs to a certain extent, will decrease during 1998 and probably for several years to come. As a portent of what is to come, Daewoo announced early in 1998 that it was putting on hold its plans to start a cathode-ray tube plant in eastern France and Hyundai decided to suspend its plans for the next phase of expansion of its Scottish semiconductor plant (*Far Eastern Economic Review*, 5 February 1998).

The European relationship with the four NIEs has been even more unbalanced than that with Japan. The economic dimension has remained totally dominant and, in part because of the peculiar international position of Hong Kong and Taiwan, the political aspects of the relationship have barely got off the ground. The methods of NIEs' exporting certainly seemed reminiscent to the Europeans of the earlier Japanese approach and, even though such comparisons have tended to be over-simplified, it has been difficult for the NIEs to avoid being typecast as 'second Japans'. The reality is that there is more diversity within the four NIEs and more divergence from the Japanese model than is often realized. European policies have rarely appreciated this fact, and the initial tendency to see all the NIEs as struggling in the current Asian financial crisis perpetuates that broad-brush categorization approach. The challenge for Europe and the NIEs is to develop a broader-based relationship which allows for such nuances of developmental character and international status.

5.   The Southeast Asian 'community'

We cannot live day to day because the world is changing so fast around us
and we had better optimise our vast potential.
(Ms Rafidah Aziz, quoted in *South China Morning Post*, 19 April 1994)

I think I'll go West.
(popular saying in Mandalay (Khin 1984, p. 96))

The NIEs themselves have been coming under challenge from the next generation of dynamic Asian Pacific economies. Leaving aside for the moment
China, which will be dealt with separately in Chapter 6, the four major
ASEAN economies apart from Singapore, already discussed previously, are
often posited in this group of so-called 'proto-NIEs' or 'neo-NIEs', which are
geographically larger and more resource-rich than the 'original' NIEs. Inevitably linked with them as part of the emerging Southeast Asian 'community'
are Brunei, Burma and the three Indochinese states, though they are at different stages in the economic development process. In the same way as with the
four Asian NIEs, there are some differences between the two more advanced
ASEAN economies, Malaysia and Thailand, and the slower-growing Indonesia and the Philippines, which make a sub-division into pairs useful.

Malaysia and Thailand have long been in competition, with relatively
similar economies: rich agricultural economies with increasing development
of manufacturing sectors with a strong export orientation. Both have also
suffered from difficulties in the political sphere; Malaysia's have mainly
derived from ethnic differences between the majority Malays and the large
minority Chinese, whereas Thailand's have derived from tensions between
authoritarian, largely military-backed forces and squabbling, often ineffective, democratic parties. While Thailand appeared to have the edge in the
early 1990s, Malaysia's growth has proved to be more strongly founded as
the end of the decade approaches.

In the early postwar years, Thailand relied on natural resource-based and
agricultural exports, especially rice, but in the 1970s it began following an
import-substitution industrialization policy based on high tariffs for imported
consumer goods. However, in the early 1980s, as a result of the second oil
shock which hit Thailand harder than the first, the government shifted its
policies towards export-oriented growth. Manufacturing has become increas-

ingly important, although some scholars argue that this sector has never played the same role as the engine of growth that it did in the South Korean and Taiwanese cases (Mackie 1988, p. 300). That assessment is less true of the 1990s, however, as export-oriented FDI has been actively solicited.

Consequently, a structural shift has been occurring in the 1990s. According to Bank of Thailand figures, if processed agricultural products are included, then more than 80 per cent of Thailand's exports are now manufactured goods, such as electrical appliances, machinery, transportation parts and chemicals; most are produced by foreign investors (including European companies) or joint ventures (World Bank 1993, p. 142; Yoshida 1997, p. 49). However, the 1990s has also seen the accentuation of some unrealistic expectations and dubious practices deriving from the fast pace of growth, with which the financial system was unable to cope. In August 1997 Thailand was forced to ask for a $17 billion bailout by the IMF; growth was expected to be either negative or zero at best in 1998, while the Thai economy underwent harsh restructuring.

Malaysia's particular racial mixture (about 48 per cent Malay, 34 per cent Chinese and 8 per cent Indian) has created political and social tensions, but has also affected its economic structure. In its early post-independence years, Malaysia still relied heavily on the plantation and mining sectors set up by the British. The limited import-substitution policy of the 1960s had to be rethought after the race riots of 1969. The resultant New Economic Policy (NEP), introduced in 1971, was intended to promote growth with equity – to reduce the economic imbalance felt by the Malays – by what became a mixture of import substitution and export promotion (World Bank 1993, p. 135). In practice, the NEP served as a kind of affirmative action programme in favour of one race: the Malays (Drakakis-Smith 1992, p. 134). Malaysia therefore lacks the same kind of development ideology found in South Korea, for example, as the rationale for Malaysia's economic policies of the 1970s and 1980s was redistributive rather than efficiency-maximizing (Mackie 1988, p. 319). Nonetheless, apart from 1985–87, when global recession caused Malaysia's first real slump in growth since independence, the economy registered steady growth, with the years 1988–96 showing an average of 8 per cent growth (Aoki 1997, p. 38).

With increasing emphasis on the manufacturing sector, manufactured products rose from 32 per cent of total Malaysian exports in 1985 to 79 per cent by 1995 (Aoki 1997, pp. 38–39). In the 1990s, although the NEP has been replaced with a successor programme, the government has become slightly more relaxed about the redistributive aspects and in recent years has gone all out to achieve the present Prime Minister, Dr Mahathir Mohammed's '2020 Vision', the achievement of developed country status by that year (*Far Eastern Economic Review*, 24 October 1996). FDI, especially high-technology-related, has become a political and economic imperative, with the Multi-media Supercorridor project at the heart of Mahathir's plans (Aoki 1997, pp. 42–44). Mahathir railed against foreign currency speculators as Malaysia came under fire in the Asian financial crisis of 1997, but, by cancelling or postponing some of his pet projects, he was able to avoid having to follow the Thai route of going to the IMF for help (*Far Eastern Economic Review*, 4 December 1997). Nonetheless, Malaysia dropped into negative growth in the first quarter of 1998, with the prospect of a hard year or two ahead.

The Philippines, given its natural resources and legacies from US colonial-ism, should have been up there with Malaysia and Thailand, but instead it has found it difficult to escape from the epithet 'the sick man of Asia'. Early promise in the 1950s under a highly protectionist industrialization policy petered out in the 1960s. The old landed elite contrived to hold on to their economic privileges, while President Ferdinand Marcos in the 1970s culti-vated a new elite through what has become called 'crony capitalism'. Extravagence and misdirection of resources occurred on a massive scale; agriculture lagged while manufacturing did not grow rapidly enough (Mackie 1988, pp. 305–310). Despite the dramatic 'people power' revolution in 1986, vested interests proved hard to reform and the export-oriented policies of the 1990s have only slowly been coming to fruition, with average GNP growth during 1991–95 only 2.2 per cent. President Fidel Ramos launched a 'Philip-pines 2000' initiative, a national campaign designed to raise economic standards to the level of its neighbours (Nozawa 1997, p. 71–72). While the Asian financial crisis has ensured that this target will not be achievable, the country has certainly entered a more positive growth cycle and, despite some jitters and declining growth, was actually able to avoid in 1997 going to the IMF for a bailout.

In Indonesia, by far the most populous of the ASEAN countries, post-independence economic policies were shaped by a strongly anti-colonial and anti-ethnic Chinese bias and were inward-looking in nature. Chaotic eco-nomic conditions helped to fuel dissatisfaction with the government; an attempted communist coup gave President Suharto the opportunity to take power and turn Indonesia on a more outward-oriented path (Mackie 1988, pp. 311–313). Indonesia undoubtedly benefited from the oil and primary commodity price booms of the 1970s, but its dependence on oil revenues was a mixed blessing. By the mid 1980s, Suharto and his group of technocrats were forced to make adjustments, which again swung the economy towards a more outward-oriented mode, especially in order to attract FDI to build up the weak manufacturing sector (World Bank 1993, pp. 136–139). Excluding processed food and raw materials, manufactured products still only consti-tuted around 32 per cent of total exports in 1996 (Araki 1997, p. 64). Indonesia, therefore, has lagged economically behind its neighbours, Malaysia and Thailand, tending to be more conservative about opening up both to its ASEAN partners, through regional cooperative projects and programmes, and to the rest of the outside world. Reluctance to change old practices made Finance Minister Mar'ie Muhammad's comparison of the Indonesian economy with the Clint Eastwood movie 'The Good, the Bad and the Ugly' particularly apposite (*South China Morning Post*, 13 October 1997). Although forced to ask the IMF for a $27 billion handout in October 1997, the Indonesian government, still subservient to an ailing Suharto and his avaricious family, dragged its heels on implementing the necessary reforms, even when faced in early 1998 by rising social discontent and a plummeting currency. Suharto was re-elected for yet another term as President in March 1998, but student-led demonstrations for greater democracy and economic transparency continued until he was finally forced to step down in favour of his deputy, B.J. Habibie, in May. With the economy in a disastrous situation (the IMF forecasts at least −10 per cent growth in 1998) and the political transition far from resolved, Indonesia remains the Asian Pacific country at the greatest danger of socio-political disruption and economic implosion.

THE EUROPEAN CONNECTION

In the early postwar or post-independence decades, European economic relations with these four countries were characterized by a strong European interest in importing natural resources and trying to export machinery and consumer goods. These economies were also, to varying degrees, recipients of overseas aid flows from Europe. Investment tended to be tied to old patterns of colonial involvement, except in Indonesia, where the 1958 forcible nationalization of Dutch investments brought an abrupt halt for many years to one source of FDI. However, the early to mid 1980s brought about a new phase of economic relations. Although the EC–ASEAN cooperation agreement, signed in 1980, was limited mainly to 'expressions of principle and intent' as far as economic cooperation was concerned (Harris and Bridges 1983, p. 24), it did provide a formal framework for consultation on commercial, technological and developmental issues and helped to symbolize the reawakening of European interest in Southeast Asia. Since then the nature of the economic relationship with these four ASEAN economies (and, indeed, with ASEAN as a whole) has changed, with trade becoming more concentrated in manufactured products than in primary or semi-processed products, with FDI and technology-transfer issues becoming increasingly important, and with aid being phased out or redirected.

Among the imports that the EC has received from the four ASEAN economies, the past predominance of raw material supply – lumber, rubber, manioc (tapioca), tin and palm oil – has been slowly declining as more manufactured goods have been imported. This change does of course reflect the shift in economic structures of these four economies themselves, as manufacturing has steadily grown in importance in their overall export profile.

For these ASEAN economies, the influence of the EU market on their primary product exports is important in many cases, not solely for specific market outlets (although that is important in one or two cases, such as Thailand's manioc exports), but also for the way in which the quantities demanded and the prices paid by Europeans can affect global market and price levels.

It is characteristic of countries pursuing rapid economic development programmes that their imports tend to consist substantially of plant, equipment and machinery. The four economies' imports from Europe therefore do tend to be predominantly manufactures, with machinery and transport equipment well to the fore.

Britain, Germany and France are the major EU trading partners of these four economies, although Britain's trade patterns still strongly reflect the influence of former colonial links, specifically with Malaysia, which has consistently been the major trading partner for Britain among the four. Even when short-term anti-British campaigns, such as the 'buy British last' movement of 1981–83, have temporarily depressed British exports to Malaysia, it has still managed to remain Britain's largest market of the four. Indeed, the tendency for many British companies to continue to focus on Malaysia (and Singapore) proved one of the driving forces behind the British government's new three-year export programme, 'South East Asia: Lands of Opportunity' campaign, launched in early 1997 to encourage British companies currently exporting to the two former British colonies to try further afield in the region (*Asia Pacific Link*, Spring 1997). France and Germany, which do not have the same colonial links with these economies, have been psychologically better equipped to approach them on a more equal basis, with differences in the levels of their trade with these four ASEAN states reflecting the nature of the economic characteristics of each particular economy rather than past colonial links. The poor state of the Philippines economy is therefore the reason why it has, since the mid 1980s, consistently lagged behind the other three economies in terms of both imports and exports with the EU.

It has to be said, however, that for the EU these four economies are still comparatively small trading partners, with barely 1.2 per cent of total EU exports going to them and only 1.3 per cent of total imports being received from them in 1995, only a slight increase over the situation even a decade earlier. Trade with the EU features more importantly the other way round for the four economies themselves, but even so the EU share is actually declining as these economies deepen their economic links with other parts of the booming Asia Pacific region and with North America. Discussions about

ways to improve the economic relationship between the EU and these economies have been largely subsumed within the parameters of the broader EC/
EU–ASEAN economic discussions and, at a further step removed, the nature
of European policies towards the developing world as a whole. It is therefore
appropriate to consider briefly both these particular aspects.

Europe and the Developing World

EU policies towards the developing world are complex and multi-layered and
have, over time, served to create what has been described as a 'pyramid of
privilege' (Mishalani *et al.* 1981, pp. 60–82). At the top are the now 70 low-
income countries, almost exclusively former European colonies, which
constitute the African, Caribbean and Pacific (ACP) countries, whose relationship with the EC/EU has been governed by a series of preferential trade
and economic cooperation agreements, usually known by the name of the
first, the Lome Convention, signed in 1975. At the bottom of the pyramid are
those developing countries which benefit only from the GSP. In between are a
range of countries and regional organizations which receive some form or
other of trade concessions. With no association agreement but only a cooperation agreement, ASEAN has tended to come towards the lower end of the
pyramid. The pyramid has, of course, not remained completely static, but the
decisions to begin negotiations with some associate Eastern European states
in 1998, which would bring about their eventual membership of the EU, and,
in the same year, to revamp the Lome Convention so that greater differentia-
tion between the richer and poorer ACP countries is achieved, are likely to be
more disruptive than anything in the past.

Association agreements, such as those given to Eastern European states,
are 'characterized by reciprocal rights and obligations, common actions and
particular procedures', whereas cooperation agreements give no special preferences, but are designed to stimulate cooperation in areas of common interest,
such as industrial development, energy and environmental protection. Unlike
association agreements, cooperation agreements contain no financial element
to support such commitments (Flaesch-Mougin 1990, pp. 35–36).

EC/EU policies towards the developing world, therefore, have combined
elements of trade stimulation, such as the extension of the GSP, and trade
deterrence, notably the imposition of tariff and non-tariff barriers, including
quotas and ceilings within the GSP. Although provision was made in the
Treaty of Rome for cooperation between the EC and developing countries
with which it had special relationships (which came to mean, for example,
the ACP countries), no explicit provisions were made for those developing
countries that had no form of association with the Community, countries that
came to include the members of ASEAN (Harris and Bridges 1983, p. 31).

The ASEAN Dimension

The GSP was introduced by the EC in 1971 for manufactured and semi-manufactured goods and a number of processed agricultural products from developing countries. However, its effect was felt among ASEAN countries only after Britain's accession to the EC led to the loss of more liberal Commonwealth trade preferences for Malaysia and Singapore. The EC accepted that other countries in the same geographical area, in practice the other three original members of ASEAN, should be treated similarly to the two former British colonies under the GSP scheme.

Needless to say, the ASEAN countries have consistently pushed for better access to the EC/EU market under the GSP scheme. During the 1970s, ASEAN obtained some concessions through negotiations with the EC, such as the addition to the list of certain processed agricultural products (coconut oil, palm oil, pepper and tobacco) and the application of the principle of cumulative origin of imports from regional groupings (primarily to help Singapore, which would, by virtue of its much higher per capita income, be excluded from some GSP benefits) (Harris and Bridges 1983, p. 32). The five original ASEAN countries became major beneficiaries of the GSP scheme, so that by 1983 they accounted for 42 per cent of all EC imports from the developing world under GSP (Wannamethee 1989, p. 25). In certain products the ASEAN countries' success was clearly at the expense of the ACP countries; for example, ASEAN's share of less developed country exports of vegetable oils and fats to the EC rose from 19 per cent in 1970 to almost 54 per cent in 1983, with Ghana and Nigeria the main losers (Langhammer 1987, p. 137). However, ASEAN too suffered in certain products, such as cocoa and palm oil, where the ACP countries got better tariff preferences, and rice, sugar and manioc, which competed directly with grains, sugar and feeds produced within the EC (Grilli 1993, p. 285). Moreover, in the second half of the 1980s ASEAN itself came under increasing competition from new producers such as China and India, so that, according to EU estimates, by 1992 the ASEAN share of all GSP imports had dropped to around 25 per cent (interview, European Commission, May 1995).

Nonetheless, the impact of GSP on ASEAN manufactured exports has been more limited than the above figures might suggest, as the majority of exports eligible for GSP treatment have still faced most favoured nation tariffs. In the early 1980s, for example, only around 40 per cent of ASEAN exports to the EC actually entered duty-free or duty-reduced (Langhammer 1987, p. 137). By 1989, as ASEAN exported more textiles, clothing and electrical goods to Europe, that share was still only 30 per cent (Luhulima 1992, p. 314). The greatly revised GSP scheme introduced by the EU in January 1995, which is intended to help the poorest developing countries, especially by encouraging industrialization, will probably work to reduce the ASEAN share of benefits under the GSP scheme, although the accession to ASEAN of low-income economies such as Vietnam, Laos, Burma (Myanmar) and, eventually, Cambodia, which should be able to expand their exports under the GSP, will probably distort any calculations taking ASEAN as a whole in the immediate future.

Another area of controversy between the EC and ASEAN has been exports of textiles and clothing under the MFA, created within GATT to regulate the international textile trade. The ASEAN textile and clothing industries have played an important part in altering the export composition of the member countries. During the 1980s, according to EU statistics, ASEAN exports of textiles to the EC increased five-fold and clothing nearly seven-fold, and by the early 1990s they constituted around 15 per cent of all ASEAN exports to the EC (interview, European Commission, May 1995). Nonetheless, ASEAN continued to object to the aspects of managed trade enshrined in the MFA procedures. However, in January 1995 the MFA was replaced by a new agreement, reached during the Uruguay Round of GATT negotiations, which is intended to restore the textile and clothing trade to GATT/WTO trade regimes over a ten-year period. The long-term effects of this new textile agreement will be favourable to ASEAN exporters.

The controversial trade issues of GSP and MFA need to be set against the broader background of economic relations between the EC and ASEAN. The EC had welcomed the establishment of ASEAN in general terms, but no concrete contacts developed until Britain joined the EC, when the ASEAN side decided to initiate some low-level contacts. Slowly, however, the level of contact was raised until the first EC–ASEAN ministerial meeting was held in Brussels in 1978. This led to the signing at the second ministerial meeting in Kuala Lumpur in March 1980 of the EC–ASEAN Cooperation Agreement. Although it contained little more than expressions of principle and intent as far as cooperation in the fields of trade, investment and development were concerned, it provided for a formal framework, including a joint cooperation committee to meet annually, within which consultation could take place (Harris and Bridges 1983, p. 24). There was no formally agreed preferential treatment for ASEAN producers (or, for that matter, for European companies going into the ASEAN market), but the aim was to encourage free enterprise between the two regions through the two communities and individual governments providing better support (Mols 1990, p. 74).

The 1980 agreement was extended several times after its initial five years, but by the early 1990s officials on both sides felt a new agreement with much broadened scope would be advantageous. But, as will be discussed below, Portugal, because of its heightened campaign against the continued Indonesian occupation of East Timor, has consistently blocked the conclusion of any such new agreement. Foreign ministerial meetings have continued regularly at approximately 18-month intervals through the 1980s and 1990s (although, because of the first ever Euro-Asia Summit in March 1996, nearly two-and-a-half years elapsed between the 1994 and 1997 meetings). At least until the end of the Cold War and the winding down of the Cambodia conflict, there had been a relatively trouble-free politico-strategic dialogue, with a considerable degree of convergence in analysis and approach. The economic dialogue has been more contentious, but apart from a one-off meeting of economic ministers in 1985 and the last-minute appearance of ASEAN trade ministers to accompany their foreign ministerial colleagues to the 1990 ministerial meeting, detailed discussions have been largely left either to foreign ministers or lower-level officials. The collective clout of ASEAN has worked to their members' benefit in these negotiations. In the assessment of one German scholar, there is some evidence that the ASEAN group has received better treatment under both GSP and MFA through negotiating together as a group with the EC than if each country had tried to bargain individually (Langhammer 1987, p. 143).

Efforts by the ASEAN side to secure better access to the European market – the standard complaint against European protectionism – has been a consistent feature of the EC–ASEAN dialogue from the late 1970s. However, direct investment – and associated technology transfer – has come increasingly to the fore since the mid 1980s. The desire of the ASEAN side to encourage greater European FDI and technology transfer has therefore become a second major theme of EC–ASEAN economic relations. Following the 1985 economic ministerial meeting, which identified European FDI in ASEAN as a 'key element in a long-term strategy to strengthen economic links between the two countries' (Luhulima 1992, p. 313), steps were taken to encourage European participation in ASEAN industrial joint ventures and other projects in the region, and joint investment committees were gradually established in all the ASEAN countries. As a result, although the EC still lags well behind the United States and Japan in historic cumulative totals of FDI in ASEAN, over the 1985–90 period EC FDI in ASEAN, excluding Brunei, reached $4.7 billion, actually outstripping Japanese and US FDI during the same period.

To sustain this FDI flow and to encourage technological collaboration, in the 1990s the EU has begun to support what it calls 'technology windows', such as the Europe–Singapore Regional Institute of Environmental Technology and the Energy Management Training and Research Centre in Jakarta, and also to establish a network of European business information centres equipped with detailed commercial, financial and legal information.

The third theme of EC–ASEAN economic discussions has been development aid. The EC has had a general commitment to provide developmental aid to the ASEAN countries as part of its policies towards non-associated developing countries, but the 1980 Cooperation Agreement set a precedent by specifically including a separate development article. However, no new budget was allocated to ASEAN and aid to ASEAN has been small in per capita terms compared with that given to the ACP countries (Harris and Bridges 1983, pp. 39–40). Indeed, the so-called 'Pisani Memorandum', a policy document conceived by the then European Commissioner in charge of development in 1982, actually served to lower the rank of the ASEAN countries in the hierarchy of EC development priorities, and aid to ASEAN nations in the 1976–88 period averaged out at barely $40 million per annum (Grilli 1993, pp. 285, 288). Some ASEAN countries, such as Singapore and Brunei (after it joined in 1984 when it decided, on independence, not to ask for ACP privileges to which it would have been entitled), have never received any EC aid because of their income levels. However, they have been able to make use of EC aid given to regional projects such as aquaculture development.

In the 1990s EU aid to ASEAN has been around the $60 million mark annually, but it is now concentrated in only three countries – Malaysia and Indonesia, both for forestry projects, and the Philippines, for rural development, family planning and environmental protection – and is all in the form of grant aid (a marked contrast with the much larger Japanese aid to the region which has an extremely high loan component). With the accession of poorer economies to ASEAN, the focus of EU aid will shift in their direction. Indeed, at the 1994 EU–ASEAN ministerial meeting in Karlsruhe, Germany, the EU side specifically asked the existing ASEAN countries to join in fostering the rehabilitation of the region's poorest countries (interview, European Commission, May 1995).

Bilateral aid from individual EU countries to individual ASEAN countries is more substantial than EU aid, having risen from around $400 million annually in the early 1980s to between $780 and $900 million per annum in the 1990s (interview, European Commission, May 1995). However, bilateral aid has proved to be extremely controversial in recent years, in some cases because of the linking of aid packages to specific human rights or environmental objectives; in others because of the overly close inter-relationship with commercial objectives.

Until the late 1980s aid from European countries might well be described as having been 'politically invisible' (*Far Eastern Economic Review*, 7 February 1991), but the end of the Cold War helped to change that. Encouraged by the democratization of Eastern Europe and aware, coincidentally, of growing popular environmental concerns, a number of EC countries, led by the Netherlands, began to look at ways of introducing human rights and environmental criteria into their programmes (Godemont 1993, p. 97). This heightened tensions with ASEAN countries, none of which feel comfortable discussing these issues, and in the case of Indonesia, Malaysia and Singapore brought forth quite strident criticism. The Indonesian government, which became increasingly upset with what it saw as patronizing Dutch 'lecturing' on human rights in the aftermath of the East Timor killings of November 1991, decided in March 1992 to disband its Dutch-coordinated international aid support group, the Inter-Governmental Group on Indonesia, and to refuse any further Dutch bilateral aid (van den Ham 1993, pp. 532–534). Indonesia then reformed the group, with World Bank assistance but without Dutch participation. This move was popular within Indonesia and had little deleterious economic impact, since Dutch aid to Indonesia in 1991 had only been $91 million. At the first meeting of the new World Bank-chaired Consultative Group on Indonesia (CGI), in July 1992, Indonesia was offered its largest ever aid package of $4.9 billion (*International Herald Tribune*, 18 July 1992).

Equally controversial has been the increased 'commercialization' of aid from some European countries, although European countries are not the only ones which try to stretch to the limits the mix of export credits and aid to support export efforts. This was to become the focus of a dispute between Britain and Malaysia over the utilization of the British government's aid and trade provision (ATP) to help secure an order for the Pergau hydro-electric project in Malaysia. In 1991, over-ruling objections from some officials from the Overseas Development Administration who had raised doubts about the project's economic viability, the British government decided to commit $435 million, the largest ATP commitment ever made by Britain, to the Pergau project. British government approval of this aid package was almost certainly linked to the 'moral obligation' to entertain Malaysian requests which derived from earlier bilateral agreements made in 1988 for Malaysia to spend over $1.8 billion on purchasing British fighter aircraft and other arms (Foreign Affairs Committee 1994a). Press reports about the Pergau scandal led to separate accusations in one British Sunday newspaper that a British company had tried to bribe Malaysian politicians to secure an order. The Malaysian government, already unhappy with the publicity given to the Pergau case, reacted strongly to the accusations, which it denied. It followed up by instituting a ban, which was to last for nine months, on public contracts for British companies (reminiscent of the 1981–83 'buy British last' campaign) (*Financial Times*, 8 August 1994).

As a result of criticism in the media and by politicians, the British government reviewed its ATP programme, lowered the per capita income limit for qualifying countries and reiterated that there should be no linkage between defence sales and aid. Replacing Malaysia as a leading recipient of new aid, ironically, was Indonesia, which does anyway purchase British arms, including fighter aircraft (Robinson 1996, p. 79), and which had become one of the largest recipients of British ATP-related aid by the mid 1990s. In 1997, however, the incoming Labour government, while resisting demands to cancel orders for Hawk aircraft and Saracen light tanks approved by the former Conservative government, made it clear that aid policy towards Indonesia would be reviewed in the light of that country's poor human rights record and, indeed, at the July 1997 CGI annual meeting in Tokyo, Britain failed to make a firm commitment of aid to Indonesia (*Independent*, 17 and 29 July 1997). Arms and aid are set to remain a controversial topic for future European relations with Indonesia, especially as the role of the army internally is highlighted under the deteriorating socio-economic conditions.

INDOCHINA AND THE ASEAN 'TEN'

The addition of Brunei to the original five ASEAN members in 1984 made little significant difference to the nature of the EC–ASEAN relationship. A small, extremely rich country (because of its oil and natural gas exports), ruled by an absolute monarch, Brunei – apart from its links with Britain through the Gurkha troops retained for security purposes and the heavy connection with the Anglo-Dutch oil company Shell (so strong that Brunei is sometimes jokingly called a 'Shellfare state') – has few ties with the rest of Europe and is firmly oriented towards the Asia Pacific in its economic and political relations.

However, more recent members of ASEAN have had a greater impact not only on the group itself, but on the nature of its relationship with Europe. Vietnam joined in July 1995, and Laos and Burma (Myanmar) in July 1997; Cambodia, whose entry was delayed because of internal political chaos, is expected to become a member late in 1998. All these are much poorer economies than the earlier ASEAN members and so involve the Europeans in a different set of problems. With the partial exception of Vietnam, trade and FDI flows with Europe have been limited, aid (or the lack of it) has been more central to the economic relationship, and political links have been either fragile or controversial. While Vietnam was the only newcomer some of these problems were left on one side, but now with the two (soon to be three) other new members, the nature of ASEAN as an economic – and political – organization and as an interlocutor of the EU is inevitably going to change. Faced with concerns about a 'two-tier' community evolving because of internal economic disparities with the newcomers, and with embarrassment over their collective failure either to talk frankly to Indonesia about its cross-border smog pollution in 1997 or to deal with the impact of the Asian financial crisis, the new ASEAN is certain to undergo a period of navel-gazing and rethinking.

The end of the debilitating and destructive Vietnam War and the reunification of the two halves of the country in 1975 did not bring peace and economic reconstruction to Vietnam. Within four years, it had embarked on an invasion of neighbouring Cambodia which turned out to be a prolonged and expensive operation, damaging not only to its economy but also to its international reputation. By the middle of the 1980s living standards in Vietnam showed barely any improvement over those that prevailed during the Vietnam War. However, desperate to try to restore the economy, the Vietnamese government began, in consultation with and under pressure from the IMF, which came to replace the ailing Soviet Union as Vietnam's 'lifeline', to introduce a range of experiments in economic reform in the second half of the 1980s under the slogan of '*doi moi*' (renovation) (Kolko 1997, pp. 31–52). Although the Vietnamese approach to reform shared many characteristics with the earlier Chinese model, it was not as clearly phased in as in China, where agriculture benefited first, with urban and industrial reform lagging behind. In Vietnam, more of the reform process came together at the same stage. However, not until Vietnam decided to pull out of Cambodia and allow a peace process to develop, which culminated in the 1993 elections there, was it able to shrug off its pariah image and begin reintegrating into the regional economy (Williams 1992, pp. 59–64).

In political terms, although Vietnam's domestic political structure – and the associated rhetoric of socialism – has remained unaltered during the 1990s, its foreign policy changed rapidly so that it could become first an observer of ASEAN and then a full member within the space of two years. Economically, it has continued its liberalization and opening up, encouraging FDI in particular, but the 'incongruous mixture of laissez faire and socialism' (Kolko 1997, p. 157) has produced a disjointed and inequitable economy. Although areas of the former South Vietnam, especially Ho Chi Minh city, are becoming prosperous, as a whole Vietnam remains a poor country with a per capita GNP of $240 in 1995.

Vietnam's land-locked and mountainous neighbour, Laos in essence remains even poorer, although it did have a higher per capita income of $350 in 1995. Heavily dependent on Vietnam after the communist takeover in 1975, Laos has been handicapped by its poor infrastructure and limited natural resources (Zasloff 1991, pp. 3–6). Only through its ability to harness the Mekong river and its tributaries to produce hydro-electric power had it been able to attract foreign investment or earn foreign currency. Around three-quarters of FDI is estimated to go into hydro-electric projects. Although the government has stuck strictly to its one-party socialist state political system, it was earlier than Vietnam in thinking about ways to reform the economy, through its 'new economic mechanism', formally adopted in 1986 but incorporating some ideas already being practised from the early 1980s (*South*, July 1988 pp. 39–41). However, industrialization has barely begun, and outside the capital of Vientiane the majority of the population is still engaged in subsistence farming.

Cambodia, like Laos, is a former French colony whose drive for independence was entangled with the struggle between the Americans and the Vietnamese, but its post-1975 communist takeover history has been very different. While Laos has remained a sleepy and widely ignored state, Cambodia has been pitched into the forefront of regional and international attention. On seizing power in 1975, the guerrilla forces of the Khmer Rouge, the Cambodian communists led by Pol Pot, embarked on a radical policy of terror and genocide. According to the latest estimates, the 'killing fields' probably accounted for more than 1 million people out of a total population of some 7 million (*Far Eastern Economic Review*, 7 August 1997). Although Vietnam invaded at the end of 1978 and installed a new Cambodian government, a prolonged civil war was the only result. China, ASEAN and the Europeans, opposed to Vietnamese intervention, ended up supporting an unholy alliance of remnant Khmer Rouge forces and supporters of the former king Prince Norodom Sihanouk. Inconclusive but bloody civil war raged throughout the 1980s until finally the Vietnamese decision to withdraw its troops in 1989 opened up the opportunity for a settlement.

Held under UN supervision (and with European involvement, as is discussed in Chapter 8), the 1993 elections resulted in another marriage of convenience, this time between the winning royalist party, headed by Sihanouk's son, Prince Norodom Ranariddh, and its close rival, the successor party to the Vietnamese-installed socialist party, headed by Hun Seni, a fractious and cumbersome arrangement (Lao 1993, pp. 393–394). Relations between the two co-Premiers deteriorated until, finally, in July 1997 Hun ousted Ranariddh in a coup which culminated in Cambodia's accession to ASEAN being delayed (*Far Eastern Economic Review*, 17 July 1997). Although the second half of the 1980s did see the introduction of a form of 'planned economy with markets', the years of civil war and international isolation have left Cambodia with an economy in a state of decay and stagnation (Wang 1994, pp. 326–327). Even by 1995 its per capita GNP was only $270. The 1997 coup, which demonstrated the inherent internal political instability, marked another setback to an economy which had just begun to show signs of recovery under the post-1993 'peace'.

The three Indochinese states had all, of course, been French colonies and France continued through a mixture of nostalgia and economic self-interest to want to play a role in bringing about some resolution of the Cambodian crisis during the 1980s. Indeed, it can be argued that the Vietnamese occupation of Cambodia and the search for a solution came to be the key element of the EC–ASEAN political dialogue throughout the decade. Until the late 1980s, the position of the EC and most of its member countries was closely allied with that of ASEAN, the United States and China. Several European governments did privately share some reservations about a policy which seemed designed to push Vietnam deeper into the arms of the Soviet Union and which also entailed a degree of support for the notorious Khmer Rouge (Williams 1992, p. 75). Nonetheless, most European governments, even the British, felt there was little that they could do while both fighting on the ground and the international diplomatic stalemate continued.

The key exception was France, which refused to ban all humanitarian aid to Vietnam and the Hun Sen Kampuchean government, and continued to talk with the Indonesians, who saw themselves as the ASEAN 'leader' on this issue, about ways to break the deadlock. France not only hosted the first substantial talks between the Cambodian factions in 1987–88 but also organized international conferences in 1989 and 1991 which finally hammered out a peace settlement. It became the first Western country to give aid to the Hun Sen government (Lao 1993, p. 389). In February 1993 French President Francois Mitterrand visited Cambodia and Vietnam, the first visit by a Western head of state since the communist victories (*South China Morning Post*, 10 and 12 February 1993). The visit was strong on symbolism but also replete with commercial overtones, for French business had been consistently pushing the government to move quicker on extending aid and economic and technological assistance for Vietnam. Total EC trade with Vietnam had grown from only $77 million in 1985 to $867 million in 1992, with France the leading trader and, having invested $490 million of FDI in Vietnam by April 1993, also the leading EU investor in the country, having overtaken Britain, which had invested earlier in the oil industry but done little else.

Mitterrand's visit also acted as a catalyst for spurring negotiations already under way between the EC and Vietnam for a cooperation agreement, designed to follow on from a textile agreement concluded in December 1992 which contained very strict quantitative limitations on Vietnam, which was not party to the MFA. The European Commission, in laying down negotiating guidelines in July 1993, made it clear that, as had been proposed for the case of any future revised EC–ASEAN agreement, the cooperation agreement should have some clause referring to human rights and democracy (*Agence Europe*, 16 July 1993). Nonetheless, economic and technical assistance provisions eventually formed the bulk of the agreement. The EC governments believed that by assisting in Vietnam's transition to a market economy, new commercial opportunities would emerge. Paradoxically, while several European governments (notably the French and the Italian) urged the Americans to ease their restrictions on IMF loans to Vietnam (Williams 1992, p. 75), European businessmen saw advantages in having US commercial rivals still excluded from doing business there. Thus the lifting of the American embargo in 1994 was viewed by them with mixed emotions. Trade, nonetheless, has continued to grow steadily, with total EU–Vietnam trade reaching $3.5 billion in 1996.

The EU–Vietnam cooperation agreement negotiations stumbled over the phraseology of the formula to cover human rights, continuing European aid for the repatriation of Vietnamese boat people (which will be discussed in chapter 8), and a German–Vietnamese dispute over the return of around 40,000 Vietnamese who had been living in the former East Germany (also to be discussed in Chapter 8). The speed-up in the timetable for Vietnam's accession to ASEAN all but overtook the negotiations, in the sense that once an ASEAN member Vietnam would become eligible to join in the EU–ASEAN Cooperation Agreement. However, both sides decided to continue with the planned EU–Vietnam agreement, which was duly signed in July 1995.

Trade and investment flows between Europe and Laos and Cambodia are extremely limited, with aid flows being almost as important. After almost non-existent trade relations during the 1980s, EU–Laos trade has risen rapidly during the 1990s, from virtually nothing ($19 million) in 1990 to $127 million in 1996, and EU–Cambodian trade has exhibited a somewhat similar pattern, from $15 million in 1990 to $229 million in 1996 (IMF (Direction of Trade Yearbook, various years) statistics), but these levels hardly qualify either to be ranked as a serious trading partner of Europe. European FDI in both countries has been extremely limited. In Cambodia only a few brave European multinationals have ventured in. The Anglo-Dutch Shell company entered Cambodia in 1992, investing $60 million in opening up over 40 filling stations, which has given it a 20 per cent market share. British American Tobacco has sunk nearly $40 million into a joint venture to improve and expand production of local cigarettes (*Asia Pacific Link*, Spring 1997). The EU has supported a number of development projects in Laos, covering food security, water supply, and energy and forest conservation, providing around $130 million in aid during the decade to 1996. The EU and its member states have been the largest contributors to the rehabilitation programme in Cambodia. By 1995 the EU had committed $72 million for short-term refugee aid, food aid and rehabilitation.

The EU has also been carrying out negotiations since 1995 with both countries to create economic, trade and development cooperation agreements, drafts of which were initialled with both countries in November 1996. Part of the economic aid envisaged under the agreement with Laos will be dedicated to anti-drug trafficking and environmental protection programmes (*Agence Europe*, 8 November 1996). Drugs and the environment are also to be covered in the agreement with Cambodia, but with additional special emphasis on mine clearance (a legacy of the civil wars), transport infrastructure reconstruction and job creation activities (*Agence Europe*, 8 November 1996). The EU–Laos cooperation agreement was approved by the European Parliament in mid 1997, but the EU–Cambodia agreement was held up by the internal political crisis in the latter.

THE BURMESE CONUNDRUM

By contrast with Vietnam and Cambodia, which had been regular topics of political discussion between the EC and ASEAN in the 1980s, Burma (Myanmar) rarely figured in European deliberations on Southeast Asia until its military government's violent suppression of pro-democracy demonstrators in 1988 brought it into the international spotlight. Since then Burma has been one of the most divisive issues in EC–ASEAN relations, and its accession to ASEAN in July 1997 has certainly done nothing to diminish that tendency.

Burma is a multi-ethnic and resource-rich country, which by its largely self-imposed isolation has missed out on the dynamic socio-economic changes which have transformed most of the other countries of Southeast Asia in the last two or three decades. From the early 1960s to the late 1980s, Burma kept itself to itself, ruled by a nationalistic military government determined to follow the 'Burmese road to socialism'; it proved to be merely the route to political repression and economic stagnation. Mounting economic discontent and political frustration ultimately led to the confrontations of 1988, when the pro-democracy movement was bloodily suppressed (Bray 1995, pp. 4–5). Since then the military government, re-titled as the State Law and Order Restoration Council (SLORC), has tried to maintain a delicate balancing act: slowly and carefully opening up the economy to the outside world while keeping a firm lid on any democratic aspirations or ethnic separatism which might undermine its rule. It has ignored the 1990 election results, which were a landslide for the democratic opposition, and harassed Aung San Suu Kyi, its charismatic leader, who was held under house arrest from 1989 to 1995 and is allowed barely any greater freedom now. In November 1997 SLORC transformed itself in name into the State Peace and Development Council, but although some personnel changes were effected at the same time, the new body remained basically the same, an unrepresentative military junta (*Asian Defence Journal*, December 1997).

Burma's economy has been in a kind of time warp; it remains the predominantly agricultural economy that it was 30 years ago, with the lucrative lumber, oil, gas and precious metals trade largely in the hands of the military and its cronies (Mya 1992, pp. 215–219). The economic sanctions imposed by foreign countries after 1988 left the Burmese government with little option but slowly to change course and try to deregulate some sectors of the economy. But the FDI which has flowed into the country in the 1990s has been mainly into oil and gas exploration and the tourist sector; almost nothing has gone into manufacturing. With the government itself doing little to foster either manufacturing development or agricultural efficiency, and allowing the currency to become vastly over-valued, the Burmese economy is once again going backwards (*Far Eastern Economic Review*, 7 August 1997). Although its semi-isolated economy has not been so directly affected by the Asian financial turmoil as its richer ASEAN neighbours, the indirect effects, mostly notably a drastic reduction in FDI from those neighbours, are further depressing Burmese growth.

After the bloody events of 1988 the EC condemned the killing of pro-democracy demonstrators and suspended aid programmes (though these had already been fairly small scale). It has persistently called on the ruling military junta to recognize the results of the 1990 general elections, has sought an official arms embargo and, on a number of occasions, has urged trade sanctions against Burma. In July 1991 the European Parliament awarded the confined opposition leader, Ms Aung San, its Sakharov human rights prize (Bray 1992, p. 292).

Putting aside concerns about human rights issues, European companies became more interested in trade and investment with Burma in the early 1990s as it began to show signs of opening up. It even began to be talked about favourably in terms of being a serious, in some ways better equipped, competitor of the newly emerged Vietnam. Nonetheless, EC–Burma trade remained at a very low level, rising from only $175 million in 1990 to $308 million in 1996, and FDI tended to be confined either to the tourist sector (hotels) or to off-shore oil and gas development projects. Of the European countries, the former colonial power, Britain, has been the largest investor, with a total of 17 committed investments valued at $643 million by the end of 1995 (*South China Morning Post*, 14 April 1996). But France is close behind, with $465 million committed in one massive project: a controversial pipeline joint venture between the French oil company Total, which is part-owned by the French government, and the US company Unocal to pipe gas from the Andaman Sea to Thailand. The project has been criticized both for its environmental impact and for the use of forced labour for construction, and some Total employees have been killed by ethnic insurgents in the area (Pilger 1996 p. 278; *Sunday Morning Post*, 26 January 1997). But Total have stayed on the project.

Not all European companies have been so resistant to European pressure group activities, and as popular feelings against the Burmese government (including threats of consumer boycotts of companies investing in Burma) have grown, and as European governments have progressively toughened their attitudes in response to the failure of the SLORC to implement political liberalization, some European companies have begun, like some of their US counterparts, to withdraw from their investments in Burma. The most well known of these are the Dutch beer company Heineken and the Danish beer company Carlsberg, both of which closed down their breweries during 1996. Heineken scrapped its $35 million for the sake of its 'corporate reputation' (Pilger 1996, p. 279).

In the early 1990s, the EC maintained a policy of 'critical dialogue' with Burma, with supposedly an emphasis on both words (Bray 1995, p. 58). However, as critics have argued, this approach has not only been rather ineffective but has allowed European companies 'undeterred and often secretly encouraged by their governments' to carry on doing business in Burma (Pilger 1996, p. 277).

Nonetheless, during 1996 a change of tone and substance was detectable in European governments' policies. Disappointed with the SLORC's restrictive policies towards the democracy movement after Ms Aung San's release from house arrest, the EU began to get tougher, instituting in the spring of 1996 strict limitations on contacts with senior SLORC officials, followed by the suspension of ministerial contacts (October 1996) and, after recognition of authenticated reports of the use of forced labour, a withdrawal of tariff preferences granted under the GSP to Burmese industrial goods (December 1996) and agricultural goods (February 1997) (*South China Morning Post*, 2 April 1996; *Agence Europe*, 28 October 1996 and 19 February 1997). Denmark had been one of the leading advocates of these further sanctions against Burma after its unaccredited honorary consul in Rangoon died in June 1996 in suspicious circumstances (*Bangkok Post*, 1 October 1996). Britain, which has been strongly supportive of Ms Aung San, who is married to a British academic, had previously argued that sanctions could only be effective if agreed at the UN level, but it too began to harden its attitude, including making it clear that a resumption of normal relations was conditional on progress in the key areas of democratic reform and human rights (Pilger 1996, p. 278).

The GSP suspension was the only means of economic pressure available within the EU framework, as the EU has no cooperation agreement with Burma. As will be discussed further in Chapters 8 and 9, Britain and the EU made it clear that even though Burma had now entered ASEAN it would not be welcome at the ASEM 2 Summit in London in April 1998, and they have suggested that the EU–ASEAN Cooperation Agreement might well not be extended to Burma in the way that it is being to other new entrants (*Agence Europe*, 19 February 1997). Burma protested that as a member of ASEAN it should have been allowed to participate in the 1998 ASEM, and Malaysia strongly supported its case, but the new British Labour government remained firm in insisting that Burma would be barred in line with EU sanctions against the country (*South China Morning Post*, 12 September 1997).

Given the downturn in its economy and the tension over its internal political situation, which is not only continuing but if anything heightening, Burma is unlikely to become an important trading and investment partner of the EU in the foreseeable future. It is likely, however, to remain a source of continuing friction in the European political dialogue with Asia.

In the postwar period, the European colonial withdrawal from Southeast Asia was accompanied by a loosening, or even in some cases a severing, of economic and commercial ties. The 1980s did, however, see a degree of commercial re-involvement which paralleled a limited, but nonetheless palpable, convergence of political and strategic concerns with ASEAN, which became the axis of Europe's relationship with Southeast Asia.

The end of the Cold War brought no fundamental change to the Europeans' basic perception of ASEAN as a relatively stable, accessible and politically compatible grouping. But as the 1990s have continued, there have been some fluctuations in the economic relationship, in part because expectations on both sides have not been matched by accomplishments, and because some new tensions, most notably over Burma, have been injected into what had been a relatively trouble-free political–strategic dialogue. Europe has tended, in the past, to take both ASEAN's political stability and its limited intra-regional economic cooperation for granted, but the changed nature of the organization through expansion and the socio-political disruptions brought to some of its member countries by the Asian financial crisis suggest that Europe needs to re-evaluate its relationship with ASEAN. ASEAN, too, will no doubt find the need to re-examine and possibly even re-invent itself, and, indeed, some voices within ASEAN are already calling for it to convert itself into a proper community. So Europe should watch carefully and be prepared to respond positively to the newly emerging regional order in Southeast Asia.

6. Coping with China

Baffled by this immensity,
I ask the vast expanse of earth,
Who, then, controls the rise and fall of fortunes.
(poem entitled 'Changsha' by Mao Zedong (Schram 1994, p. 225))

Clearly China, as a major political and strategic power and an increasingly important economic power, deserves some special consideration in its own right in terms of Europe's relations with the Asia Pacific region. The course of Sino-European relations since 1949 has seen ample evidence of the complex interplay of political and economic elements in that relationship.

Although Europe has been going through important transformations during that time, including, of course, the development of the EC and the rise and fall of the Cold War, the most dramatic impacts on the relationship have tended to come from the changes taking place within China and in the nature of that country's leaders' perceptions of the outside world and Europe's place in that worldview. After Mao Zedong's guerrilla armies defeated the Nationalists in the civil war, new land and industrial policies were introduced along Soviet lines, but Mao could not resist the tendency to go for more radical approaches. The 'Great Leap Forward' of the late 1950s and the decade-long 'Cultural Revolution' from the mid 1960s did untold damage to the Chinese economy and society, and kept China effectively isolated from the outside world. However, the re-emergence of Deng Xiaoping and a coterie of pragmatic reformers in the late 1970s enabled China to experiment with a new model of development, 'a mixture of planned economy and market socialism' (Wang 1994, p. 24). Reform began in the agricultural sector and moved on to the industrial and financial sectors, but left pockets of the planned economy, notably the near-bankrupt state enterprises, behind. The country moved from import substitution to active engagement in foreign trade and inward investment, particularly through special economic zones, as an engine of growth.

In contrast to his enthusiasm for economic reform, Deng was resistant to real political reform, and was prepared to call in the military to crack down on the pro-democracy students in Tiananmen Square, Beijing, in 1989 to prevent what he saw as a threat to Communist Party supremacy. His approach has been characterized as 'soft economics and hard politics' (Wong 1997, p. 51). Nonetheless, his programme of economic reform continued and, at one stage in the early 1990s, was even speeded up. Although the current leadership under President Jiang Zemin and Prime Minister Zhu Rongji have put a priority on socio-economic stability, which in practice has meant a slowdown of the pace of economic reform and growth (and, indeed, they did succeed in 1996–97 in constraining over-heating in the economy), they are not fundamentally opposed to the direction in which Deng has set the country. At the 1997 15th Party Congress, the new leadership even took the first steps to bite the bullet of reforming the state enterprises, by announcing plans effectively to 'privatize' (although that word was not used) most of them (*Far Eastern Economic Review*, 2 October 1997).

The results of Deng's economic modernization have been impressive. China began to generate consistently good growth rates in the 1980s, and in the first half of the 1990s it was the fastest-growing economy in the world. Economists differ over ways to calculate per capita growth levels and rates accurately for an economy as large and, increasingly, as decentralized as China's. Its official per capita GNP of $750 (at the end of 1996) actually rises to three or five times that level in the coastal regions such as Shenzhen, Guangdong and Shanghai. In terms of purchasing power parity, China's per capita income could be as high as $2200. But some economists doubt whether the high growth rates and high incomes can really be attributed to other than the booming coastal regions, leaving much of the inland in a much less dynamic mode (*Asia Inc.*, August 1997). Whatever the validity of the Chinese statistics concerning domestic growth, the external sector is quantifiable. China has rapidly risen through the ranks of the world's trading nations. In 1978 it was ranked 32nd in world trade, but by 1995 it was 11th; over the same period its share of world trade had risen from 0.8 to 2.9 per cent (Findlay and Watson 1997, p. 108). More significantly, the structure of China's exports had changed from a primary product focus to manufactured products, which by 1994 made up some 85 per cent of its exports (Findlay and Watson 1997, pp. 110–111). China has also become a massive absorber of FDI, certainly in the 1990s, when it has attracted more FDI than any other developing nation.

These economic statistics can be matched, though not in so easily quantifiable a form, by the apparent growth of China's political and strategic importance, as shown by its steady growth in military expenditure, its greater willingness to assert itself over regional issues (such as Taiwan and the South China Sea), and its higher profile in the UN and other international organizations. This combination of economic and political power has led some observers to conclude that 'the world has never seen a power rising as fast, or on such a scale, as China is doing in the late twentieth century' (Segal and Goodman 1997, p. 5). This chapter examines what this rise means for Europe and for Sino-European relations.

Drawing on the analysis of Michael Yahuda (1994, pp. 268–270), who posits four phases to Sino-European relations, it is possible to distinguish some broad characteristics in the relationship since the People's Republic of China (PRC) was established in 1949. The first phase, covering the 1950s and 1960s, was marked by Chinese preoccupation with internal revolution and problems on its immediate borders. Although cursory diplomatic ties were established with a few European states, the formation of the EC was treated with 'relative indifference' (Kapur 1986, p. 4) and the apparent breakthrough in relations with France petered out. Above all, the relationship was constrained by bipolarity, namely the US–Soviet superpower struggle (Yahuda 1994, p. 268). With the Cultural Revolution winding down, however, the 1970s saw a new phase of Chinese interest in Europe, as the Chinese saw the EC as a potentially important trading partner and Western Europe as a whole as a useful 'ally' in its attempt to develop an anti-Soviet international united front, even though China was never able to cement such an 'alliance' (Yahuda 1994, pp. 268–269).

Differing here slightly from Yahuda's chronological division, the third phase can be dated from the late 1970s, as the EC–China preferential trade agreement was signed and China began its open-door policy of economic reform and modernization. A solid economic base to the relationship was established, which made possible the subsequent senior-level political exchanges as China moved towards its 'independent' foreign policy in the early 1980s (Kapur 1986, p. 47; Yahuda 1994, p. 269). Consequently, the relaxation in East–West and Sino-Soviet relations in the second half of the 1980s led China to down-grade its assessment of the strategic value of Western Europe (Cabestan 1990, pp. 216–219). A fourth phase, however, began with the Tiananmen Square massacre in 1989. Although European business soon returned to the Chinese market, the 1990s have been marked by greater friction in Sino-European relations, both over economic issues and over political issues such as human rights, Taiwan and Hong Kong. As will be argued below, the 1997 handover of Hong Kong to China marks the beginning of a new fifth phase of Sino-European relations.

OPENING UP THE CHINESE ECONOMY

In the 19th century, the Europeans had been attracted by the potential of the Chinese market, a dream which was never fully realized despite the European encroachments into certain coastal regions. Civil war, Japanese invasion and internal political turmoil dampened commercial prospects for much of the 20th century, but the late 1970s did see the rebirth of the European dream. However, as will be shown below, this time too the dream has yet to be fully realized.

Although Britain, Denmark and the Netherlands recognized the new PRC government almost immediately in 1950, France did not follow until 1964 and the remainder of the EC states not until the early 1970s when the 'diplomatic revolution' which was to see Taiwan replaced by China at the UN occurred (Kapur 1986, p. 32). Economic relations between China and Western Europe were as low level as the political contacts, and not until the mid 1960s did total two-way trade even begin to approach $1 billion. The Cultural Revolution did nothing to boost trade ties. However, the change of international environment in the early 1970s, with the EC not only enlarging but also needing new trading opportunities to sustain employment and China rebuilding relations with the United States, encouraged both sides to look at each other anew. In 1975 a visit by a senior commissioner to Beijing and a visit by Deng to France broke the ice (Kapur 1986, pp. 33–37). The third phase of Sino-European relations set out above was about to begin.

The result was that a new basis for EC–China trade was established, though not without some hard negotiating on the first two accords: a preferential trade agreement was signed in 1977 and a textile agreement in 1979, after which, finally, in 1980 the EC unilaterally extended its GSP benefits to Chinese industrial goods and certain agricultural products (Kapur 1986, pp. 47–54, 59–64). Total trade, which had been around $2.5 billion in 1976, doubled by the year 1980, when it broke the $5 billion barrier. This was due not just to the agreements with the EC, which in particular helped to foster exports to the EC, but also to what has been described as the 'Great Leap Westward' – the sudden and often indiscriminate import of capital machinery and technology from the West, especially from Western Europe, during the 1977–79 period (Chen 1989, pp. 175–177). The inevitable readjustment in Chinese import policy in the first half of the 1980s to cope with the foreign currency drain led to a slowdown in the growth of European exports. According to IMF figures, this resulted for the first time in a trade surplus, albeit a very small one, for China in its trade with the EC in the years 1980–82 (Grant 1995, p. A.7); it should be noted that Chinese figures claim that China was still in deficit to the EC in those years (Chen 1989, p. 177). It should be noted here that discrepancies between European and Chinese trade statistics have been a recurring phenomenon – and the source of much controversy between the two sides in the 1980s and 1990s – but can certainly be explained in part by differences in how both sides account for re-exports through Hong Kong in their statistics, with the role of goods produced in China under 'outward processing' activities and then exported to Europe being particularly difficult to handle. However, almost certainly, as has been documented in the case of Sino-US trade (Kueh and Voon 1997, pp. 73–76), both China and the EC have a tendency to under-report their exports to each other and to over-state their bilateral trade deficits.

In fact, throughout the 1980s there were fluctuations in the trade balance, but since 1988 there has been a persistent and increasingly large trade surplus for China which, as shown in Table 6.1, hit a peak of $10.8 billion in 1992, before stabilizing around that level through into the mid 1990s. However, from 1995 the Chinese trade surplus began to rise again, to $13.1 billion that year; by the following year it had risen to $16.2 billion. Comparing the start year of China's open-door policy (1978) with the situation 15 years later, it is clear that in terms of EC import share China has overtaken both Hong Kong and Taiwan in importance as a source, although as a destination for Chinese exports the EC has retained roughly the same degree of importance to China through the period (round the 10–12 per cent mark). Although the percentage of EC exports going to China has also increased over the period, overtaking Taiwan and drawing level with Hong Kong in importance, from the Chinese side the EC has become a less important source of imports, with the EC share slowly but steadily declining, from 18 per cent in 1978 to 14 per cent in 1993 (Ferdinand 1995, pp. 27–28). It could be argued, however, that this is still an assymetrical trade relationship, not in the sense of surpluses for one side or the other, but because compared with the relative importance of the EU in both China's exports and imports, China, even in 1995, accounted for only 1 per cent of the EU's total exports and 1.6 per cent of the EU's total imports.

China's main imports from the EC have been chemicals and related products, semi-manufactured goods and machinery, and transport equipment. Although chemicals have declined in importance in the 1990s, mainly be-

Table 6.1   EC/EU trade with China

	Exports to China (US $million)	As per cent of total EC/EU exports	Imports from China (US $million)	As per cent of total EC/EU imports
1980	2478	0.36	2753	0.36
1985	5484	0.84	2971	0.45
1990	7373	0.49	13289	0.86
1991	7719	0.52	18160	1.15
1992	9604	0.61	20995	1.28
1993	14301	1.00	23730	1.70
1994	16246	0.99	27644	1.74
1995	19237	0.96	32333	1.69
1996	18407	0.90	34608	1.77

Source: IMF, *Direction of Trade Statistics Yearbook*, 1987 and 1997 editions (Washington: 1987 and 1997).

cause several of the major European chemical producers have set up joint venture plants inside China, electrical machinery and transport equipment have remained important. However, the switch in the commodity structure of China's exports has been more noticeable than in its imports. In the 1970s and early 1980s Chinese exports to the EC still consisted mostly of food and crude materials and textiles/clothing, including silk; in 1985 textiles accounted for almost 30 per cent of China's exports to the EC (Chen 1989, p. 183). But in the 1990s, although clothing is still the largest export item (20 per cent in 1993), toys and consumer electronics have become important too; foodstuffs have all but disappeared (Commission 1995, Annex 2).

The trade surplus increases were undoubtedly due to the more rapid increase in Chinese exports to the EC as compared with EC exports to China. The Tiananmen Square massacre undoubtedly caused European companies to 'shun' the PRC market for a while (Ferdinand 1995, p. 28), in part because of governmental and EC-level sanctions imposed on China; in part because of the companies' own fears about political instability inside China. Although by about 1991 that reticence had largely disappeared, the Europeans seemed to be unable to capitalize on the new high growth in the Chinese economy to increase their market share. They were barely able to hold their own against their Japanese, American and overseas Chinese competitors.

European companies complained that they still found exporting to and doing business in China difficult. In 1991 the EC began a periodic series of trade experts' meetings with China, intended to examine specific problems hampering trade and market access, such as transparency of regulations, foreign exchange controls, limitations on financial services, IPRs and tax regimes. From 1994 special sectoral groups started work on financial services, IPR and agriculture. The EC/EU approach was governed by two important considerations: to maintain pressure on the Chinese authorities to ease the existing problems and to avoid any discrimination that might result from China's deals with other trading partners, in particular the United States (Commission 1995, Annex 3).

But more crucial in the trade relationship than problems of market access for European goods in China has been the determined push by the Chinese to export to Europe. This was particularly noticeable in the late 1980s–early 1990s as, according to IMF figures, Chinese exports to the EC grew dramatically from $2.9 billion in 1985 to $13.3 billion in 1990 and $18.2 billion in 1991. By 1996 Chinese exports to the EU had nearly doubled again, to $34.6 billion (see Table 6.1).

These rapid increases have meant that China has come to be viewed by the Europeans as yet another Asian exporter posing a serious threat in certain industrial sectors. Even as early as 1984, before the great rise in Chinese exports to the EC, the European side was adopting a cautious attitude to

Chinese exports. The 1984 textile protocol was, on the whole, more restrictive than the 1979 textile agreement, and the new Trade and Cooperation Agreement, signed in 1984 to replace the 1978 trade agreement, offered no new liberalization of trade restrictions on Chinese products (Kapur 1986, p. 79). However, Chinese goods did continue to benefit from the GSP system and, according to EC calculations, these rose from $2.5 billion in 1988 to $8 billion in 1992 (out of total Chinese exports to the EC of $21 billion that year). By the latter year, China had become by far the biggest beneficiary of the EC's GSP system, receiving 22 per cent of the total benefits accorded to the developing world, three times greater than the second largest beneficiary (Commission 1995, Annex 2).

As was the case with the earlier waves of Asian exporters, the EC resorted to various measures to try to stem the flow of imports from China. Even in the first half of the 1980s anti-dumping measures were taken on some Chinese products of limited importance, such as lithium carbonate, magnesite and alarm clocks (Kapur 1986, pp. 79–80). A World Bank study estimated in the early 1990s that EC protection using non-tariff barriers such as quantitative restrictions and MFA quotas covered about 30 per cent of all EC imports from China and, if manufactured goods only are considered, that share rose to 48 per cent (Acharya 1995, pp. 61–62). It has been estimated that nearly a quarter of all EC anti-dumping duties imposed on third-country imports during the 1988–95 period were actually targeted at Chinese goods (Dent 1997, p. 11). Certainly, by the mid 1990s EU anti-dumping actions and duties were being imposed on Chinese goods ranging from shoes and handbags to bicycles and ferro-silico-manganese (*South China Morning Post*, 29 January 1997). But, as evidence of the way in which China's manufactured exports to the EU are being upgraded, consumer electronics have now come under the watchful eyes of the Europeans. In early 1997 the European Commission announced its first ever anti-dumping investigation of imports of personal fax machines from China (*Agence Europe*, 5 February 1997). There was therefore a tone emerging in Sino-European trade disputes that was ominously reminiscent of earlier European trade disputes with other Asian Pacific states. The sense of *déjà vu* has become pronounced.

INVESTING IN CHINA

A key facet of China's opening up to the outside world at the end of the 1970s was the attraction of FDI, as a way to speed up modernization, technology transfer and export growth. Beginning with the four 'special economic zones', the encouragement of FDI was allowed to spread to other coastal zones in the early 1980s and later in the decade to inland areas as well.

In the early years of China's opening, FDI from the EC was very important, accounting for 41 per cent of all FDI going into China in the years
1979–82 and totalling $315 million over those years. However, this relatively
significant presence can be attributed to the conclusion of oil exploration and
energy development contracts, mainly with French companies (Chen 1989,
p. 187). Although this tendency remained strong into the mid 1980s, including the agreement in 1986 on the investment by French and British companies
in the Daya Bay nuclear power plant in south China close to Hong Kong
(Taylor 1990, p. 77), the Europeans did slowly begin to put more emphasis
on manufacturing FDI. Nonetheless, the Europeans appeared to be much
more cautious than other overseas investors. In the 1983–85 period, EC FDI
dropped to only 9.8 per cent of all FDI going into China (Chen 1989, p. 187).
The EC share dropped further to 5.5 per cent in 1985–87 and 2.6 per cent in
1990–93 (data from the Commission Office, Hong Kong).

The EC has continued to hold a relatively poor position in China, despite
the boom in FDI in the country since the early 1990s. Indeed, by 1993,
although cumulatively the EC countries had invested nearly $2.5 billion over
the 1979–93 period (pledged amounts actually totalled $7.3 billion) in some
3000 projects, the EC share of total FDI into China was only around 4 per
cent (Commission 1995, p. 9). EC FDI represented less than half of the FDI
of either US or Japanese companies and was, of course, well below that of
the Hong Kong-based companies. As shown in Table 6.2, Britain has generally been the largest EU investor (even though it is not the largest EU trader
with China). Although the average size in terms of capital investment of the
EU projects tends to be larger than that of its competitors, a characteristic
which has been true since the late 1970s (Chen 1989, p. 187), clearly the
number of companies, particularly the smaller and medium-sized companies,
committing themselves to the Chinese market has been much smaller.

Table 6.2   European FDI in China (utilized amounts in US $million)

	Germany	France	United Kingdom	Netherlands	Italy
1985	24.1	32.5	71.4	0.1	19.4
1990	64.3	21.1	13.3	16.0	4.1
1991	161.1	9.9	35.4	6.7	28.2
1992	88.6	44.9	38.3	28.4	20.7
1993	56.3	141.4	220.5	84.0	99.9
1994	259.0	192.4	688.8	111.1	206.2
1995	386.4	287.0	914.1	114.1	263.3

Source: *Almanac of China's Foreign Economic Relations and Trade, 1996/97* (Beijing: China
Economics Publishing House, 1997).

Both national governments and the EC/EU itself were aware of this unsatisfactory FDI record compared both with EC–China trade shares and with rival advanced country FDI in China. The European Commission has undertaken a number of initiatives to promote business and FDI links through sectoral seminars, sponsoring a China–Europe Business Forum, information diffusion, management training for Chinese (specifically the China–Europe International Business School (CEIBS) launched in 1994 in Shanghai to replace the less successful China–Europe Management Institute), and extending the European Community Investment Partners scheme to China. National governments have also become more active, as businessmen put pressure on their respective governments to help show the flag and, through high-level visits, assist in gaining preferential access for infrastructural and industrial projects. Several European leaders, headed by German Chancellor, Helmut Kohl (November 1995) and French President Chirac (May 1997), have therefore visited China in recent years. A May 1995 delegation led by Britain's Deputy Prime Minister, Michael Heseltine, was described as the largest British trade mission to China for over 200 years (Whitla, Bridges and Davies 1995 p. 5); encouraging British investment was one of its main objectives.

While appreciating that investment decisions are ultimately up to individual companies, with or without national governmental support, the European Commission has nonetheless been disappointed by the lack of coordination among the rival European companies. Although cross-frontier cooperation does occur among European companies, such as in the aerospace or power generation sectors (Maclean 1995, p. 46), insistence on going it alone at a national level, when a cross-European bid for major investment projects might have been more effective, has surely worked to the advantage of other non-European rivals.

One issue which affects all European companies and where the EU has been able to play a useful role on behalf of all has been IPR. The US government has consistently taken a harder line than the EU on this particular issue, even though it is of equal importance to European companies and, in some cases, a serious deterrent to them in committing themselves to FDI in China. In 1994–95, indeed, the US Trade Department threatened to implement huge tariffs on certain Chinese exports before the Chinese relented and came to a bilateral IPR agreement with the Americans in early 1995 (Whitla, Bridges and Davies 1995, p. 5). This agreement was worrying to European businessmen, who warned that the EU's 'softer and less sabre-rattling stance [should] not give any undue advantage to US companies' (Maclean 1995, p. 49). There was a marked reticence from the Chinese to agree to the equal applicability of this agreement to the EU and it took a visit to Beijing by EU Vice-President Brittan in April 1995 to secure a Chinese guarantee of its extension to European companies (*Eastern Express*, 20 April 1995). Of course, to the Americans the EU attitude smacks of the Europeans riding on the coat-tails of the Americans, who get all the flack for the hard negotiating (Whitla, Bridges and Davies 1995, p. 5). European diplomats admit that there has been a tendency in the past for such a European approach, both over IPR and over Chinese membership of the GATT/WTO (discussed below), but argue that in recent years the Europeans have been more forthright in their own way (interview, German Foreign Ministry official, May 1997).

Nonetheless, despite the efforts of the European Commission and member governments, the EC record on FDI has not improved significantly. According to Chinese figures, utilized FDI flows from the EU increased from $670 million in 1993 to $1.54 billion in 1994 and $2.14 billion in 1995. Although the EU share of Chinese incoming FDI rose from 2.4 per cent in 1993 to 5.7 per cent in 1995, it is still less than not only Japan and the United States but now also ASEAN. Singapore's FDI alone into China in 1995 was more than double that of the largest European investor that year, Britain (Fung and Lau 1997, pp. 217–218).

DEVELOPMENT AID

European aid to China has been even more low key than European FDI, but the Europeans have put increasing stress on the economic cooperation aspects in recent years.

The European Commission has itself admitted that its own aid to China has 'remained small' given the vast needs of China (Commission 1995, p. 13). The very limited programmes in place in the 1980s were anyway suspended after the 1989 Tiananmen Square crackdown. Even after resumption, in the 1991–94 period less than $24 million a year was used for China, barely a quarter of the budget set aside for India. The first project in China to be financed by the EC came in 1984, but the real aid programme did not begin until 1985 after the Trade and Cooperation Agreement was signed. During the 1985–94 period a total of 25 developmental projects were begun under the rubric of technical and financial assistance. Most of these projects have been based in rural areas, a dairy developmental project being the largest. By contrast with some other donors to China, most notably the Japanese, the EU's aid to China is in the form of grants not loans, although since the end of 1995 the European Investment Bank has been empowered to provide loans to China.

The EU's own aid programmes towards China during the 1990s have tended to operate in parallel to an emphasis on economic cooperation, in particular four aspects: human resources, economic and social reform, business and industrial reform, and the environment (interview, European

Commission official, June 1996). These have resulted in initiatives for cooperation in higher education, such as an agreement signed in May 1996 to promote European studies in China and the establishment of a programme to have European managers trained in China, as well as special seminars in China on IPR enforcement and village governance. Not all the European-level initiatives have been successful. A programme in the late 1980s to support the modernization of Chinese companies was abandoned within a couple of years as there was little evidence of a knock-on effect throughout the country, and the China–Europe Management Institute, set up in 1985, suffered from infrastructural and administrative problems until it was effectively superseded by the CEIBS (Commission 1995, Annex 4, p. 2). However, the CEIBS, as well as several of the other initiatives of the mid 1990s mentioned above, is still too new to allow for an effective assessment of whether they will be more successful than earlier programmes.

Individual EU member countries do, of course, have their own aid programmes for China but, as has often been the case with European aid to other Asian Pacific developing countries, these have been mostly, either directly or indirectly, tied to commercial activities. For example, when France extended a loan of FFr 1 billion (approximately $200 million) to China in 1995 it went to a series of projects such as water and sewage treatment plants, telephone systems and hospital equipment in which French companies were involved (*Eastern Express*, 5 December 1995). Since the mid 1980s, when France began to extend these loans to China, over $2.9 billion has been disbursed (Godemont and Serra 1997).

Britain, too, has extended export credits to China to help British business, with the largest of these agreements, for $1.5 billion, being extended to industrial projects in Wuhan in October 1994 (*Sunday Morning Post*, 15 January 1995). Britain has made use of its controversial ATP system (discussed in Chapter 5) for contracts with China, and in the period 1986–93 provided $340 million to British companies undertaking projects in China, which made China the second largest ATP recipient in the world after Malaysia, whose figures were of course inflated by the massive Pergau dam provision (Foreign Affairs Committee 1994a, Vol. II, p. 20). Since 1993 British ATP to China has been running at around $30–40 million per annum (British Consulate-General, Hong Kong, statistics). British officials have argued that the ATP has been particularly beneficial in opening up the Chinese market to British suppliers of project goods (Foreign Affairs Committee 1994a, Vol. II, p. 342). In 1993 China was the top recipient of Italian overseas aid, but since 1995 budgetary constraints in Italy have meant that both financial aid and mixed credits have slowed to a trickle (Dassu 1997).

The use of mixed credits and semi-concessional tied aid covers a grey area in aid funding and, despite several international conferences in the early

1990s to clarify and coordinate definitions and practices, aid figures are almost as slippery to deal with as FDI figures. Nonetheless, while Japan clearly remains by far the largest supplier of overseas aid to China, though admittedly almost exclusively in the form of loans, the Europeans do play a useful, if auxiliary, role as suppliers as far as the Chinese authorities are concerned.

WTO MEMBERSHIP

One of the more contentious issues in Sino-European economic relations in recent years has been the Chinese application to join – or, in the Chinese definition, re-join – GATT and its successor, the WTO. China, then under the Kuomintang, had been one of the original signatories of GATT in 1947, but withdrew in 1950. However, in the early 1980s, as mainland China (the PRC) began to become increasingly open to the international economy, it also began to show an interest in GATT operations and started to send observers to GATT-related meetings (Harris 1997, pp. 134–135). In July 1986 China formally applied to resume its membership of GATT and, after a working party was set up the following year to consider entry terms, negotiations have been proceeding ever since.

China's hopes of a speedy accession were dampened first by the political fall-out from the 1989 Tiananmen Square massacre and second by the complications of the 1990 bid by Taiwan, admittedly under a carefully phrased application as an autonomous customs territory of 'Taiwan, Penghu, Kinmen and Matsu'. In July 1991, significantly a few days after US President George Bush had come out openly in favour of Taiwan's bid, the EC welcomed the Taiwan application (Chiu 1993, p. 212). China has not directly objected to Taiwanese membership as such, but has insisted that Taiwanese accession should not precede its own (Harris 1997, p. 136). In 1992 Taiwan, under pressure from China, did agree to add 'Chinese Taipei' to its application title and later the same year it was granted observer status in GATT (Hsieh 1996, p. 98). About the same time, China began a renewed push for its own membership, hoping, in vain as it turned out, that it might become one of the founding members of the new WTO, which came into operation in January 1995 (Harris 1997, p. 136).

There are clearly advantages for both China and the world trading community, including the EU, in China being part of the WTO. China could receive a considerable reduction in tariff and non-tariff barriers imposed on its exports to Europe and elsewhere, while the Europeans and others would benefit to some extent from a more orderly export expansion by China (Acharya 1995, pp. 54–55) and from a greater transparency and predictability in

China's own import and inward investment regimes (Harris 1997, p. 143). The GATT has had to deal with, and did admit in the past, state trading nations, despite the considerable incompatibility between GATT principles and the practices of such nations (Acharya 1995, pp. 56–57). However, the sheer size of China and its rapidly growing involvement in the international economy in recent years have raised an important set of legal, institutional and economic issues which have complicated, and therefore delayed, the processing of the Chinese application. The transition to the WTO, which by covering additional areas such as services and agriculture has a wider brief than the GATT, did also slow the issue-by-issue negotiating process.

But perhaps by far the most serious problem has been the inevitable role that the United States has taken in the accession negotiations and the way in which bilateral tensions in Sino-American relations have impinged on these negotiations. The Europeans have of course shared many – if not all – of the US concerns about Chinese trading practices. The 1995 EU strategy paper on China listed many areas of concern: reduction or elimination of import tariffs and quotas, foreign trade liberalization, adherence to international procurement agreements, industrial policy reform, traded services reform, and acceptance of the basic principle of non-discrimination (Commission 1995, pp. 10–11). Although it has been argued that there are subtle differences between the EU and US demands on China, in that the United States tends to put more emphasis on obtaining access to the Chinese market (reflecting 'the US domestic political emphasis on exports') while the EU is more interested in 'securing liberal safeguard provisions against imports from China' (Noland 1997, p. 286), it is nonetheless true that the EU concerns about China's trading practices, as listed above, are not dissimilar to the US wish-list.

However, differences in the means to achieve these ends have emerged more openly between the Europeans and the Americans. Although the initial EC position on conditions for China's entry was very similar to that of the United States (Acharya 1995, p. 61), when serious negotiations resumed in 1992 the EU began to differentiate its approach slightly from the tough line taken by the United States. While the United States continued to insist that China enter effectively as an 'industrialized' or 'developed' nation, with correspondingly stricter requirements, the EU appreciated that the variegated nature of the openness and development of the sectors of the Chinese economy made it unrealistic to describe China either as 'developed' or as 'developing' in the usual senses of the words (Acharya 1995, p. 68). During 1993, therefore, European leaders and Commission officials began to talk about using the technique of transitional periods. Their basic position was that while most of the commitments that China would have to make on entry into the GATT/WTO would have to be implemented at the date of accession, some could be implemented under multilateral surveillance over a fixed period of time after entry (Commission 1995, p. 10). But, as EU Vice-President Brittan explained when receiving the Chinese Trade and Industry Minister, Mrs Wu Yi, in October 1995, and again when he visited Beijing in November 1996 on the eve of the first WTO ministerial meeting in Singapore, Europe has been looking for China to make 'down-payments' on its tariff reduction plans and to agree on a 'precise and reliable calendar' for the fulfilment of the various criteria in order to sell this transitional period approach (*Agence Europe*, 11 October 1995; *Asiaweek*,13 December 1996).

Despite these words, however, undoubtedly the EU approach has been 'progressively altering the course of China's accession proceedings' (Elgin 1997, p. 494). As the European approach began to find favour with the WTO's China working party, the United States too came round to accepting the general principle of a transitional period, but the exact definition of that period in terms of time and whether it would apply selectively on a sector-by-sector basis has remained a contentious issue. After negotiations stalled again in 1995–96, the Europeans tried to get them restarted by sending a high-level delegation to China in January 1997; negotiations did recommence in the spring of 1997.

China has, of course, consistently argued that it should be considered as a 'developing' country and that therefore, although it has done much through successive reforms to meet the basic requirements of WTO membership, it will still require a long transition period to meet all of the WTO requirements (Fung and Lau 1997, p. 227). In the Chinese view, the membership fee has to be consistent with the level of the country's economic development. Consequently, Chinese negotiators have preferred the European approach to the US approach, which they see as being motivated by political rather than purely economic considerations. Mrs Wu at one stage described the European initiative as 'kind-hearted', but pointedly added that, as far as China was concerned, it was Washington rather than Brussels which would be decisive in deciding on Chinese admission (*Asiaweek*, 13 December 1996). In fact, the 'conciliatory' role taken by the EU, which must take credit for defusing one of the major sticking points (China's status as a developed or developing nation) in the negotiations, may well not be all that it seems. It has been suggested that the EU has a hidden agenda: to try to arrange a 'quick deal' on entry in return for some 'discriminatory measures' against Chinese imports (Elgin 1997, p. 508), though any such terms would actually be a breach of WTO rules.

The Europeans have been careful not to blame the Americans in public for being overly tough. Indeed, they have continued to stress, as EU Vice-President Brittan has argued, that the onus is on China to provide 'convincing offers' to which the negotiators can give 'a positive, flexible response' (Brittan 1997). Six months later, he was still talking about China having 'a long way to go' before admission (*Hongkong Standard*, 25 September 1997). The comparatively warm summit meeting between President Jiang and President

Clinton in October 1997, coming on the back of fresh Chinese offers of tariff reductions and market liberalization, did however open up the prospect of China finally gaining admission during 1998 or 1999. Whenever China manages to gain accession, then, as tacitly agreed by the Europeans and other major trading nations several years ago, Taiwan will soon follow, possibly even as close as a few minutes later (Tseng 1995, p. 55).

THE POLITICAL RELATIONSHIP

The economic relationship between Europe and China, for all its importance, however, cannot be seen in isolation from the political relationship. As Yahuda has argued, China's political relations with Western Europe, at least until the end of the Cold War, have been heavily influenced by developments in the international system and by China's fluctuating relationships with the two superpowers (Yahuda 1994, p. 268).

In the early years after 1949, apart from the few initial breakthroughs in diplomatic recognition mentioned earlier in this chapter, political contacts with Western Europe were constrained, not least by China's close relationship with the Soviet Union, which laid down a critical line against Western Europe and openly denounced the EC when it was established (Kapur 1986, pp. 3–4). The deepening Sino-Soviet rift did encourage China at least to look anew at Western Europe in the 1960s, but Mao's preoccupation with an anti-American stance over the Vietnam War and the convulsions of the Cultural Revolution (which had as a concomitant a Chinese interest in the student upheavals in Western Europe) meant that little was achieved in practical terms (Yahuda 1994, p. 269).

However, the first half of the 1970s did see a renewed Chinese push towards Europe, as China tried – and succeeded – to gain diplomatic recognition from those Western European states still linked with Taiwan and tried – and failed – to incorporate the Western Europeans into its anti-Soviet international united front. Despite some weapons sales to China and a few intemperate remarks by some European politicians (and, on one occasion, noted in Yahuda (1994, p. 270), by Britain's most senior military authority), a real common or coordinated position on the Soviet Union failed to materialize. In the 1980s, as China itself began to adopt what it described as an 'independent' foreign policy, it began to take a more realistic view of the EC and its member countries. It viewed the growing autonomy of the Europeans as a beneficial development, but came better to understand that there were still limits to how 'united' and independent Western Europe was becoming and that completion of such an ideal would be a 'hard task' (Kapur 1986, p. 83; Cabestan 1990, p. 219).

The EC and its member countries, in turn, seemed better prepared to supplement what had been their strong economic interest in relations with China with a political dialogue. Apart from the particular cases of Sino-British political contacts over Hong Kong, which culminated in the Joint Declaration in 1984, and the subsequent Sino-Portuguese contacts, resulting in the 1987 agreement on Macau, there were an increased number of contacts between senior political leaders on both sides.

This pattern of slowly intensifying political exchange was shattered by the Tiananmen Square massacre in June 1989. This dramatic event came at a time when Western Europeans had already begun to become more critical of China's human rights record (the European Parliament from 1987 onwards had begun passing critical resolutions (Yahuda 1994, p. 272)). Arguably, the emotional European response was tinged with 'a sense of guilt' that past policy towards China had been overly naive in its faith in the proposition that assisting China's economic reforms would inevitably promote democracy (Cabestan 1990, p. 221). But there was also a very real sense of revulsion in Europe, especially given the way in which the Eastern European states were coping much more peacefully with the emerging signs of democratic movements and political instability in their countries.The EC agreed to institute sanctions against China, such as the stopping of high-level ministerial visits, the freezing of arms and military technology sales, and the suspension of soft loans. Some countries, most obviously France, offered sanctuary to Chinese dissidents forced to flee China in the aftermath of the crackdown (Yahuda 1994, p. 273). Britain sought to reassure a nervous Hong Kong by introducing a Bill of Rights and offering a limited number of passports to selected citizens. China inevitably protested against the European actions but, with the exception of some vitriolic attacks on France, the Chinese leadership confined themselves to 'regretting' European sanctions rather than using the stronger term of 'condemning' which was reserved for US moves (Cabestan 1990, pp. 222, 229).

Although European businessmen returned to the Chinese market within months or even weeks (Cabestan 1990, p. 227), the political rehabilitation of China took much longer. Only slowly, over a number of years, were the various sanctions relaxed, and one, the ban on weapons sales, remains in force in 1998. Official and then ministerial visits were resumed, with British Prime Minister John Major, forced to make a gesture in order to secure a deal over the construction of a new airport in Hong Kong, finding himself in the personally distasteful role of being the first Western European leader to meet the 'butchers of Beijing' (Dimbleby 1997, pp. 70–71).

However, human rights had arrived on the Sino-European political agenda. This could only in part be ascribed to the Tiananmen Square massacre. In part it also reflected a greater European interest – including public interest –

in human rights after the collapse and democratization of Eastern Europe as well as a feeling that, with the collapse of the Soviet Union, issues in the Sino-European relationship which had previously to be played down because of an overall need to keep each other on the same side could now be given greater rein (Ferdinand 1995, p. 31).

As European member states grappled with the process of relaxing their individual sanctions while maintaining some private pressure on China over human rights in the early 1990s, the European Commission itself came round to thinking about ways to deepen the political dialogue with China. As a result, in June 1994 an ambitious new framework for bilateral political dialogue was set up, under which the EU *troika* would hold regular ministerial meetings with China, supplemented by *ad hoc* EU–China foreign ministerial and foreign minister–EU ambassadorial meetings. The final step in upgrading the dialogue was the inauguration of an EU–China summit, the first one of which was rather hastily arranged to be held in the margins of the ASEM 2 in London in April 1998; short on substance, it was nonetheless an important occasion for new Premier Zhu to give the Europeans the impression that he was a man with whom they could do business.

Bi-annual meetings of officials specifically devoted to human rights issues were also launched, ironically at China's initiative (Commission 1995, pp. 4–6), although these were suspended in the spring of 1996 and only resumed in November 1997. The EU also tried to encourage the international community to retain an interest in human rights through the sponsoring from 1995 onwards of an annual resolution in the United Nations Human Rights Commission (UNHRC). The February 1995 resolution noted Chinese efforts at legal reform, but argued that repeated instances of violations of human rights in Tibet and elsewhere showed that China still had room for improvement. The EU drew satisfaction from the level of international support for that resolution (Commission 1995, p. 6), even though China mobilized enough support of its own to ensure that it did not pass.

The result was the same with the 1996 resolution, but by then some cracks in European unity were beginning to appear as some EU member countries argued for doing a deal with China in which, in return for dropping the resolution, China would ratify one important international covenant on civil and political liberties. The deal was not struck in the end, but the French in particular were becoming increasingly impatient to adopt a different approach to the human rights issue. By the end of 1996 they were telling their EU partners that they preferred dialogue to a 'ritual condemnation' of China. Several other EU member countries, such as Germany, Italy, Greece and Spain, came round to the French line of thinking and blocked a joint EU sponsorship for the April 1997 resolution. In the end Denmark, a consistent supporter of human rights, with strong support from Holland and Britain, took on the task of sponsoring the resolution (*South China Morning Post*, 17 April 1997). But with China mobilizing developing country support around its position, the resolution failed even to be debated.

The Chinese no doubt felt that their divide-and-rule tactics had successfully undermined European unity. China has used the carrot of commercial orders combined with the stick of economic weapons as a reprisal for what are seen as unfriendly actions by Europeans. The strategy was clear in the aftermath of what one European diplomat described as the 'debacle' in Geneva. The Chinese praised France for its 'discerning' and 'just' move (*China Daily*, 2 April 1997), postponed a planned visit to four of the sponsoring European nations by then Vice-Premier Zhu and cancelled planned visits to China by the Dutch Economics Minister and by Danish officials. After Denmark appealed to its European colleagues for sympathy and support, several European countries, as well as the EU's own officials, went out of their way to explain to China that it should not victimize any particular European state and that an 'attack' on one state was an attack on them all (*South China Morning Post*, 26 April 1997).

The French move undoubtedly helped to set the seal on the visit by President Chirac to China in mid May; he cancelled his own visit to Hong Kong but insisted on going to China, despite the parliamentary election campaign going on at home, and was rewarded with some lucrative business contracts, primarily for the Airbus aircraft, which, while it is constructed by a European consortium, is primarily built and headquartered in France (*South China Morning Post*, 17 May 1997). The Dutch, who held the revolving EU presidency in the first half of 1997, were angry at the move by France and others, and the Dutch Foreign Minister wrote to his colleagues in other member countries accusing them of double standards on human rights in China (*South China Morning Post*, 12 April 1997). The British were very disappointed that, in the year that Hong Kong was due to revert to China of all years, the Europeans were sending the wrong message to the Chinese. The head of the EU office in Hong Kong too expressed his dismay at the Europeans losing their credibility by falling into public disarray and thereby not helping to further the cause of human rights in China (*China Post*, 18 April 1997). In 1998, however, the Europeans restored a measure of unity and decided, though not without some grumblings from some member states, that since a united front in support of a critical resolution could no longer be maintained, no UNHRC resolution would be proposed at all and that recourse instead would be made to the 'quiet diplomacy' of encouraging greater Chinese respect for human rights.

THE HONG KONG DIMENSION

From the late 1980s, therefore, human rights within China have been a particular concern of the Sino-European political dialogue, whereas Hong Kong was not. However, the rolling down of the British flag at midnight on 30 June 1997 and the raising of the Chinese flag immediately after, not only represented the end of one era and the start of another for Hong Kong and its people. For Britain too, which has in previous cases prepared its former colonies for independence rather than for handover to another sovereign power, this marked a new stage in its relationship with both China and Hong Kong. But the departing colonial power was also a member of the EU and for Europe, too, a new phase is about to begin. There will not only be continuity – predominantly in the ongoing commercial interests of the Europeans in Hong Kong – but also some new areas of involvement, particularly in political affairs, which Europeans have tended to leave to the British in the past. This will impact on Sino-European relations in a significant manner.

Chapter 4 discussed some of the key features of the trade and FDI flows between Europe and Hong Kong, but it is worth noting here that not just Britain but all of the major EU states have a significant commercial involvement in Hong Kong. There are many hundreds of European companies operating in the manufacturing, trade, finance, insurance, retailing and other service sectors in Hong Kong. The British Chamber of Commerce in Hong Kong alone claims over 500 member companies; the German Consulate-General in Hong Kong estimates a similar number of German companies operating there. More Europeans live in Hong Kong than in any other Asian city and over a million Europeans visit every year. Hong Kong also plays a role as a financial and service centre not just for China but for the whole Asia Pacific region; currently 94 British and an overall total of some 250 European companies have their regional headquarters in Hong Kong.

The Sino-British Joint Declaration allows for a 'high degree of autonomy' for the Hong Kong Special Administrative Region (HKSAR) after the handover, but the concept lacks a clear definition and examples from other parts of the world suggest a wide variation in the powers available to autonomous regions in practice (Davis 1990, pp. 131–135). On paper, the Joint Declaration grants a range of powers to the HKSAR which are more extensive than is usually the case for autonomous regions and are certainly greater than those powers allowed to any other province or region of China, where a certain degree of decentralization in economic policy-making has not been accompanied by anything like the same degree of loosening of political control. The test, of course, lies in the implementation of the HKSAR's powers. The historical tradition of strong central control combined with rivalry among various Chinese ministries and organizations is likely to limit the scope for the new HKSAR really to be master in its own house.

The approach of the EU and its member countries through the 1990s has generally been to 'hope and believe' that the high degree of autonomy will be maintained. But as the Chinese attitude to the democratic proposals put forward by Governor Patten hardened, culminating in the Chinese decision to end the 'through train' for legislative councillors, the European Commission began to look for ways to 'underscore' Hong Kong's autonomy (Brittan 1996). The various statements made by the HKSAR Chief Executive-Designate, Tung Chee-hwa, and the China-backed Provisional Legislature in the first half of 1997 served only to reinforce that feeling within EU officialdom. In April 1997, in launching its new strategy paper for Hong Kong, Brittan argued that the EU should continue to make it clear that it intended to deal directly with Hong Kong in those policy areas in which it had been given responsibility under the Joint Declaration and the Basic Law (Commission 1997). One policy initiative being discussed within the EU is to put trade, investment and cooperation relations with the HKSAR on 'a more permanent footing', possibly by concluding a formal agreement similar to the one which has existed between the EU and the neighbouring Portuguese enclave of Macau since 1992.

Europeans frequently speak about the virtues of open, accountable and democratic institutions. Developing such institutions takes time, but undoubtedly the pace with which Britain has moved in the past decade or two has been far too laggardly. Even the proposals introduced by Patten, which did ensure that the 1995 Legislative Council was the first entirely elected legislature in Hong Kong's history, were, in his own words, 'fairly modest' (Foreign Affairs Committee 1994b, p. 195). The British were not only slow at introducing democratic reform but preferred to go it alone in their dealings with the Chinese, only belatedly waking up to the potential usefulness of mobilizing European support.

The other European governments have largely watched from the sidelines, neither taking steps to urge Britain to introduce greater democracy earlier in the 1980s nor subsequently committing themselves publicly and explicitly to the Patten proposals. In part, this apparent indifference stemmed from the view that Hong Kong was after all primarily a British problem, but, partly, no doubt Britain's own poor record under the Conservative Prime Ministers (especially under Mrs Thatcher but even under Major) of genuine sensitivity to other European concerns did little to encourage support (Segal 1993, pp. 182, 191). But, most importantly, it reflected a desire to keep political controversy out of their own business dealings with China. However, this posture of studied non-interference may no longer be so easily maintained.

No place can stay unchanged for 50 years, so, as China tries to bring Hong Kong more closely into the folds of the motherland, Hong Kong too will inevitably change. What does that mean for future European interests in both Hong Kong and China? Hong Kong has the potential to act both as a positive catalyst in Sino-European relations – as a facilitator – and as a source of conflict – a spoiler.

As mentioned above, the EU's long-term strategy towards China, as enunciated in its 1995 policy paper, has two basic objectives: to involve China as a full and responsible partner in the international community and to develop business opportunities for Europe in China's vast market. Clearly, Hong Kong can play a positive role in both these undertakings.

Undoubtedly China will continue to grow stronger economically and militarily and its sheer size and geographical spread will ensure its deep involvement in Asian Pacific regional affairs. Indeed, the Asian financial crisis since mid 1997 has only served to underscore the comparative economic stability of China and to enhance its status within the region. But it is also becoming an important global player in certain respects, particularly through its increasing export penetration of world markets and through its membership of the UN Security Council. The Europeans basically support Chinese involvement in international and regional organizations, but they want to see this Chinese involvement being a constructive one. Therefore, Hong Kong, as an international city, can help to play a role in increasing contact with, and exposure to, the outside world for Chinese officials and policy advisers. This in turn could encourage those leaders within China who are more open to a moderate approach to international affairs. European officials tend to characterize their own approach to China as one of 'constructive engagement', drawing China out into the international community and encouraging it to open up to a freer flow of ideas and cooperation. Hong Kong can play a catalytic role in this endeavour.

After the initial euphoria over the potentially new markets in newly democratized Eastern Europe subsided and the introspective preoccupation with completing the single European market flagged in the early 1990s, European companies began to turn to the booming Asia Pacific for new commercial opportunities. Within this region, the hugely populous and rapidly growing Chinese market has had a particular attraction. The European Commission's strategy paper spoke enthusiastically about the Chinese market becoming 'the largest in the world in many high tech sectors, from telecommunications to aircraft and from computers to energy' (Commission Communication to the Council of Ministers (1995)). Although many European companies do go directly into the Chinese market, the route through Hong Kong remains an effective and often more comfortable mode of entry. The continuing opening up of China in all directions will inevitably mean that Hong Kong will not be quite as pre-eminent in the Chinese market by the early 21st century as it is today, but, whatever the degree of Chinese interference in the Hong Kong economy, its role – and its importance in Sino-European trade and investment – will certainly not disappear overnight.

While Hong Kong's commercial role in Sino-European relations will continue to be important, a new dimension is set to emerge: political issues inside Hong Kong will almost certainly intrude into the future Sino-European relationship in a way that they have not done before. However, the extent to which these issues disrupt the Sino-European relationship will depend on the attitudes of the Chinese, at both the local and the central level, towards Hong Kong's autonomy and the willingness, and ability, of the British and other Europeans to defend the provisions of the Sino-British agreements.

Immediately prior to the handover, the British upped their rhetoric in response to concerns then being expressed in Hong Kong about the future. This was most clearly seen in Prime Minister Major's comments about pursuing 'every legal and other avenue available' in the event of a Chinese breach of the Joint Declaration while visiting Hong Kong in March 1996 (*Eastern Express*, 5 March 1996) and in Patten's last major policy speech in October 1996, when he laid out certain 'benchmarks' against which future Chinese conduct should be measured (Dimbleby 1997, pp. 368–369). Robin Cook, the Foreign Secretary in the newly elected Labour government in Britain, made it clear in one of his very first policy pronouncements that human rights would be at 'the centre of our policy concerns' (Cook 1997a). But the new Labour government has also been looking to re-establish good relations with China, so its post-handover comments have gone little further than expressing 'unhappiness' with the scrapping of the Patten system and the imposition of new electoral arrangements in Hong Kong.

In the early months after the handover, admittedly, China went to particular lengths to demonstrate a 'hands-off' approach to the governance of the HKSAR. It was astute enough to avoid any dramatic move such as arresting democrats or banning demonstrations, but it is having a more subtle impact on the political culture of the territory. As such, an incremental approach by the Chinese towards slowly reducing the parameters of civil and political liberties inside Hong Kong over time, an early example of which has been the rewriting of the electoral rules for the May 1998 legislative council elections so as to disadvantage the democrats (who took 42 per cent of the popular vote but received only 22 per cent of the seats), is unlikely to rouse the ire of either politicians or the public in Europe. For the moment, the 'spoiler' role for Hong Kong seems the less likely of the two possible roles in Sino-European relations.

MACAU

By contrast with its brash and bustling neighbour, Hong Kong, Macau has always seemed a sleepy backwater with nothing much to offer except gambling. Although, as noted in Chapter 2, the Portuguese arrived in Macau long before the British 'discovered' Hong Kong, Macau's golden age passed away long ago in the 17th century (Porter 1996, p. 74), so that during the 20th century it has always lagged behind Hong Kong, which has become a major regional and international port, and financial and service centre. Although, after China embarked on its open-door policy at the end of the 1970s, a special enterprise zone was created at Zhuhai, just across the Pearl River estuary from Macau, specifically to tap into Macau's international contacts, this has not worked in the same integrative way as the Hong Kong–Shenzhen model. If anything, Zhuhai has begun a process in recent years of at best competing with Macau for trade and inward FDI and at worst of sabotaging Macau's own efforts to heighten its international economic profile (Ngai 1996).

Although the Portuguese twice tried to return Macau to China, once after the domestic political revolution in Portugal in 1974 and again in 1977, China preferred to keep the Portuguese administration in place at least until after the Hong Kong problem had been settled. When Sino-Portuguese negotiations did begin in 1985, they were much less sensitive than the Sino-British ones; the resulting agreement was patterned closely on the Sino-British one in providing for Macau to enjoy a separate lifestyle after December 1999 under the 'one country, two systems' concept (Edmonds 1995, pp. 227–228). However, the Portuguese took a much more relaxed attitude than the British in Hong Kong to the development of democracy in Macau – even the Tiananmen Square massacre did little to affect the political situation in Macau. The Portuguese authorities were at pains to demonstrate that they did not intend to follow what they saw as the 'conflictual' approach of Hong Kong's Governor Patten, and the Chinese adopted a policy of trying to demonstrate – for the benefit of Hong Kong – that Portugal's compliant policies in Macau could be rewarded with positive support on, for example, infrastructure projects (Macau's international airport was approved and constructed much faster than Hong Kong's new one) and less overt pressure for the localization of the administration (Leung 1997). But with the Hong Kong transition completed, China is now focusing more clearly on Macau and increasing the pressure to run the enclave as it wants. The Portuguese presence in Macau is in danger of becoming 'languid and increasingly irrelevant' (Porter 1996, p. 189). Indeed, in the face of a rising 'war' between triads and police, some within Macau have even begun to call for an earlier involvement of the Chinese as the only way to maintain law and order.

How will Macau preserve its identity after 1999? Some within the Macau administration believe that it should play on its Portuguese cultural heritage so as to carve out a new role as a 'gateway' for China to develop links with Latin American countries (Ngai 1996). But if Macau's Portuguese-speakers leave after 1999 (around one-quarter of the total population of 450,000 has Portuguese passports with the right of residence in Portugal), then this vision will be difficult to realize.

Visiting Macau in February 1997, the Portuguese President, Jorge Sampaio, argued that the two transitions – Hong Kong's and Macau's – were 'being witnessed throughout the world' (*Hong Kong Standard*, 18 February 1997). However, in reality, few of Portugal's European partners have taken any interest in Macau's transition; cooperation even with Britain has been minimal in the past, although both countries have recently taken some steps to improve consultation. The Portuguese did push the EC into agreeing a Commercial and Cooperation Agreement with Macau in 1992 (something which Hong Kong does not have), but, apart from setting up a Euro-Info Centre in Macau, there has not been a great deal of new Europe–Macau–China links deriving from this agreement. An eminent persons group was established in early 1998 to consider the future of EU–Macau relations, but the fear remains in Macau that as international media interest in Hong Kong fades, Macau will become little more than a small Chinese city at the beck and call of larger forces on the mainland and that the Portuguese will have little success in interesting their European partners in its political or the commercial fate. Almost certainly, Macau's transition and its post-handover situation will fail to attract the same degree of political sensitivity as the Hong Kong issue has done in Sino-European relations.

THE TAIWAN PROBLEM

The Chinese see the return of Hong Kong and the planned return of Macau as steps along the path to the final stage of reunification with Taiwan. The strong Chinese desire to reunify with Taiwan and its consequent reluctance to consider Taiwan as anything more than a renegade province temporarily outside the fold have complicated the political relations of the European states with Taiwan and, of course, with China itself. Chapter 4 dealt in some detail with the strong economic links between Western Europe and Taiwan, and suggested that the weak diplomatic position of Taiwan *vis-à-vis* the European states certainly did nothing to help it in economic and commercial negotiations. The aim here is to look more specifically at the political and strategic issues.

Even from the early 1950s the Western European states adopted a fairly low profile on relations with Taiwan, but China's 'diplomatic revolution' of the 1970s left the Vatican as the only European state still officially recognizing Taiwan. Although the Vatican has from time to time thought about approaching China, doubts about the treatment of the Catholic Church inside China have always stymied a switch in representation (Hsieh 1996, p. 79). The other European states have worked through a process of establishing Taiwanese trade or cultural offices in the second half of the 1970s and early 1980s into a gradual, even incremental, upgrading of these operations in the late 1980s and early 1990s. By 1991 some 15 European countries had 'private' institutions in Taiwan for dealing with business, technological and educational exchanges. Some of these, such as the French, British, German and Spanish offices, have been authorized to issue visas (Hsieh 1996, p. 89). Taiwan, in return, by the same year had trade and cultural offices in 16 European states, using a bizarre variety of titles (see Chapter 4). Taiwan has been quite flexible in granting what would normally be considered the usual diplomatic privileges to the European offices in Taipei, primarily, as one Foreign Ministry official has admitted, in the hope (so far largely unfulfilled) of obtaining 'reciprocal benefits' for Taipei's representative offices in Europe (Chiu 1993, p. 205).

After the Tiananmen Square massacre, the Taiwanese hoped that European revulsion against Chinese action would bring direct diplomatic benefit to them. It is true that the Europeans did seem prepared to be more flexible on certain issues such as visa issuance, but there was certainly no reverse diplomatic breakthrough. However, it was of some comfort to the Taiwanese that in 1991 the French Industry Minister broke the lengthy ban on European ministerial visits to Taiwan by undertaking a 'private' visit to Taiwan (Chiu 1993, pp. 213–214). The following year, the German Economics Minister, clearly in pursuit of orders for German technology for the planned new high-speed train project linking Taipei and Kaohsiung, made an official visit to Taiwan (Hsieh 1996, p. 89). Taiwan also began from the early 1990s to entertain a series of distinguished former politicians from Europe, including former French President Valery Giscard d'Estaing and former British Prime Minister Margaret Thatcher. Some countries, such as Britain, which was also undoubtedly concerned about the Hong Kong factor in its relations with China, preferred to concentrate on more substantive contacts at the junior minister level rather than the more symbolic higher-level visits. Indeed, in the 1992–96 period 15 such sub-Cabinet-level visits occurred, which put Britain ahead of all other European states in numerical terms (interview, British Trade and Cultural Office, Taipei, January 1997).

While the visits by the former politicians tended to be more symbolic than anything and largely concerned with discussions of a broad political nature, the visits, whether private or otherwise, by serving ministers and officials were much more clearly linked to commercial opportunities. Indeed, the Taiwanese seem to have dangled the 'carrot' of lucrative orders under the

massive infrastructure development programme of the first half of the 1990s
with the intention of enticing diplomatic concessions out of the Europeans. In
some cases this approach seems to have worked. The success of the French
company, Matra, in obtaining the contract to build Taipei's monorail system
(a technology that the company was not well known for) is commonly attributed to the earlier decision by the French government to sell military
technology to Taiwan (interview, Chung-hua Institute of Economic Research,
Taipei, January 1997).

The Taiwanese interest in the acquisition of European military technology,
which mirrored a Chinese interest, has indeed become one of the most controversial aspects of the Europe–China–Taiwan triangle. In diplomatic terms,
the Chinese have devoted much time and energy to laying down with their
European interlocutors that they should not do anything to create 'two Chinas'. This has meant a strict watch for any sign that the Europeans might be
attempting to move to full diplomatic relations with Taiwan, but, in practice,
has meant little more than perfunctory protests at the incremental upgrading
of the functions of European offices in Taipei and even at the private ministerial visits by European politicians.

However, China has been less relaxed about visits to Europe by Taiwanese
officials and ministers, especially after Taiwanese President Lee Teng-hui's
visit to the United States in June 1995 and the almost simultaneous visit by
Taiwanese Prime Minister Lien Chan to Austria, Hungary and the Czech
Republic threatened to mark the beginning of a new wave of Taiwanese
'visitational diplomacy' around the world. In fact, the initial euphoria felt by
the Taiwanese over those path-breaking 1995 visits was misplaced, because
the furore aroused – triumphalism by the Taiwanese and criticism by the
Chinese – made the Europeans reluctant to endorse anything more than
transit-style visits by Taiwanese ministers. But by 1997 the European mood
was changing again. Lien was allowed to visit Ireland and the Vatican (with
which Taiwan has official relations anyway) in January 1997 (*Free China
Journal*, 24 January 1997), but, most notably, Taiwanese Foreign Minister,
John Chang Hsiao-yen, visited Strasbourg to address the European Parliament in May 1997, the first ever such address by a Taiwanese. Chang's calls
for full international recognition for Taiwan were immediately denounced by
China as a 'premeditated provocation' against the Chinese people (*South
China Morning Post*, 24 May 1997).

Despite the rhetoric of such criticisms, China has reserved its most vehe-
ment responses, which have included imposing or threatening to impose
economic and even diplomatic sanctions, for any signs that military technology was being sold to the Taiwanese. Nonetheless, a contrast in both modalities
and results can be drawn between the Chinese actions against the Netherlands, which agreed to sell submarines to Taiwan in 1980, and those against

France, which went ahead with fighter aircraft sale contracts with Taiwan in 1992.

In 1980 the Dutch government had given permission for a Dutch ship-building company to supply two upgraded submarines to the Taiwanese as part of a larger order for non-military equipment (this paragraph draws heavily on Houweling 1997). The Dutch Foreign Ministry was concerned about the probable political fall-out but the Economics Ministry, keen to support an ailing ship-building industry, won the day. China imposed economic sanctions against Dutch firms operating in China and reduced the level of diplomatic representation. So when Taiwan tried to secure a follow-up order, the Dutch Foreign Ministry mobilized support from Dutch firms hit by the earlier sanctions to prevent agreement. Although the two original submarines were finally delivered in 1986, the Dutch have been reluctant to follow that path again and, in 1991, a new order from Taiwan for submarines was quashed. However, according to Henk Houweling, the Dutch emphasis on 'commerce first' was not particularly successful: the original Taiwanese order did not save the Dutch ship-building industry from near bankruptcy and the later primacy given to the Chinese market (the argument deployed for refusing any subsequent orders from Taiwan) has not been rewarded. Needless to say, however, the Taiwanese considered the original submarine sale as a breakthrough: 'the first political interaction with a European country since 1949' (Hsieh 1996, p. 90).

In 1991 and 1992 the French government decided, apparently mainly for commercial reasons (to help reduce the trade deficit with Taiwan and to provide employment at home), to accept Taiwanese orders first for six La Fayette frigates and then for up to 60 Mirage 2000–5 fighter aircraft (this paragraph draws heavily on Godemont and Serra 1997). China retaliated by imposing economic sanctions (France's bid for an underground railway construction project in Guangdong failed) and diplomatic sanctions (the French consulate in Guangdong was closed). But by 1994 relations had recovered and, indeed, managed to reach new heights of friendliness in 1997, even though the frigates were finally delivered to Taiwan and the first of the 60 Mirage fighters began to arrive there in the same year. This was in marked contrast to Sino-Dutch relations, which were again troubled in 1997, this time by human rights issues.

It has been argued that the differences in the Chinese approach to these two cases can be explained by the 'reduced leverage' of China in the post-Cold War world, especially as its economic involvement in the global economy increased the likelihood that economic sanctions could be counter-productive (Yahuda 1995, p. 57). However, it may be more significant to consider the economic strength of the two European powers involved and the attractiveness of their civilian and, above all, military technology. Put bluntly, there was little that the Chinese really wanted from the Dutch, whereas the Chinese interest in getting access themselves to French weaponry (including, it is rumoured, a French aircaft carrier (*Foreign Report*, 3 July 1997)), coupled with the French desire under President Chirac once again to raise French status in China and Asia generally (Godemont and Serra 1997), if necessary by playing down 'hurtful' issues such as human rights, helped to restore French economic and political interests in China.

The Taiwanese have clearly hoped that the 'bait' of their economic power, their consumer market and their massive projects, under the rubric of the Six-Year Plan in the first half of the 1990s, could tempt Western European countries not only to intensify their trade and investment links with Taiwan but also to develop more official-level links (Chiu 1993, pp. 216–217). While the Europeans are still interested in commercial opportunities in Taiwan, the factor of the Chinese political veto has worked substantially to constrain anything other than a slow incremental build-up in the working level of Euro-Taiwanese political contacts. The process is one of a slow 'chipping away' by the Taiwanese at the political 'blockade' imposed by China, but there are no signs of an impending collapse of that blockade as far as Europe is concerned. While certain developing nations in Africa, Central America and the Pacific seem to be playing the game of recognition as a way of gaining financial favours alternately from both China and Taiwan, the Western European states are certainly not going to indulge in those kinds of manoeuvre. In that sense, China does not have to worry that any EU member state is seriously going to consider switching recognition to Taiwan.

A COMMON EUROPEAN POLICY TOWARDS CHINA?

The disappointment of many Europeans over the UNHRC resolution split in the spring of 1997 was not just over the human rights dimension but also over the failure of the Europeans to adopt a coordinated policy. Of course, policy towards China is by no means the only example of such tensions and contradictions in EU-level policy-making, which can be found in many other areas of the EU's external relations with the Asia Pacific and, indeed, other areas of the world. The differences in policy towards China, however, may reflect not so much differences over what the Europeans should try to achieve but over how to achieve it. Certainly, there is a fair degree of agreement between the EU member countries about what they wish to achieve in the longer term: a more open, responsible China, a more beneficial commercial relationship with both China and Hong Kong, and a smooth and fairly implemented transition for both Hong Kong and Macau. The problems come over how to achieve these objectives.

In this respect, there are considerable differences over approach. Miguel Santos Neves has suggested a five-category classification for examining EU member states' policies towards China (Neves 1995, p. 82). Here a slight modification is made to the two last categories when using his basic categorization: countries with important economic interests but less political motivation (e.g. France, Germany and Italy); countries with strong economic and political interests (Britain); countries with strong political interests but limited economic interests (Portugal); countries with equal but limited political and commercial interests (Holland and Denmark); and countries with moderate but growing economic interests and very limited political involvement (Spain and Belgium). These differing degrees of interest play out in the ways in which countries approach the existing and potential economic and political problems.

These differences are grounded not just in historical legacies (such as in the British and Portuguese cases) or in structures of external trade policy-making, but also reflect complex internal political situations in certain countries where rival political parties (such as inside the German coalition government) or strong political personalities (such as French presidents) can affect positions.

The result is a lack of consistency and an occasional tendency to adopt *ad hoc* policy positions. Despite the tentative moves the EU made towards the implementation of a CFSP at the conclusion of the inter-governmental conference in Amsterdam in the summer of 1997, it is clear that such differences will continue to feature in European policy towards China and Hong Kong for the foreseeable future.

In the case of Europe's relations with China, in contrast with European relations with other parts of the Asia Pacific region, politics have played almost as important a role as economics. After 1949, indeed, communist politics and the European reaction to them ensured that for nearly three decades commercial contacts were limited; indeed, during some periods, such as the Cultural Revolution, contacts of all kinds almost disappeared. Deng's pragmatic opening up of China from the late 1970s revitalized old European dreams of the great Chinese market, and economics became the driving force of the relationship until 1989, when internal Chinese politics cut a deep wedge into the developing relationship.

But from the mid 1990s Europe began another reassessment of China. Its booming economy, the approaching handover of Hong Kong and the EU's own reconsideration of its Asian policies (driven in part by Vice-President Brittan's own personal interest in China) awakened new interest in China. China's actions in the cross-straits crisis and its comparative economic stability in the face of the Asian financial crisis served as additional notice to the Europeans of China's expanding economic and strategic status and weight in the Asia Pacific. As a result, China has now become the most important actor in Europe's Asian Pacific panorama, with significant economic, political and even strategic components to the relationship.

7. Regionalism at work

The direction of multilateralism, both in Asia and in Europe,
must never swerve into closed regionalism.

(from speech by Matsunaga Nobuo, 1994)

The development of European relations with Japan and the other dynamic economies of the Asia Pacific region has become increasingly entangled with two phenomonena associated with the rise of 'regionalism': the EC's efforts to revitalize itself through the creation of a single internal market and the embryonic attempts by the Asia Pacific countries to create cooperative economic organizations and mechanisms. Regionalism has become a more complex issue than early postwar analyses, which were able to posit regionalism – or regional economic integration – as being positive if it was trade-creating and negative if it was trade-diverting, would suggest (de Melo and Panagariya 1993, pp. 6–7). In particular, as will be seen in the case of Europe and the Asia Pacific, the realities of inter-regional interactions – and in some cases merely the perceptions of the process and policies of integration in other regional groupings – can affect the intra-regional dynamics of the process within particular regional groupings.

The EU has, of course, developed a long way from the vision of the founding fathers back in the 1950s, which led to the creation in 1957, through the Treaty of Rome, of a European Economic Community (EEC) of six members (France, West Germany, Italy, Belgium, Holland and Luxembourg). With the exception of iron and steel and atomic energy, for which separate 'communities' were developed, the EEC took care of all economic matters. The postwar politicians who set out to build a new Europe through a process of economic integration worked within the framework set by Soviet hostility and US sponsorship (Wallace 1990, p. 20), but membership was intended to be open to all the countries of Europe. By the end of the 1960s the main outlines of a 'common market' were in place and in the early 1970s the new EC went through a period of expansion as Britain, Ireland and Denmark joined.

However, the steady but determined progress of the first decade of the EC's existence began to founder in the 1970s and early 1980s, as what has been characterized as 'Eurosclerosis' – a hardening of the arteries of European dynamism and flexibility – set in (Swann 1996, pp. 38–39). This meant not

121

just a decline in European competitiveness, combined with high unemployment and low growth, but also a slowing down in the development of the EC's policies and institutions. The admission of new members – Greece in 1981 and Spain and Portugal in 1986, representing the so-called 'Mediterranean enlargement' – and the changing international context (particularly the rise of Japanese technological might and the shifts in US–Soviet relations) also contributed to a new impetus to re-evaluate the progress achieved in approaching the goals of European integration.

The EC's attempts from the mid 1980s to initiate and then complete the move to a single internal market by the end of 1992 provoked a mixture of interest and consternation among its trading partners. The purpose behind the single market programme (which will hereafter be called the '1992 process') was to encourage trade and competition by removing obstacles within the EC to the free flow of goods, services and labour (Pelkmans and Winters 1988, pp. 3–4), but there were clearly linkages with external trade and investment. It was these aspects, which do not seem to have been covered sufficiently in the early thinking and policy pronouncements from within the European Commission, which brought most concern to external trading partners, including, of course, the Asia Pacific countries. This led on in the late 1980s to a perception outside of the emergence of a 'Fortress Europe'. Despite determined campaigns subsequently by the Europeans to dispel this image, they have been unable to completely shake it off. Indeed, as the Europeans approach the second stage of their immense project, economic and monetary union (EMU), which is scheduled for implementation in 1999, there seems to be a sense of *déjà vu* about the Asian Pacific reactions to this next stage, although probably more in the sense of being rather late to wake up to its imminent arrival than in the sense of an overtly suspicious attitude towards it.

But before analysing in detail how Asian Pacific governments have reacted to the 1992 process and how in practice it has affected the Euro-Asian economic relationship, it is necessary to set out briefly the character of, and background to, the EC's attempts to formulate a common commercial policy towards external partners and the philosophy and policies behind the 1992 process.

SEARCHING FOR A COMMON COMMERCIAL POLICY

Fundamental to any EU-wide strategy towards the Asian Pacific economies is the creation of a coherent commercial policy. However, a number of factors have historically hampered such a possibility. First, are the shifting limits to the EC's competence over trade policy. In theory, the nature and scope of the EC's common commercial policy are defined by Articles 110 and 113 of the

Treaty of Rome. However, according to a senior European bureaucrat, the EC's competence has been 'evolving all the time as jurisprudence progresses and implementing regulations are adopted' (House of Lords Select Committee on the European Communities 1989, p. 44). Some actions, such as any negotiation for a trade treaty with Japan or any other Asian Pacific country, must be undertaken by the Commission. Others, such as encouraging inward investment, are more for member governments to decide. Inevitably, there are a number of 'grey areas' where the dividing line over competence is unclear.

Second, there has been, and continues to be, a diversity of approaches to external trade policy among the EC countries. At the risk of exaggeration, there has been near open competition between two distinct trade philosophies within the EC: the northern 'free trade' versus a southern 'protectionist' dichotomy. Certainly at the governmental level, West Germany, Denmark, the Netherlands and, usually, Britain have tended to fall into the first group, and Italy, Spain and Portugal into the second. France, the one country which geographically straddles this north–south divide, has often sided with the southern group (Colchester and Buchan 1990, pp. 182–183). Arguably, the January 1995 so-called 'Scandinavian enlargement' brought in three new members who tend more towards the liberal end of the trade policy spectrum. But the positions of the individual member states, whether new entrants or old hands, are somewhat arbitrary and can change depending on the sector or issue involved.

Third, by extension from the second factor, divergences and cross-cutting tendencies exist within the EC decision-making process. Such divergences occur not just between and within the European Commission and the member governments, but also involve European and national parliaments, industry and trade union pressure groups, and even consumers. Thus, for example, the Dutch government has generally acted in favour of a more open external trade policy, but the largest Dutch multinational company and Europe's largest electronics maker, Philips, has long portrayed itself – and indeed has often acted – as the foremost bulwark against Asian Pacific technological domination. Typically, one Philips executive went so far as to outline his 'domino theory' of one European industry after another falling under Japanese control (*Far Eastern Economic Review*, 18 May 1989). The company has also been a leading recipient of EC subsidies and trade protection.

In theory, when the single market has been completed, the EC's common commercial policy will have matured to the point where it will have displaced member governments' commercial policies, but in practice, however far EC/EU competence may extend, it is extremely unlikely to be all-inclusive. There is, nonetheless, a complex inter-relationship between the development of the EC's commercial policy and the 1992 process. Certainly, many Asian Pacific states have conflated the two together. It is necessary to examine, therefore, some of the key parameters of the 1992 process.

EUROPE'S ADVENTURE: THE 1992 PROCESS

The 1980s had opened with a pessimistic future facing Western Europe. Unemployment was rising steadily, industries appeared unable either to utilize new technology effectively or to create their own, international oil crises and monetary instability had had a debilitating effect and, in general, Europe seemed to be slipping behind its main competitors, the United States and Japan. 'Europessimism' and 'Eurosclerosis' became the catchwords of the moment. This sorry state of affairs affected both European competitiveness in Asian Pacific markets as well as Asian Pacific perceptions of Europe as a partner. European industrialists and European politicians began slowly to realize that the EC and its member states needed to make a significant psychological breakthrough if this disturbing downward cycle was to be broken (Colchester and Buchan 1990, pp. 26–29). After much discussion and debate, the net result was a decision to try to go back to some of the original goals set out by the founding fathers of European integration in the 1950s. The socio-economic and political contexts of the late 1980s/early 1990s did differ, of course, from those of the late 1950s. But it was believed that by spelling out in detail the processes by which goals would be achieved and by setting a deadline for their implementation, the earlier dynamism could be recreated.

These policy objectives were enshrined in the broad guidelines set out in the 1987 Single European Act (Swann 1996, pp. 51–74). Although all the EC's internal tariff barriers were removed in 1968, many non-tariff barriers remained. These were basically physical (border controls, etc.), technical (varying national standards) and fiscal (different national indirect taxes). The intention was to remove all these by the end of 1992. The 1992 process, however, was to be deeply affected by two developments in 1989–90.

First, the April 1989 Delors Committee Report, endorsed after much argument at the Rome European Council Summit in October 1990, set out the transitional stages towards European EMU (Swann 1996, pp. 83–85). Like all EC economic blueprints, it had powerful political overtones with consequences for national sovereignty. The British, under the Conservative governments of Margaret Thatcher and John Major, fought a largely ineffective rearguard action against the form and timing of EMU and finally opted out of the third stage as set out in the Maastricht Treaty, but in reality instabilities in international financial markets and the reluctance of several European governments to effect unpopular fiscal rigour have been more potent in delaying progress.

Second, the collapse of the communist system in Eastern Europe in 1989, culminating in the reunification of Germany in 1990, presented an unexpected new challenge for the Western Europeans. The initial reaction was to quicken the pace of European integration, in order to bind the united Germany into the EC more tightly and to present a coherent response to Eastern European instability and rising expectations (Wallace 1989). But subsequently the EC became entangled in lengthy discussions over the long-standing dilemma of deepening versus widening which has by no means been resolved. This issue and its impact on Euro-Asian relations will be discussed in more detail later in this chapter.

Two further points need to be considered, as they complicate assessments of the impact of the 1992 process on Euro-Asian relations. First, the creation of the single market has been, and still is, a lengthy process; there was no sudden and dramatic change at the end of 1992. Many of the measures were in place before that date; others were adopted but only implemented on a piecemeal basis, and a few measures have either been effectively frozen or not yet finally decided. By the middle of 1994, however, 262 of the 282 directives envisaged by the 1985 White Paper had been adopted by European institutions; by June 1995 the vast majority of the items of Community legislation had been transposed into national legislation (84 per cent of them in Finland at the worst and 98 per cent in the best, Denmark). Some sectors, such as telecommunications, energy and air transport, have lagged behind in having their directives decided; others, such as insurance and public procurement, have suffered from slow transposition or poor implementation (Wallace and Young 1996, pp. 141–147).

Moreover, the process of European integration has not ceased. The 1992 Maastricht Treaty, which reincarnated the EC as the EU, with formal effect from November 1993, modified the objectives and guiding principles of the original Treaty of Rome in important ways which implied that, above all, the EC would move forward from the old aim of a common market to a new destination of EMU through a staged but automatic process of transition (Swann 1996, pp. 96–102). At the same time, the competence of the EC/EU was also extended into a number of new areas in economic and social policies, while the European political cooperation mechanisms were to be subsumed into a new inter-governmental CFSP framework and cooperation on judicial and home affairs was to be improved. The Maastricht Treaty was concluded only after considerable controversy, not least among the voting populations of several member countries, and its implementation has continued to be difficult. That treaty itself was reviewed at an inter-governmental conference which began in March 1996 and ended at the Amsterdam European Summit of June 1997, when a few more modifications were made to the overall process of integration.

Second, running parallel to the 1992 process were protracted negotiations to complete the Uruguay Round of the GATT, which was finally concluded in 1994, and later the follow-up negotiations under the auspices of the new

WTO. The EC went into the negotiations believing in the need for a strong multilateral system based on a balance of rights and obligations (the opening up of the markets of Japan and other Asian Pacific states was implied) which would obviate the need for bilateral deals such as the US–Japan agreements). The EC continued to support differential and more favourable treatment for developing countries, but envisaged a process of 'graduation' under which these countries undertook more obligations as their economies developed (this was undoubtedly aimed at the Asian Pacific NIEs and proto-NIEs) (Woolcock and Hodges 1996, pp. 306–307). The lack of a sustainable, coherent position on agriculture undoubtedly hindered the EC negotiating role, but in the later, more political, stages of the GATT negotiations the EC became more proactive and can be said to have contributed to the strengthening of multilateralism (Woolcock and Hodges 1996, p 323). These extended GATT negotiations therefore did impact on several issues which came up in Euro-Asian negotiations, not least in areas such as anti-dumping, where the EC was strongly resistant to the GATT's general desire for tighter discipline.

THE ASIAN PACIFIC REACTION

The Asia Pacific countries, which had grown used to the repeated failures of the Europeans during the first half of the 1980s to live up to their rhetoric of trying to restore industrial competitiveness, had initially not fully appreciated the seriousness with which the Europeans were taking first the 1985 White Paper and then the subsequent 1987 Single European Act. Indeed, if anything it was the Americans who first woke up to the significance of these European initiatives and who began to suspect that protectionist motives lay behind them. During 1988, however, the 'Fortress Europe' debate really began to take off – and Japan and the NIEs became actively involved. The tone of that emerging Asian Pacific debate is well reflected in a cover story of the *Far Eastern Economic Review* from that period entitled, 'Europe: Asia's Friend or Foe?' (*Far Eastern Economic Review*, 5 May 1988). The Asians – led by the Japanese – suspected that the single market project was at least partly aimed at them, because they were formidably competitive in those products, such as cars and electronics, which the European governments were most likely to protect (Colchester and Buchan 1990, p. 197).

This initially critical reaction, even if rather delayed, from the Asians, nonetheless made the Europeans themselves concerned about the image being created. The December 1988 European Council Summit in Rhodes was forced to issue a communiqué under the rubric of '*L'Europe ni fortresse ni passoire*' (Europe: neither fortress nor sieve). The message was that Europe would be a world partner not a bloc closed in upon itself (Colchester and

Buchan 1990, pp. 193–194). Underlying this message to the world, undoubtedly, was also a warning to some within the EC about the necessary commitment to free trade.

The EC moves to reassure the Asians were only partially successful. By 1989 some Japanese observers had begun to notice that initially exaggerated fears in Japan of 'Fortress Europe' had begun to subside somewhat (Inoguchi 1993, p. 79). But other Asian Pacific states remained unconvinced. Symbolic of continuing Asian concerns, for example, was the unexpected appearance of ASEAN trade ministers accompanying the foreign ministers to the 1990 Kuching EC–ASEAN ministerial meeting. EC representatives were forced to take considerable pains at that meeting with ASEAN to try once again to dispel the myth of 'Fortress Europe'. The South Korean government's Economic Planning Board produced a report in February 1991 which, while admitting that there would be trade-creating advantages as well as trade-diverting disadvantages for Korea, argued that the 1992 process would turn the EC into 'a formidable trading bloc with strengthened negotiating leverage', which would mean in particular that Korea would 'face greater pressures for reciprocal market opening' (Economic Planning Board 1991).

The Issues for the Asians

The Asian countries' fear of 'Fortress Europe' seems to have arisen mainly from their perception that their manufactured exports to the EC would be adversely affected by the 1992 process. This fear had both a general and a specific component. Generally, the creation of the single market, in that it was intended to make the European companies more competitive, was expected to affect non-European firms adversely, including Asian Pacific ones, simply by providing more competition (Kreinin and Plummer 1992, p. 1357). But more specifically, as Ishikawa Kenjiro has argued, widespread scepticism emerged in Japan (and similarly elsewhere in the Asia Pacific) that, by converting national quotas and other restrictions into EC-wide ones, the single market would create barriers to commerce and investment that were 'broader, more systematic and more damaging than the scattering of measures that already hinder some aspects of trade' (Ishikawa 1990, p. 6). Clearly, the nature of the issues raised by the 1992 process is not exactly the same for all the Asian Pacific countries. In particular, there are some differing concerns for Japan and the NIEs than for the ASEAN members or China. However, a number of key issues can be considered in detail as representing the broader spread of concerns.

Automobiles
For Japan, the automobile issue ranks above all other issues as the litmus test of the EU's free-trading resolve. It is also important to the Koreans and, to a

much lesser extent, to the Malaysians, the only other Asian Pacific car exporters to the EU. The world motor industry is in a state of flux and nowhere
more so than in Western Europe. The EU car sector has traditionally been
riddled with barriers to trade and competition, so the array of quantitative
restrictions (QRs) and VERs against Japanese cars were not totally out of
character. The Japanese response to the European desire to achieve restraint
seems to have been conditioned by the wish to 'accommodate these protectionist forces in order to avert more blatant protection' (Woolcock and Yamane
1993, p. 16). By the late 1980s Japan's share of the EC car market was about
10 per cent, but with large differences depending on the country market,
ranging from around 43 per cent of the Irish market to less than 1 per cent in
Spain. France, Britain, Spain, Italy and Portugal all maintained either QRs or
VERs, limiting the flow of Japanese cars to a share of their home market or to
a fixed number.

During 1988 the Commission began to consider quite restrictive measures,
such as keeping Japanese car sales in the EC proportional to European car
sales in Japan, as advocated by the Brussels-based Committee of Common
Market Automobile Constructors. But more liberal commissioners, such as
Martin Bangemann, the industry commissioner, argued that no EC-wide QRs
on cars should be permitted after 1992 (Ishikawa 1990, p. 123). But in return
for the elimination of national restrictions, the Commission decided to negotiate some kind of 'transitional restraint' (a VER by another name) during
which the EC and Japan would 'monitor' the level of car exports to the EC.
The member governments were split: some, such as Britain and West Germany argued for a short transitional period; others, such as Italy, France and
Spain, argued for ten or more years. France, which feared that its national
market would be undermined by a Britain acting as a Japanese 'Trojan horse'
within the new single market, wanted to count cars made at Japanese-owned
plants within the EC into the intended limits, but Britain, host to more
Japanese car plants than any other EC country, obviously did not. After much
intra-EC haggling and some difficult talks with the Japanese, a 'deal' was
reached in July 1991 (*Agence Europe*, 16 January 1992; Lehmann 1992,
pp. 47–50). The transition period was long, until the end of 1999, after which
the EU market would be completely open. The overall number of Japanese
cars to be directly exported to the EU in the final year (1999) would be only
1.23 million, only a marginal increase on the amount exported in 1990. Since
the five member-country markets with restrictions on Japanese car imports
agreed to abolish them from 1993, in effect Japanese car exports to other EC
member-country markets would have to decrease to compensate for sales to
the newly opened markets.

The issue of 'transplants' – Japanese cars manufactured inside Europe –
was fudged. There was no explicit restraint on production and sales inside

Europe, although the Japanese government agreed to warn the Japanese car-makers not to concentrate their transplant sales on any one particular market. The agreement is subject to half-yearly monitoring and annual haggling over the exact import levels for the following year this has not been easy as consumer demand within the EU has weakened. The Japanese side console themselves with the thought that the mechanism's ultimate dismantlement will occur on the last day of 1999, but the crucial issue for the Europeans is whether their car manufacturers will have made themselves competitive by then. That the fear of some observers that European car-makers may still be wedded to old mind-sets is not unrealistic can be seen from comments such as those by Jacques Calvet, the President of Peugot, in the spring of 1996 that Japanese car-makers were simply 'preparing for a new offensive' against Europe (*International Herald Tribune*, 5 March 1996). However, in reality, the Japanese share of the EU car market had dropped to 11 per cent by 1996, compared with a peak of 13 per cent in 1991 (*Korea Herald*, 11 December 1997), and there have been few signs of a resurgence since then.

The high political visibility of the car industry in several EU member countries means that 'protectionist' sentiment is likely to be higher than in other industrial sectors. Malaysian car exports to Europe are still small at around 12,000 in 1993, mostly to Britain, but concern is beginning to grow within Europe about Korean cars (M. Calvet mentioned this 'threat' at the same time as he was criticizing the Japanese (*International Herald Tribune*, 5 March 1996)). This is, of course, symptomatic of a general stereotyping of the Koreans as directly copying earlier Japanese tactics. Exports of Korean cars and vans to Europe have grown steadily from 40,000 in 1991 to 120,000 in 1994. Some observers have predicted that the annual total could reach 200,000 by the year 2000 (probably close to half the level of Japanese exports by then) (*Nihon Keizai Shimbun*, 23 June 1995). But the Koreans have also begun to follow the Japanese precedent of investing inside the Union too. Kia became the first Korean car company to do so, with a decision in 1994 to set up a plant to manufacture sports-utility vehicles at Osnabruck in Germany, but early in 1995 Daewoo announced plans for a much larger car plant in Britain, with the aim of producing around 100,000 cars annually by the time the EU car market becomes fully liberalized on the expiry of the EU–Japan car agreement. Although the South Korean economic crisis in late 1997 led to concern that the Korean car companies' FDI into the EU would be adversely affected, in this particular sector it is more likely to mean a postponement of new investment plans rather than a withdrawal of existing investment.

Local content

Rules of local content are one way of writing a rule of origin. In certain industrial sectors, some EC member countries have required foreign-owned manufacturing companies to use a minimum percentage of locally produced inputs before the goods could be classed as EC-made and open to free circulation within the EC. These arrangements have usually been determined on a bilateral basis between national governments and the investing foreign company. For a long time, the EC Commission was vague about percentages, preferring to talk generally about the 'last substantial manufacturing process' taking place within the EC. However, in the late 1980s regulations were introduced specifying 45 per cent of EC-origin parts for televisions and video recorders.

In June 1987, the EC Council adopted the so-called 'screwdriver plant' regulation, which set a maximum of 60 per cent for parts coming from the country of origin to be used in assembly operations at new plants established following the imposition of anti-dumping duties. This provision, for example, affects most Japanese electronic typewriters made in Britain. Britain itself negotiated a form of local content arrangement with the Japanese car company Nissan (initially 60 per cent, rising to 80 per cent in 1990) in return for generous inward investment incentives. However, when in the autumn of 1988 Nissan began to export its UK-made Bluebird cars to the rest of the EC, both France and Italy objected, saying that the local content was too low. The British government strongly supported Nissan. The row, in which the Commission after some wavering basically supported the British line, was not solved until the spring of 1989, when France and Italy backed down (Ishikawa 1990, pp. 76–81).

Nevertheless, the *ad hoc* basis of EC-level rules of origin has provided uncertainty for Japanese and other Asian investors. The result has been covert pressure, which has made it politically advisable for the Asian companies to increase local content continually, even where there have been short-term cost and quality difficulties. This has often led on to subsidiaries or associated companies of the Asian manufacturers also coming to invest inside the EC. One survey of Korean electronics manufacturers in 1990 revealed that they found locally acquired parts and components to be less than satisfactory; as a result, more than three-quarters of the responding firms said that they were planning more investment to localize production of parts and components (Han 1992, pp. 24, 48).

Reciprocity

One of the few references to external trading partners in the 1985 White Paper argued for the consolidation of the Community's commercial identity in such a way that external trading partners 'will not be given the benefit of a wider market without themselves making similar concessions' (Han 1992, p. 28). As the 1992 process began to take off, the Commission began to make it clear that it would seek 'reciprocity' from non-EC countries as a condition of access to the newly integrated markets in services, investment, government procurement and other areas not covered by GATT. Typical of the EC view was the statement by Andreas van Agt, speaking in 1988 as the EC ambassador to Japan, that the EC did not have a political, legal or moral obligation to 'just open all the gates in 1992 to goldmine opportunities without asking any fee for entry tickets' (El-Agraa 1988, p. 7).

The vagueness of the term 'reciprocity', as it appeared in some of the draft financial legislation, and the tendency for some senior EC officials to make over-optimistic pronouncements on its reach undoubtedly contributed to the unease in the United States, Japan and other parts of the Asia Pacific. The United States made the running in criticizing the EC's usage, but undoubtedly the Asia Pacific states benefited from US pressure and lobbying during the EC's deliberations, especially over the Second Banking Coordination Directive, which was finally adopted in December 1989. France, with the support of some European Commission officials, wanted to have a reciprocity provision included in this directive, but the more 'liberal' EC states combined with the external trading partners to ensure that a much weakened provision found its way into the final version (Woolcock and Yamane 1993, pp. 21–22). The EC was forced to clarify that it was not trying to obtain sectoral reciprocity, identical particular legislation or quantified economic benefits. Rather, the aim was an 'across-the-board multilateral balance of economic advantage' (House of Lords Select Committee on the European Communities 1989).

Financial services were a key area at dispute, since the deregulation and integration of financial services were an important element of the 1992 process. Regulatory structures and banking development differed widely among EC members and, until the late 1980s, some EC countries also imposed legal obstacles to the establishment of foreign bank subsidiaries and to the acquisition of firms by foreign banks. The EC's Second Banking Directive, however, provided mutual recognition within the EC, so that a Japanese (or any other foreign bank) established in, say, London would in theory be able to supply the whole of the EC with banking services (Woolcock and Yamane 1993, pp. 20–22). Needless to say, there were diverging views within the EC about how far to push for reciprocity of such financial advantages in overseas markets. The British, concerned to maintain the presence of Asian financial institutions in London, saw the retention of an open market in London as more important than reciprocity. After much hard bargaining within the Commission and among member governments, the banking directives came to use a reformulated version of 'reciprocity' encapsulated in the expression 'effective access' for EC financial institutions to non-EC markets. This was taken by the EC into the Uruguay Round negotiations, when the EC argued forcefully for a general agreement on trade in services which would provide for 'equivalent competitive opportunities'.

Anti-dumping

Although revisions in the EC's anti-dumping code could well have taken place anyway, regardless of the 1992 process, in the minds of many Asians, the EC's anti-dumping policy – and what is perceived as a greater anti-Asian bias in that policy – have become inextricably tied up with the 1992 process. The issue will therefore be discussed here, although earlier chapters dealing with individual or groups of countries have touched on it already. The EC's anti-dumping regulations have been modified several times since they were first introduced in 1968, but the EC has always maintained that they were in conformity with GATT codes.

Anti-dumping is one area where European industry rather than member governments takes the initiative. The Commission is required to act on any complaint of dumping brought by EC producers of the product concerned, when they consider themselves to have been injured – or threatened – by dumped imports. The procedures for calculating the margins of dumping are extremely complex and controversial. Some observers argue that they appear to be tilted in favour of finding that dumping has occurred; that the 'creative dumping-inquisitor can demonstrate just about anything' (Colchester and Buchan 1990, p. 201). The EC, needless to say, denies this, arguing that duties are only imposed after thorough and systematic investigation. EC statistics suggest that during the 1980–87 period, out of 281 investigations concluded, 69 per cent resulted in either the imposition of a definitive duty or the acceptance of a price undertaking by the non-EC producer (National Consumer Council 1990, pp. 13, 49).

Although other EC statistics show that during the same period more anti-dumping cases had been launched against Eastern European producers than against Asian Pacific producers, in the second half of the 1980s the weapon seems to have been pointed with greater force against Asian Pacific targets. Between 1987 and 1991, around half the 169 anti-dumping cases initiated by the EC were against Asian countries (*Far Eastern Economic Review*, 8 October 1992). Investigations were instigated against Japanese products ranging from VCRs, computer printers and compact-disc players to electronic typewriters and other office equipment. Often simultaneously, investigations were increasingly launched against South Korean electronic goods. For example, the EC initiated 19 anti-dumping investigations against South Korean products in the 1985–90 period – more than twice the total number of cases in the 1972–84 period (Han 1992, p. 28). Indeed, in the 1990s, as anti-dumping cases against Japanese products declined significantly, investigations of Korean, Taiwanese, Singaporean, Hong Kong and even Chinese products have increased. The Koreans have been particularly vocal about the investigations of their exports, arguing that they are being victimized by being drawn into EC actions against Japanese products at a time when Korea itself is still much less developed economically and, therefore, in a different situation to Japan.

Apart from the number of cases against its manufactured goods, Korea is also in a unique situation in that one company, Hyundai Marine, had action taken against it in 1988 by the EC for dumping in the service sector, on the grounds of 'unfair pricing' on its liner shipping services between Europe and Australia because it allegedly received subsidies from the Korean government (*Financial Times*, 13 July 1988). However, this precedent has not yet led to any follow-up cases.

The United States has even been drawn into these Euro-Asian dumping disputes, after the EC decided to check products exported to Europe from Japanese – and other Asian – factories set up in the United States. The most blatant case of this type of EC anti-dumping action was against photocopiers being exported to the EC from the Japanese company Ricoh's US plants (Colchester and Buchan 1990, p. 200).

Post-1992 anti-dumping actions and decisions against NIEs' products have included computer diskettes from Korea and Hong Kong (March 1994), colour televisions from Korea and Singapore (October 1994), hydraulic excavators from Korea (January 1995), and fax machines from Korea, Singapore and Taiwan as well as four other Asian Pacific countries (February 1997). The accession of three new members to the EU in January 1995 actually worsened the situation for several Asia Pacific countries, as the new members, which had previously been more moderate in their trading actions, began charging the same anti-dumping duties as the existing members. Hong Kong was not alone in arguing that the expansion of the EU altered its industrial and market structure, so that a new assessment of dumping injury rather than an automatic extension of the existing duties was needed (*Eastern Express*, 28 October 1995).

China has emerged rapidly as the newest threat to the EU. In 1994, indeed, it shot to top position as the trading partner of the EU that had had the most anti-dumping and anti-subsidy measures initiated against it during the year (*South China Morning Post*, 9 August 1995). Chinese trading patterns, particularly the use of Hong Kong as an export outlet, have threatened to drag Hong Kong into EU–Chinese trade disputes. Indeed, in late 1995 the EU began its first ever action under new anti-circumvention legislation to investigate imports of computer diskettes coming from Hong Kong which were believed to originate in China. The anti-dumping duties imposed on Chinese diskettes are much larger than on those of Hong Kong origin. Hong Kong trade officials agreed to cooperate with the EU investigation but warned that if the EU were to decide that some or all of the Hong Kong disk manufacturers should be subject to the specific higher Chinese duties then the case would be taken to the WTO (*Eastern Express*, 23 October 1995). Hong Kong was therefore relieved when the EU decided to drop its investigation after finding insufficient evidence to support European companies' complaints (*South China Morning Post*, 31 July 1996).

The use of the EC's anti-dumping code has been affected by, and indeed has itself affected, negotiations within the GATT to produce a uniform anti-dumping code. For example, Japan took the EC to the GATT over its 'screwdriver plant' regulation; the first time that Japan had taken such an action against the EC on a major issue at GATT (Woolcock and Yamane 1993, p. 17). To the embarrassment of the EC, in May 1990 the GATT panel found against it, but the Commission made it clear that it would not amend its rules until the broader Uruguay Round negotiations on anti-dumping were concluded. This case naturally encouraged the Japanese to press for tighter rules in the negotiations on anti-dumping in the Uruguay Round. A group of developing countries, 'piloted' by Hong Kong, have also made strong criticisms of EC anti-dumping policies in the GATT Round negotiations (Davenport and Page 1991, p. 13).

Impact on Asian Economies

The actual impact of the 1992 process has varied depending on the particular Asian Pacific country and its industrial and export product mix. Prior to the completion of the 1992 process, studies looking at the ASEAN countries suggested that the net effect for Singapore and Malaysia would be negative, while the other three main ASEAN economies would gain, though only Indonesia to a significant degree (Davenport and Page 1990, pp 96–100; Kwarteng 1992, pp. 223–239). With the exception of Singapore, the ASEAN countries have not been major exporters of services, so the main effect of the 1992 process was expected to be in the realm of non-tariff barriers on commodity exports to Europe (Kreinin and Plummer 1992, p. 1353).

However, early studies of the post-1992 impact have proved less pessimistic. After reviewing some of these studies and adding his own calculations, Richard Pomfret suggests that there is 'little or no evidence' that the 1992 programme has damaged Asian exports to Europe (Pomfret 1996, p. 19). However, as he points out, perceptions have proved powerful in the Asia Pacific region – and the perception remains in the region that Asian exports have suffered. The continuance of Asian complaints about specific sectoral arrangements or particular policy actions, such as anti-dumping investigations, testify to the resilience of these perceptions.

WIDENING AND DEEPENING THE EU

The long-standing dilemma of European policy-makers, whether to enlarge the community further or whether to deepen its functions, or even whether to try to attempt to do both, has by no means gone away. The EU did expand by adding three members, Austria, Finland and Sweden, in January 1995, after a fourth potential entrant (Norway) turned down the opportunity to join in a national referendum. But these three members were broadly comparable with the existing members in levels of economic development and political structures. Much more difficult to manage will be the probable entry of the former communist countries of Central and Eastern Europe over the coming decade or so. Formally, there are 11 accepted candidates waiting to apply for EU membership; negotiations with a selected few began in 1998, but it seems impracticable to expect any of the new aspirants, led by Poland, Hungary and the Czech Republic, to gain admission before 2002–3. What kind of Europe will eventually emerge and how policy-making will be managed among the ever-growing EU, which could end up with anything between 20 and 30 members, remain fundamental issues for European leaders. In turn, EU enlargement has implications for how Europe interacts with the Asia Pacific and how the Asians in turn view Europe. A prolonged and difficult enlargement process, with existing members arguing over budget and institutional reforms, would cause disillusionment among the immediate applicants and the watching wider world, including the Asia Pacific.

Deepening too, especially in the context of the planned move to a single currency, the euro, in January 1999 under the EMU plan, also holds significant implications for the EU's relationship with the Asia Pacific. On 1 January 1999 an irrevocable fixing of the conversion rates, the definition and execution of a single monetary policy, and the redenomination of public debt and foreign exchange operations in the euro will take place. Actual euro coins and banknotes will come into use in January 2002. In much the same way as the original 1992 process was intended to be about enhancing economic competitiveness but contained a strong political flavour, so too are the EMU process and timetable 'essentially driven by politics' (Munchau 1997, p. 1). It is an economic project designed to bring net economic benefits, but it will also bring political benefits, particularly in reducing uncertainty and suspicion among members.

While European business is enthusiastic about this move forward, not least because it will eliminate currency conversion costs, the European public is much less so (even, or perhaps especially so, in Germany where the German public seem reluctant to lose their precious deutschemark). Governments, too, have displayed markedly different degrees of enthusiasm, with the British of course being the most recalcitrant. Although the Labour government installed in May 1997 has adopted a more positive attitude towards the EU than its Conservative predecessor, Britain is still not ready and willing to join in the first core group of member countries starting the EMU in January 1999.

As had been the case nearly a decade before when the single market was first mooted, the Asians have been rather slow to wake up to the implications of EMU. Again there was a tendency towards a 'knee-jerk' type of reaction until, during 1997, first the Japanese and then other Asian Pacific governments and research organizations began to carry out surveys and investigations on how the EMU might impact on their business environment. These reports tended to be less 'scare-mongering' in their conclusions than had originally been expected. A Bank of Korea report in late 1997 concluded that on balance EMU would be beneficial for Korean companies in the medium and long term (interview, EU delegation, Seoul, November 1997). Asian companies, or at least the larger ones which are heavily exposed in the European market, have also begun to study the likely impact of the euro on marketing strategies. Two of the largest Japanese investors in Europe, the electronics companies Sony and NEC, set up study teams during 1996 (*Nihon Keizai Shimbun*, 14 December 1996).

This time, compared with the birth of the single market programme one decade earlier, the European Commission itself has been much more proactive, arranging seminars and briefings on EMU and its likely implications for Asian Pacific companies at various capitals around the region. At the first ever ASEM finance ministers' meeting in Bangkok in September 1997, a meeting held at a time of major concern throughout the Asia Pacific region about exchange rate fluctuations, the Europeans tried to reassure their Asian counterparts that the single currency would not be manipulated to protect European jobs from cheap Asian exports (*Korea Herald*, 20 September 1997).

Significantly for Asian companies and countries, the British role has taken on more importance in the EMU debate than might otherwise have been expected as Japan, Korea, Taiwan and, to a lesser extent, the other Asian Pacific economies have significant investments inside Britain which might be adversely affected by Britain staying outside EMU. The controversial statement by Okuda Hiroshi, the President of Toyota, in early 1997 that his company would shift its production facilities from Britain to another EU member country if Britain were to fail to join the EMU (*Nihon Keizai Shimbun*, 22 February 1997) not only reflected some concerns of Asian companies about the marginalization of Britain but also acted as a trigger for a number of British companies to be more open in expressing their own concerns about Britain being left outside EMU. As such, the advent of the Labour government in May 1997, with its seemingly more positive attitude towards Europe, undoubtedly helped to give some reassurance to both Asian investors and

British companies. But even the change of government in Britain did not prevent Toyota from deciding in late 1997 to set up its second European manufacturing plant in France. Okuda claimed that the euro problem did not influence the company's decision (*Korea Herald*, 11 December 1997), but given his earlier comments it is difficult to believe that it was not a factor in the final decision.

The overall picture, however, suggests that the Asians on the whole have been slow to appreciate that, for political if not for pure economic reasons alone, the momentum moving the EU towards a single European currency has been too strong for individual members to resist for long. By focusing on British objections, a tendency no doubt reinforced by the almost inevitable predominant means of access for Asians to the intra-European debate being through the medium of the English language, the Asians tended to underestimate the determination of the key EU players, France and Germany, to advance to this next stage in regional integration. While monetary union is not, of course, political union, EMU naturally introduces a new set of constraints on policy-making and as such represents a crucial step on the way to greater integration.

ASIAN PACIFIC REGIONAL COOPERATION

By comparison with the European integration process, the Asian Pacific experience has been both more laggardly and more multi-layered, with more varied examples of regional and sub-regional cooperation. There is also a difference in kind between the European model, which is built on a highly institutionalized, highly legalistic form of supra-nationality, and the Asian experience so far, which has tended to informality, minimal institutionalization and, if anything, national sovereignty enhancement.

Although the concept of broad Asian Pacific regional cooperation can be dated back to the Pan-Asian ideas of the early part of the 20th century or even to the Japanese wartime 'Greater East Asia Co-Prosperity Sphere', it was the mid 1960s which saw the first flowering of regionalist ideas within the Asia Pacific region. Undoubtedly the establishment of the EC, and its subsequent impact on international trade and investment patterns, spurred this development. One of the earliest ideas, for a Pacific Free Trade Area, was floated by a Japanese academic, Kojima Kiyoshi, in the mid 1960s. His intention, that the five most advanced Pacific nations, including Japan, should form a grouping, was neither politically nor economically acceptable at the time, but it did stimulate thinking in the region and indirectly led to businessmen in these five countries setting up the Pacific Basin Economic Council in 1967. This business grouping has met regularly since, but its influence has been limited.

The next stage of cooperative discussions began in the late 1970s, with a Japanese prime ministerial study group, a major US Congressional report and an Australian initiative to hold an international conference. The result was the creation of the Pacific Economic Cooperation Conference, which has met bi-annually since 1980. The characteristic of this organization is tripartite business, academic and unofficial government delegations (Drysdale 1988, pp. 204–228).

Until the late 1980s the running on regional cooperative ideas had been made by academics and businessmen, with governments giving only background encouragement. However, the third phase of regional integration initiatives began at the governmental level, with Australian Prime Minister Bob Hawke proposing and subsequently hosting in November 1989 the first Asian Pacific Economic Cooperation (APEC) conference. Ministerial meetings have been held annually, alternately being hosted by an ASEAN and a non-ASEAN member, and since 1993 a summit-level meeting has been held at the same time.

APEC has, like the EC/EU, had its own debates about widening and deepening. Membership has grown from 12 at its foundation in 1989 to what will be a total of 24 when the 1998 annual meeting is convened in Malaysia. Significantly, all three Chinas – China, Taiwan and Hong Kong – are represented, as are two South American states (Chile and, from 1998, Peru). Faced with the same kind of magnetic effect that the EU has had for the countries of Eastern Europe and peripheral Europe, APEC has taken a more determined line on expansion. Much to the disappointment of the waiting eight other applicants, led by India, the APEC summit in Vancouver in 1997 decided to impose a ten-year moratorium on new membership (*Far Eastern Economic Review*, 4 December 1997).

The deepening of APEC has proved more contentious, however. Early debates within APEC were driven by an Eminent Persons' Group, which pushed for wide-ranging trade liberalization measures as a way to encourage free trade within the APEC area (not quite the same as a 'free trade area' (Bergsten 1994, p. 23)), but not all member states were ready to move so fast. The November 1994 summit meeting in Bogor endorsed ambitious plans for free and open trade and investment in the region by 2010 for developed economies and 2020 for developing economies. This was followed up in Osaka in 1995 with an 'action agenda' under which all members were to present specific lists of measures for reducing tariff and non-tariff barriers. However, progress on these programmes has been rather limited. Compliance is voluntary, at the strong insistence of some members such as Malaysia, and the offers put on the table have been generally rather restricted and self-serving. The Canadians, who hosted the 1997 Vancouver meeting, therefore were keen to start on a sectoral basis, and agreement was finally reached on nine sectors which would be liberalized from 1999, but again only on a voluntary basis (*Far Eastern Economic Review*, 4 December 1997). Inevitably, however, the financial turmoil in the Asia Pacific in the second half of 1997 threatened to make member countries less rather than more inclined to open up their markets to the outside world.

One further regional initiative needs to be considered, which involves only Asian Pacific states. In December 1990 Malaysian Prime Minister Mahathir proposed an East Asian Economic Grouping (EAEG), which deliberately excluded both the Australians and the Americans and was specifically conceived of as a regional counter-weight to the emerging North American Free Trade Area (NAFTA) and the EC's 1992 programme. The ASEAN countries, Japan, China and South Korea were seen as the initial participants. Ironically, this grouping had a close geographical similarity to the much-hated wartime Japanese Greater East Asia Co-Prosperity Sphere (Korhonen 1997, p. 359). Several Asian Pacific states which were proposed as members had doubts about the wisdom of trying so blatantly to exclude the Americans and the Japanese, and the South Koreans in particular came under pressure from the United States to prevent this grouping from ever getting off the ground (US Secretary of State James Baker was vehemently against its creation). Even within ASEAN (especially in Indonesia, which did not like being upstaged), there were some reservations and so in 1991 Mahathir watered down his proposal into an East Asian Economic Caucus (EAEC), which could meet on an *ad hoc* basis (*Far Eastern Economic Review*, 25 July 1991). This meant that the concept retained the central point that, as some critics have charged, it is 'a caucus without Caucasians' (Godemont 1997, p. 282), but it also made it less problematic for the Japanese and South Koreans.

Nonetheless, for several years it looked as if in practice the Malaysian initiative was being slowly talked into the ground. No formal meeting of the EAEC took place, despite Malaysian efforts to call such a meeting. Ironically, it was the ASEM process that brought a renewal of life to the concept, since the Asian side participation at ASEM I was almost exactly that envisaged by Mahathir at the beginning for his EAEG concept (only Vietnam had been added). Indeed, this significance was not lost on the Malaysians, who made some efforts to build on this fortuitous precedent. The ASEAN summit meeting in December 1997, together with leaders from Japan, China and South Korea, in practice also came close to accepting the EAEC's existence, although not in formal nomenclatural terms. It is likely that in future there will be *ad hoc* meetings of ministers or leaders from time to time, but that the EAEC will not take on any form of institutionalization or even regular consultations.

SUB-REGIONALISM IN THE ASIA PACIFIC

Variously described as both a regional organization and as a sub-regional organization, depending on the geographical area in the mind of the speaker or writer, comes ASEAN. Devised as a way to overcome the Malaysian–Indonesian confrontation through broader regional reconciliation and built on earlier stillborn concepts, ASEAN was founded in 1967 with five original members (Indonesia, Malaysia, Thailand, the Philippines and Singapore). The ASEAN Declaration signed in August 1967 assigned top priority to cooperation in the economic, social and cultural fields; although it steered away from sensitive political issues, ASEAN benefited from the convergence in political outlook between the individual members. Although the organization appeared to do little more than survive in its early years, external pressures from the changing regional environment were felt strongly enough to keep it together (Harris and Bridges 1983, pp. 5–8).

The end of the Vietnam War, the communist takeovers in the other two Indochinese states and, subsequently, the Vietnamese invasion of Cambodia pushed ASEAN into a second phase of development. ASEAN emerged internationally as an organization with an important voice on both regional and global issues, particularly in the management of the politico-security order in its part of the Asia Pacific region. Gradually ASEAN became enmeshed in a series of regular dialogue mechanisms with the major powers, including the EC. (The political dimensions of ASEAN's relations as a group with Europe will be discussed in Chapter 8.) Coordination of policy on external economic issues improved, in part because (with the exception of Singapore) there was a considerable degree of complementarity on the kinds of issue the members wished to raise with external partners; this enabled ASEAN to speak forcibly with one voice (Shibusawa, Ahmad and Bridges 1992, pp. 99–101). However, intra-ASEAN economic cooperation still failed to take off, despite the introduction of a number of schemes for regional import-substitution industrialization during the 1970s and 1980s. The ASEAN record in that respect indeed remained 'insignificant', until finally, and again partly inspired by the changes in the external international economic environment (which included Europe's 1992 process), in 1992 ASEAN embarked on the ambitious programme to create an ASEAN Free Trade Area (AFTA) through progressive tariff cuts (Lim 1996, pp. 19–25).

The shift in emphasis away from bureaucratic-led negotiated cooperation to a more informal, private sector-led form of regional cooperation, combined with the way that ASEAN quickly moved to shorten the deadline for achievement of AFTA from 2003 to 2008 after APEC began its own broader regional process to set targets for trade liberalization, give more grounds for optimism about AFTA than previous efforts at intra-ASEAN cooperation. Nonetheless, economists in the region remain sceptical about its implementation prospects given the past poor record of intra-ASEAN economic cooperation, and argue that its impact, even if achieved on target, is 'likely to be quite limited' (Lim 1996, p. 24). The recent financial crises in several ASEAN member countries have added a further dampener to the enthusiasm of the member countries for signing away their protective practices.

GROWTH TRIANGLES

Much less contingent on state-to-state negotiation, and therefore more flexible in adapting integrative strategies at the firm level, is an increasingly popular form of sub-regional economic cooperation which can be seen at a much more local level and can even be described as sub-sub-regional in nature, namely the emergence of zones, popularly called 'growth triangles', in the Asia Pacific region. Three waves of growth triangles can be identified in Southeast Asia: the South China economic zone, involving China, Hong Kong, Taiwan and Macau, from the late 1970s; the Sijori (Singapore, Johore, Riau) triangle of the late 1980s; and the newer plans of the 1990s, such as the Northern Growth Triangle, the East ASEAN Growth Area and the 'Golden Quadrangle', or Greater Mekong area. Northeast Asia has really seen only one such zone emerge, in the 1990s, in the Tumen river area. Even when it may not be geometrically accurate, the term 'growth triangle' essentially applies to contiguous geographical areas under different sovereignties which link together across their borders to maximize their varied factor endowments and exploit their comparative advantages (Yeung 1995). It is a form of transnational production 'bloc' within which labour, capital and technology can move freely.

This particular phenomenon of transnational production activity is not solely confined to the Asia Pacific region; arguably the United States–Mexico borderlands and the Franco-German boundary zone display some similar characteristics. But in the Asia Pacific region, the growth triangles can be distinguished from comparative developments in other parts of the world by their incorporation of more than two countries/regions, their spatial separation (in several cases they stretch overseas), and the complex mix of ethnic and socio-political backgrounds involved. Moreover, they began to be developed in what was, at least until 1997, a region of dynamic economic growth, with traders and investors constantly searching for new business opportunities. In practice, of course, these economic zones have grown through a mix of both private sector initiative and government intervention, although the balance between these two forces varies in each individual case. Yeung Yue-man has classified these economic zones under three broad types, depending from where he sees the main impetus deriving: government-led (which can be seen in the Sijori case), private sector-led (the South China economic zone fits this category best) and UN development programme-led (Yeung 1995, pp. 62–63, 75–76). Yeung uses the third category to describe the Tumen river project in Northeast Asia, for which there is no direct equivalent in Southeast Asia, although if the Greater Mekong concept develops with a leading role for the Asian Development Bank, then this third category might be usefully redefined as 'international organization-led'. A fourth category might also be postulated, drawn from the efforts to create economic exchanges among cities bordering on the Japan Sea (or East Sea), in which it is local governments which take the initiative (Taga 1994).

EUROPE'S INTERACTION WITH ASIAN PACIFIC REGIONAL COOPERATION

What do these varying types and varying degrees of economic integration mean for the Europeans, both at the company or commercial level and at the institutional or governmental/EU level? Much of the early debate in the late 1970s and early 1980s in Europe about Asian Pacific cooperation and integration was coloured by the stuttering in the European integration experience and the apparently embryonic and extremely rudimentary nature of the early Asian Pacific experiments. Even ASEAN, with which the Europeans came into frequent contact (as described in Chapter 5), was recognized among the Europeans – as indeed among the Asians themselves – as having had only a limited degree of success in promoting intra-ASEAN regional cooperation, let alone integration. While the EC steadily crept towards levels of intra-EC trade as making up more than 50 per cent of total EC trade, intra-ASEAN trade hovered around the 20 per cent mark out of total ASEAN trade with the world. Europeans noted that trade and investment promotion delegations from individual ASEAN countries visiting Europe would stress the comparative advantages of their own particular national economic environment and would rarely, if ever, mention the ASEAN dimension. This led at best to a European tendency to underestimate the Asian Pacific cooperation movement and at worst to dismiss it as a non-starter.

This rather jaundiced view of Asian Pacific economic cooperation undoubtedly coloured early European views of the APEC process, but by 1993 a more sinister view of APEC was beginning to emerge as the Americans moved first to upgrade APEC activities with the first annual leaders' summit and then proceeded to use APEC as a tool to beat the EU during the closing stages of the Uruguay Round of the GATT negotiations. In the words of one senior French researcher, some people in Europe began to see APEC as a 'war machine', which when linked with the emerging NAFTA would act as a way of 'economically encircling' Europe (*Nikkei Weekly*, 11 April 1994). It was undoubtedly true that the 1993 Seattle summit was the high point of US attempts to use APEC as a new leverage against the EU to reduce its trade barriers, especially in the area of agricultural goods, then a major sticking point in the GATT negotiations. When the Europeans were upset by this 'bullying', the Americans subsequently back-tracked slightly and indeed admitted to the Europeans that they had sent out the wrong diplomatic signals (interview, European Commission official, 4 February 1994).

Although one EC Commissioner went as far to suggest that the EU should be given at least observer status at APEC, the EU's general policy response to the revamped APEC was to request in the spring of 1994 some opportunities for dialogue with the organization, or at least with the organization's trade and investment committee (*Straits Times*, 24 April 1994). Although the South Koreans were supportive, the majority of APEC members were non-committal and the Americans distinctly cool (interview, European Commission official, 4 February 1994). The result has been not only that neither observer status nor formal dialogue status has been accorded by APEC to the EU, but also that the EU has taken the opportunity, instead, to deal directly with the Asian members of APEC through the ASEM process, which will be discussed in more detail in Chapter 9.

At the same time, the Seattle and Bogor meetings of APEC probably helped to give the impression to the Europeans that the United States was drifting towards Asia. So in parallel with the emerging ASEM process, the Europeans also began to debate among themselves and with the Americans the future of the transatlantic relationship, with some discussion of the concept of a Transatlantic Free Trade Area occurring from early 1995 (Dieter 1997, pp. 30–31).

TRILATERALISM, REGIONALISM AND MULTILATERALISM

The discussion above of the role of the United States and of NAFTA in the context of EU–APEC links is a salutory reminder that the Euro-Asian relationship does not exist in a vacuum. It is inevitably affected by the inter-linkages with the United States and the broader international economic and political system. Back in the 1970s, as the Trilateral Commission was launched, indeed, Europe, the United States and Japan seemed to be the three poles of the non-socialist industrialized world economy and there seemed to be grounds for expecting trilateralism to emerge in a more formal inter-governmental context (Shibusawa 1984, pp 164–165). That has not occurred.

Although the Trilateral Commission, a group of senior businessmen, politicians and intellectuals, has continued to meet, its work has become overshadowed by changes in the international system, not least the economic emergence of the Asia Pacific region apart from Japan.

In the subsequent decades, Europe or the EC/EU, North America or NAFTA, and the Asia Pacific region have, through growing economic interdependence and corporate globalization, become closer together, but the inter-linkages have invariably resulted in shifting two-against-one tactical coalitions on particular sectoral issues. For example, the Europeans have supported US attempts to open up the Japanese market as bringing benefits for European as well as US companies, but they have been wary of a tendency to unilateralism on the part of the United States and the apparent Japanese preference to respond to US pressure by giving 'special' concessions, such as in the infamous semiconductor agreement. The Europeans felt the same reaction to US deals with the South Koreans and the Chinese at different times in the 1990s over IPRs.

Divergent views have fuelled the debate among economists about whether regionalism, as shown by the EC, NAFTA and APEC processes, is beneficial to trade and investment flows and to improving the living standards of the peoples concerned, and whether regionalism advances or hinders multilateral processes for economic liberalization such as the GATT/WTO (these debates are outlined in Cable and Henderson 1994). Regionalism and multilateralism are not necessarily mutually exclusive. To take just one example, the political momentum given by the Americans to both NAFTA's creation and APEC's ambitious liberalization programme undoubtedly had a positive impact on the GATT negotiations and Europe's approach to those negotiations. Moreover, the evidence about trade diversion and trade creation (and investment flows too) is rather ambiguous. The EC example suggests differences across sectors, with trade creation effects in manufacturing (from which the Asians have benefited) and trade diversion effects deriving from the common agricultural policy (which has impacted on a few Asian agricultural exporters to the EC market) (Smith 1994, pp. 28–30). In addition, while intra-regional trade and investment flows have increased, EC–Asia Pacific trade flows in the 1980s, for example, grew faster than intra-EC trade (Cable 1994, p. 11). It should also be noted that, according to IMF figures, in 1990 for the first time EC trade with the Asia Pacific countries being covered in this study exceeded the EC's trade with the United States. By 1995 EU–Asia Pacific trade was more than 30 per cent larger than EU–US trade (author's own calculations from IMF data).

However, in the case of regionalist developments, perceptions have often been as important – indeed, arguably more important – than realities. The above review of Asian views of the 1992 process and European views of Asian regional cooperation suggests that scepticism has alternated with mutual suspicion in the reactions and responses of each region to the other's attempts to move towards regional cooperation and even integration. This phenomenon has been reinforced by the almost complete lack of region-to-region interaction at the organizational or institutional level. Much has been left to individual governments and companies to find their way around the maze of new integrative and cooperative movements. Growing realization of this problem by the mid 1990s, however, led to efforts to remedy this particular deficit, through the creation of a new process which would directly involve for the first time region-to-region contacts and dialogue, the ASEM process, discussed in Chapter 9.

8. Developing a political partnership

Now is not the time to be concentrating on economics,
    but rather on politics.
            (From a speech in 1989 by Aung San Suu Kyi (Aung San 1995, p. 222))

As the earlier chapters have suggested, the postwar relationship between Western Europe and the Asia Pacific has been a distant one and predominantly an
economic one, marked by a strong element of commercial contention. However, although the level of political dialogue and political interaction has been
far less intense, it has not been non-existent. Some examples have been noted
in the earlier chapters, but the intention here is to try to draw these together in a
way which demonstrates that quietly and gradually the political dimension of
the relationship is becoming both more complex and more important.

THE COLD WAR UMBRELLA

The Western European states have a general interest in peace and stability in
the Asia Pacific region. But if we are to take the term 'interest' more specifically, then the Western European states no longer have vital interests in the
region in the sense of interests which, if threatened, would directly or immediately affect their own survival, or interests which they would defend or
promote by force of arms if no other means were adequate.

  Nonetheless, this does not mean that the Europeans are unconcerned about
political and strategic developments in the Asia Pacific countries. During the
Cold War era, even though Western European eyes tended to be focused on
Eastern Europe and the Soviet Union, the ties with the United States and the
rivalry with the Soviet Union drew them into commitments in the Asia Pacific
which went beyond immediate and admittedly declining colonial involvement. The concern was more obvious during the early years of the Cold War,
when forces from several Western European states participated in the Korean
War in support of South Korea (ten states sent either military forces or
medical units) and in the formation of the rather nebulous and largely ineffective Asian equivalent of NATO, the Southeast Asian Treaty Organization
(SEATO), of which Britain and France were members (Segal 1990, pp. 204,
238). Even then, as the British, for example, made clear over their participa-

tion in the Korean War, the European involvement had more to do with helping to ensure that the Americans remained committed to Western Europe's defence than with a deep belief that they could usefully defend the stability of the whole Asia Pacific region. Indeed, a constant concern of the Europeans was to prevent the United States from overcommitting itself in Korea at the expense of European security (Risse-Kappen 1995, pp. 42–57).

The limits to the European commitment had become clearer by the 1960s and especially by the 1970s as SEATO faded away. Despite US attempts to cast its cause as a 'free world' crusade against communism, the Europeans contributed virtually nothing to the US struggle in Vietnam, with only Spain sending a handful of troops (Larsen and Collins 1975, pp. 22–23). Indeed, in a neat reversal of the situation in the Korean War, European perceptions of their declining military power in the face of the Soviet build-up and of US unwillingness to be involved absolutely everywhere caused some European governments actually to oppose US intervention in Vietnam because it might 'jeopardise NATO's ability to cope with the Soviet threat in Europe' (Godemont 1993, p. 107). The last European troops to see serious action in the Asia Pacific region were British troops involved on Malaysia's side in 1963–65 in its *konfrontasi* (confrontation) with Indonesia, and even then the British needed to call on Australian troops to help ensure success in the jungle battlefields (Thompson 1994, pp. 91–94).

As the Cold War continued into the 1980s, however, it was possible to distinguish a number of broad objectives which underpinned European thinking about the Asian Pacific political and security scene: to discourage the spread of communist ideology; to encourage stable and democratic governments; to reduce existing intra-regional tensions in 'hot spots' such as the Korean peninsula and Cambodia; to prevent the proliferation of weapons of mass destruction; and to ensure that no hostile power either controlled the whole region to the Europeans' disadvantage or interrupted international trade at vital choke-points such as the Straits of Malacca or the South China Sea. The end of the Cold War eliminated the Soviet Union as a player in the region – and the Russian role subsequently has been much more subdued – but it did not change substantially these broad objectives. Of course, in some cases, as was certainly true during the early decades of the Cold War, these objectives have not always been compatible with each other, especially when advocating anti-communism resulted in supporting some far from democratic governments (South Korea, South Vietnam and the Philippines in the 1960s and 1970s and even into the 1980s come easily to mind).

However, these objectives have not always been sufficiently widely recognized or firmly enough articulated by the Europeans. From time to time, and with varying degrees of emphasis depending on the government or country concerned, they have become part of the rhetoric of European ministerial pronouncements but invariably without the backing of policy actions or real commitments.

If the Europeans can be rightly accused of not doing enough in the past to create substance out of rhetoric in their expressed concern for Asian Pacific political and security issues, then the reverse is even more the case. Asians were concerned about tensions that arose from the lengthy Cold War, not least because these tensions found expression in two 'hot wars' which were fought in the Asia Pacific region itself. But with the European political and security scene set solid for so long, resulting in minimal movement between the two blocs in Western and Eastern Europe, there seemed little that Asian states could do or, indeed, needed to do. Even in the 1980s, Asian support for Western European positions on issues of importance to the Europeans was usually given as a *quid pro quo* for European support on an issue of signifi- cance to Asians rather than because of any deep-seated identification with the European need. For example, the EC–ASEAN ministerial meeting in 1980, which produced a joint political declaration for the first time, outlined ASEAN support for the EC's opposition to the Soviet occupation of Afghanistan only in return for EC support of ASEAN's opposition to the Vietnamese invasion of Cambodia (Harris and Bridges 1983, p. 53). In certain cases, where the Asians saw no such coincidence of interests, such as the Falkland islands dispute in 1982, when support from Asia Pacific states for the British view- point was divided at best (Leifer 1989, p. 144) and non-existent at worst, the Asians seemed reluctant to be drawn in at all.

The Asians' broad political concerns as far as Europe was concerned could therefore be summarized as: to prevent the confrontational split between Western and Eastern Europe having any undue repercussions in the Asia Pacific; and to try to keep the Europeans engaged, not so much in the sense of maintaining troops and bases in the region, but as a means of possibly moderating excesses by the two superpowers. The comment of one Singaporean scholar that the ASEAN states did 'not see the Europeans as participants in the strategic equation in South-East Asia' (Lau 1989, p. 73) could apply with equal force to the whole Asia Pacific region.

The Asians did watch with interest as the dramatic changes in Eastern Europe, the reunification of Germany and the final collapse of the Soviet Union panned out during the 1989–91 period. But they were interested by- standers and, indeed, have remained that way, with the exception of the involvement of a few Asian states, predominantly ones with significant Mus- lim populations, in the chaotic political maelstrom of the former Yugoslavia, specifically with peace-keeping and other forms of humanitarian support for the beleaguered Muslims of Bosnia.

The series of financial crises spreading across the Asia Pacific from the middle of 1997 helped to concentrate European as well as Asian minds on the linkages between socio-economic and political stability. While the initial reactions of many within and without the region were to treat these problems as purely economic ones, the impact on domestic politics became increasingly clear as the financial problems contributed to the switch to a new Thai Prime Minister, the election of an opposition candidate for the first time ever in South Korea, and the most serious anti-government demonstrations in Indonesia for more than 30 years. While the Europeans could do nothing but watch from afar as these political changes worked their way through, they were not averse to privately urging economic reconstruction and reform policies and hinting that cleaner, more open and, by implication, more democratic political processes would also help.

RUDIMENTARY POLITICAL DIALOGUE MECHANISMS

As a result of the low level of mutual interest in non-commercial matters, the mechanisms for political and security dialogue remained fragmentary, uncoordinated and largely bilateral – confined to the individual state level – during the Cold War period. Indeed, the record of EC-level political interactions with Asia Pacific regional states was a disappointing one and even the end of the Cold War only brought about a slow realization of the need for better mechanisms.

As noted in Chapter 3, the EC–Japan political dialogue had little real substance during the 1980s, and even after the conclusion of the 1991 EC–Japan Declaration progress has been uneven and unexciting. The EC/EU's political dialogue with South Korea, as shown in Chapter 4, has barely begun. Chapter 6 showed the mixed record on political discussions with the Chinese too, though for different reasons. A high degree of mutual wariness over political issues has been the main characteristic, especially where, for example, in the 1970s the Europeans felt themselves under undue Chinese pressure to join an anti-Soviet front, and in the 1990s, conversely, the Chinese have perceived themselves as being consistently on the receiving end of European pressure on human rights issues.

The EC–ASEAN political dialogue is actually the longest running in institutional terms. As discussed in Chapter 5 in primarily economic terms, the EC–ASEAN dialogue evolved out of concerns about British accession to the EC but were formalized through the personal efforts of the German Foreign Minister, Hans-Dietrich Genscher. Regular foreign ministerial meetings began in 1978 and political issues have always been prominent. Since the mid 1980s EC representatives have also regularly attended the dialogue sessions following the annual ASEAN foreign ministers' meetings (known by the acronym of ASEAN-PMC for post-ministerial conference), at which both political and economic issues have been discussed. The Europeans saw ASEAN as a basically stable, accessible and 'anti-communist' grouping which could be a compatible partner for political dialogue. The ASEAN side felt better able to sustain an equal stature in the political discussions by comparison with its inevitably weaker position in economic tasks (Luhulima 1992, pp. 317–318, 322).

However, there were some signs from the mid 1980s that the content of these political discussions was beginning to 'stagnate', that, for example, the reported conclusions on topics such as the Vietnamese occupation of Cambodia were becoming repetitive (Regelsberger 1989, pp. 84–86). Attempts were made to broaden the range of topics and themes discussed, but these were only partially successful as some of these issues were ones on which a consensus could not easily be achieved, even within the European membership.

As the Cold War order began to crumble, the overall basic convergence in EC and ASEAN views in the politico-strategic sphere began to waiver slightly. With Germany, so often the lead country in the dialogue with ASEAN, overwhelmed by its reunification problems, intra-European policy differences became more visible. So too did differences with ASEAN. France made more of the running on the Cambodian problem, as discussed later in this chapter, while Holland and Portugal became prominent in the politicization of aid and economic cooperation policy. These states were not always supported whole-heartedly by all the other EU member states. The tendency to focus more on 'new' issues on the international agenda such as human rights, coupled with the winding down of the Cambodian problem and the emergence of the Burma problem, has produced more lively, but also more contentious, political discussions in EC/EU–ASEAN meetings in the 1990s. This trend became apparent as early as the May 1991 Luxembourg meeting and the October 1992 Manila meeting (*Far Eastern Economic Review*, 20 June 1991; *Straits Times*, 24 September 1994). The two sides actually decided to reduce the frequency of the ministerial-level meetings, not least because of the problems of getting so many ministers together at one time, but at the same time to introduce more frequent and more efficient contacts between senior officials. In recent years the timing and purpose of the EU–ASEAN dialogue have been affected by the new ASEM process, which has 'taken over' some topics of political concern. Nonetheless, it is the changing character of the topics being raised which has done more to affect the character and depth of the political dialogue than any institutional changes.

The ASEM process is an important one and will be discussed in detail in Chapter 9. ASEAN, through extending the logic of its ASEAN-PMC meetings, has developed since 1994 the ASEAN Regional Forum (ARF), which involves EU membership with most of the Asia Pacific states, and this will be discussed later in this chapter. Only one other forum has regularly brought together European and Asian Pacific states (albeit only one, Japan) to discuss political questions formally: the annual seven-power summits (known generally as G-7 or, from 1997 when Russia became broadly involved, as G-8). These summits had begun as economic meetings with foreign policy being raised only incidentally, but by the early 1980s political issues had become a regular and occasionally preoccupying theme (Putnam and Bayne 1987, p. 241). The French had been initially resistant to focusing on political issues and Japan, as the only non-member of NATO, seemed uneasy too.

Initially feeling rather outnumbered and uncomfortable in this Western 'club', Japan has always tried to portray itself as the representative of Asia at these summits (Saito 1990, pp. 43–116). Other Asia Pacific countries have sometimes had reservations about this approach, despite Japanese attempts to incorporate other Asians' ideas by consultations prior to the annual meetings. Indeed, on occasions, such as the Indonesian intervention with the British hosts on the eve of the 1984 London summit, they have felt it necessary to ensure a more direct input for their views. Nonetheless, Japan has helped to concentrate the minds of the Europeans on Asian issues, such as the situation on the Korean peninsula and the plight of Vietnamese refugees, especially when it has been taking its turn to act as host. In turn, Japan has been forced to contribute more to the discussion and resolution of global political issues, especially after Nakasone became Prime Minister in 1983. Indeed, according to two historians of the G-7 summit process, 'the most durable achievement of the summits was to bring Japan firmly into the circle of Western consultation and co-operative action' (Putnam and Bayne 1987, p. 242).

THE SECURITY DIMENSION

Despite the rhetoric of European declaratory statements, it is clear that the broad political interests delineated earlier in this chapter have been translated into only a very limited military and strategic role in the Asia Pacific region.

Europe has no more than a handful of minute residual commitments. Britain effectively withdrew militarily from 'east of Suez' in the late 1960s– early 1970s, but did of course retain a presence in Hong Kong until June 1997. The closing down of the British bases – or, to be more precise, their takeover by the Chinese People's Liberation Army – effectively marks the end of the historic British military presence in the Asia Pacific. The British do have an ongoing commitment in Brunei, despite its independence in 1984, but it is an ambiguous and low-key one. A small detachment of British troops (invariably Gurkhas and numbering normally about 1000) is kept there at the specific request of the Sultan of Brunei under an agreement renewed at five-year intervals under which the Sultan pays most of the costs, an estimated $6 million per year (Leake 1989, p. 143). This deployment has as much to do with maintaining internal order as it does with discouraging external enemies. Next due for renewal during 1998, this agreement is expected to remain in force for at least another five years. In addition, a token British colour-guard presence is maintained in South Korea on attachment to the Commonwealth liaison force, and the senior British military attache at the British embassy in Seoul acts as one of the UN representatives on the Military Armistice Committee.

Britain also has obligations to its former colonies of Malaysia and Singapore under the semi-dormant Five-Power Defence Arrangement (FPDA). Set up in 1971 as a way of reassuring these two states after the planned British withdrawal from east of Suez, Britain, together with the other two partners, Australia and New Zealand, is required only to 'consult' with Malaysia and/ or Singapore should they be subject to attack (Chin 1991, pp. 194–195). There is no automatic defence commitment. The British withdrew their last small ground troop detachment from Singapore in 1976 and the Australians and the New Zealanders similarly reduced their deployments progressively during the 1970s and 1980s. In the late 1980s, however, Australia tried to revamp the FPDA, and joint military training and exercises have subsequently been conducted on a more regular basis. These joint exercises enable the British to send naval forces to Southeast Asia on an occasional basis and, as such, allow them to act as a symbol of the British interest in the region's security (Chin 1991, p. 198). The extended 'Ocean Wave' Asian Pacific tour which British naval forces undertook in the first half of 1997, including visiting Japan and South Korea as well as participating in the FPDA exercises in April 1997, was a clear example of this desire. In fact, the FPDA 'Flying Fish 97' naval exercises off the coast of Malaysia were the most ambitious ever held under the FPDA's auspices (*South China Morning Post*, 19 June 1997). With naval visits to Hong Kong now proving to be much more restricted (the first post-handover naval visit to Hong Kong did not occur until December 1997), British naval forces are likely to call in more regularly to Singapore. Indeed, early in 1997 Britain signed an agreement with Singapore to facilitate naval training and exchanges (*South China Morning Post*, 27 April 1997).

In 1991 for the first time ever a meeting of defence ministers of the FPDA member countries was held, and at a subsequent meeting in Singapore in 1994, the defence ministers actually agreed to strengthen their decision-making procedures (*South China Morning Post*, 21 September 1994). Although the defence ministers argued that the FPDA was still relevant to the developing regional security framework, any major change to its membership or mission seems unlikely. Given that the FPDA is 'an unobtrusive but uniquely

Commonwealth arrangement' (Chin 1991, p. 200), occasionally in the years since it became independent, Brunei has been mentioned as a possible new member. Although Singapore, which has close ties with Brunei (and sends its troops there for jungle training), has hinted that it is in favour of such an expansion, the Brunei government has never made any formal approach for membership. Inhibitions about unnecessarily upsetting Indonesia, which saw the FPDA as originally targeted against itself, have probably acted as a restraint (Wanandi 1995, p. 442). FPDA defence ministers met again in April 1997, when a subtle change in the wording of the arrangements, from 'coming to the defence' of Malaysia and Singapore to 'assisting' in their defence was agreed (*South China Morning Post*, 27 April 1997). This reflected the better economic and military capabilities of these two Southeast Asian states to defend themselves, but, nonetheless, the FPDA ministers still saw the need for both British and US forces to show their presence in the region from time to time. For the two Southeast Asian states the continuing involvement of Britain is useful not just for additional security for their own countries, but also as a way of keeping the US interested, but not obsessively overbearing, by demonstrating that US allies are also doing something to help in maintaining a peaceful regional order (*South China Morning Post*, 27 April 1997).

Britain did once, but only once, in 1986, participate in the multinational Rim of the Pacific (Rimpac) naval exercises, at the time that New Zealand was at the height of its dispute with the United States over nuclear weapon-carrying ships and hence excluded from such exercises (McIntosh 1987, pp. 142–144).

Other European forces are barely on the map in the Asia Pacific region. France has only limited military deployments in its South Pacific territories of Polynesia and New Caledonia, though it has also used Muraroa atoll near Tahiti as a site for its underground nuclear tests, which were controversially resumed in 1995–96. Portugal has no armed forces deployed in its last remaining territory in the region, Macau.

The Western Europeans, therefore, have looked to the United States in the first instance to protect their interests in the Asia Pacific region, a fact which the Americans feel is not always sufficiently appreciated by the 'ungrateful' Europeans. During the Cold War era, despite their inevitable preoccupation with the European theatre, the Western Europeans were not unaware that both their ally, the United States, and their potential adversary, the Soviet Union, had Pacific seaboards and alliance relationships with various Asia Pacific states. The Soviet Union was allied with North Korea and Mongolia, and the United States with Japan, South Korea, the Philippines, Thailand and, on the edge of the region, Australia and New Zealand (Segal 1990, pp. 235–257).

In general, however, the Western Europeans have tended to underestimate the linkages between security issues in Europe and Asia, feeling that out of sight means out of mind (I am indebted to a former colleague, John Roper, for this suggestion). This tendency was indeed shared by the Asians, too. Only occasionally did particular crises, such as that during the mid 1980s over how to respond to the deployment of Soviet SS-20 missiles and how to deal with their potential transfer between the European and Asian theatres of the Soviet Union, really bring the Western Europeans and the Southeast Asians close together. In that one particular case, lobbying efforts by Europeans, Japanese, South Koreans and Chinese ensured that the final Intermediate-range Nuclear Forces (INF) Treaty, signed by the United States and the Soviet Union in 1987, reflected these shared concerns (Kirby 1988, pp. 236–247). By 1991 all SS-20s and all other US and Soviet weapons in the INF category had been completely eliminated (Findlay 1996, p. 222). A common position was reached between the Europeans and the Asians on the basis of an understanding that any deal which might temporarily improve the European security situation would adversely affect Asia, and could in time once again threaten European security as Soviet missiles were first moved one way and then the other (Takahashi 1993, p. 107). But such instances were few and far between.

The post-Cold War world, however, has given rise to some new challenges to old conceptions of security and security linkages around the globe. It is therefore helpful to examine a few cases to see whether the new global and regional context has helped to stimulate any new thinking or policy-making about Euro-Asian political and security links.

The Cambodian Crisis

The prolonged attempts to resolve the crisis brought about by the Vietnamese occupation of Cambodia and the continuing civil war there during the 1980s provided an interesting test case of Euro-Asian political and security cooperation. The winding down of the US–Soviet and Sino-Soviet rivalries in the late 1980s altered the stakes for the major powers involved in the Cambodian embroglio and helped to facilitate moves towards a settlement. As discussed in Chapter 5, among the Europeans it was successive French governments, which, given their strong feeling of 'responsibility' for bringing peace and stability to their former colonies, tried to discuss possibilities and propose initiatives to break the diplomatic and military deadlock, particularly by forming close links with those states within ASEAN, notably Indonesia, which felt the need to try harder to resolve the problem. With the approval of ASEAN, France hosted meetings between Cambodian faction leaders and then an international peace conference in 1989, but not until a further international conference was held in 1991, with the UN Security Council P-5 group becoming more actively involved, were the finer details of the peace plan hammered out and agreed.

The comprehensive political settlement committed the UN to taking over transitional administrative responsibilities in the country. By the end of 1991 a small advance UN guard, principally consisting of French and Australian troops and headed by a French general, had arrived in Cambodia (Roberts 1993, pp. 71–76). The degree of eventual participation in the UN Transitional Authority in Cambodia (UNTAC) operations by European countries represented a new example, albeit one which will not often be repeated, of European involvement in Asia. By the eve of the May 1993 Cambodian elections, ten Western European countries had either military forces or police stationed in Cambodia (*Asiaweek*, 30 October 1992; 15 March 1993). The French had by far the largest contingent among the Europeans, with 1362 soldiers and 139 police, followed by the Netherlands with a total of 831 soldiers and police. When the security situation inside Cambodia began to deteriorate in late 1992 the French actually sent in a battalion of its famed foreign legionnaires (Peou 1997, p. 249). Even Germany, which had balked at sending troops to the multinational forces fighting in the 1990–91 Gulf War because of constitutional constraints, found it possible to send 149 military and 76 policemen to Cambodia. The EC and its constituent member countries, collectively, were also the largest provider of funds – $230 million pledged in 1992 – to the UNTAC operation, although, in practice, like many other donors, they were dilatory in actually supplying the funds.

Not all the Europeans and Asians were in complete agreement with how UNTAC carried out its operations, particularly when the Khmer Rouge proved intransigent about meeting pre-election cease-fire and disarming provisions. In July 1992 French General Jean-Michel Loridon, the second-in-command of the UNTAC forces, who was angry at repeated Khmer Rouge violations, was relieved of his command after his arguments in favour of forcibly disarming the Khmer Rouge, even if it cost UNTAC lives, set him against his UNTAC superiors (Peou 1997, p. 249). Other senior UN officials complained that the French were not acting as 'team players', and they disliked the requirement for all UNTAC activities to be conducted in French as well as English (*Foreign Report*, 3 December 1992).

Nonetheless, the Europeans felt that the May 1993 elections, which were not held in perfect conditions but at least were the fairest in Cambodian history and received a high voter turnout, provided satisfactory justification for their commitment. ASEAN, in turn, appreciated the European commitment. With the elections over, the French strongly asserted their anti-Khmer Rouge policy and, with more lukewarm support from Britain, they showed themselves prepared to turn a blind eye to Hun Sen's party forcing a power-sharing coalition arrangement provided the Khmer Rouge were kept out of power (Peou 1997, pp. 253–254). Several European governments committed themselves to infrastructural reconstruction funding and the French sent army experts to assist the new Cambodian government in rebuilding its armed forces (Peou 1997, p. 254).

The particularities of the Cambodian situation and the UNTAC operation did provide a special case for European and Asian political and security cooperation. Although some military strategists are arguing for the major European powers to sustain a limited military capability capable of global reach and able to cooperate with the forces of Asian countries and the United States (Eberle 1998, p. 39), in the immediate future there are unlikely to be many similar cases to the Cambodian one in which the imperatives for cooperation are so clear. Nevertheless, the symbolism of European forces again being committed to the security of an Asia Pacific country, albeit under a UN flag and wearing UN 'blue helmets', was an important one for both Europe and its Asia Pacific partners.

The North Korean Nuclear Crisis

While the Cambodian crisis was struggling towards resolution, another crisis was emerging in Northeast Asia over suspicions that North Korea was trying to develop nuclear weapons.

From the late 1980s the US and South Korean governments had become suspicious that North Korea might be secretly reprocessing nuclear fuel and even producing nuclear weapons. North Korea prevaricated over opening up its nuclear reactor sites to the International Atomic Energy Agency (IAEA), threatened in the spring of 1993 to withdraw from the Nuclear Non-proliferation Treaty (NPT) and practised brinkmanship coupled with the occasional inflamatory statement (such as threatening to turn Seoul into a 'sea of fire') during a long series of negotiations with the United States during 1993–94. Talk of sanctions and even pre-emptive military strikes against the suspect sites hovered over the negotiations, and at one stage in mid 1994 the situation did seem to be close to war (the US ambassador in Seoul later admitted as much in the *Korea Herald* of 31 January 1997). But a US–North Korean framework agreement was finally signed in October 1994 after the personal intervention of the former US President, Jimmy Carter. This agreement provided for international assistance from a newly created consortium for North Korea to build and develop two nuclear power plants and to supply much-needed oil in the interim (Oh and Grubel 1995, pp. 97–116). The Korean Energy Development Organization (KEDO), as the international consortium became known, was formally inaugurated in January 1995, with the United States, South Korea and Japan as the three initial members of the 'board of governors' or executive committee. A series of further negotiations to fill in the details about the site of the nuclear reactors, their type, design and construction schedule dragged on through 1995–96, but construction of the first reactor began with the formal ground-breaking ceremony in August 1997 (*Nihon Keizai Shimbun*, 20 August 1997).

Although none of the EU states have an alliance relationship with South Korea, European troops did fight on South Korea's side during the Korean War. Despite their dislike of the authoritarian leaders of South Korea over the subsequent decades, the Western Europeans maintained strong diplomatic and commercial links with the South. Of the EU states only Denmark and Portugal of established relations with the North as well, back in the 1970s, and trade links have remained at a very low level (Hindley and Bridges 1996, pp. 75–77). Although France toyed with the idea of recognizing the North in the early 1980s and the British normally adopt a policy of recognizing an established government regardless of its political hue, in reality none of the other EC states gave serious consideration to approaching the North (Bridges 1986, pp. 85–86). That is, at least until the end of the Cold War allowed South Korea to expand its diplomatic horizons with recognition by the North's allies in Eastern Europe, the Soviet Union and finally China. But the North's erratic behaviour and response to losing out in the diplomatic competition with the South did little to encourage the Europeans to consider breaking the diplomatic isolation of the North. Apart from a German interests section, inherited, as it were, from the pre-unification East German embassy in Pyongyang (Morris 1996, p. 91), there is no European diplomatic presence in North Korea (both Portugal and Denmark operate out of their Beijing embassies).

It was against this background of strong links with the South and distinct suspicion of the North that the Western Europeans became involved with the nuclear weapon crisis. The Europeans were kept informed by the Americans and the South Koreans about the mounting evidence from intelligence sources and from the IAEA itself about the suspicious activities going on at North Korea's nuclear site at Yongbyon. The two UN Security Council states, Britain and France, together with other EU states, made it plain that they deplored both North Korea's threat to leave the NPT and its failure to open up its sites to full inspection. However, the Europeans were divided over whether sanctions should be imposed to force North Korea to accept its obligations. The French took a strong line and clearly advocated the imposition of sanctions if North Korea failed to comply within a certain deadline, but others took a more conciliatory line. There was certainly collective relief among the Europeans when the 1994 framework agreement was concluded.

It was at this stage that the Americans, Japanese and South Koreans began to look for more substantial support, primarily in terms of financial contributions to KEDO, which had been set up specifically under the terms of the US–North Korean framework agreement. Britain earned some good points with its Asian partners by becoming the first European state to offer financial support, with an offer of $1 million in June 1995. But it was far more difficult to get a European consensus, despite some enthusiasm from within the European Commission itself. The Danes and the Swedes were worried about the nuclear safety angle, the Germans about the potential liability problems, the Austrians about compromising their neutrality and the French about the exact budget details (*Agence Europe*, 22 November 1995; *Korea Herald*, 2 October 1996). The KEDO members tried to persuade Britain to push its European partners, but the British were reluctant to use up too much political capital on this issue when there were, to them, more crucial issues which required bargaining with other EU members. The British nonetheless did try to show the way by offering to give a second tranche if necessary (interview, British Foreign Office, June 1996).

The situation became complicated, however, as towards the end of 1995 the Europeans decided that they would ask for a seat on the existing tripartite executive committee as part of the reward for contributing financially. This was received with mixed feelings by the Asian members: the Japanese felt that the role that the EU could play should depend on how much the Europeans decided to contribute (*Eastern Express*, 15 January 1996), while the South Koreans, initially at least, made it clear that they did not want the EU to hold 'equal power' with the three original executive members (*Korea Herald*, 16 January 1996).

The haggling over this point, within KEDO's tripartite leadership and between KEDO and the EU negotiators, slowed down decision-making. Finally, in May 1997 the EU and KEDO agreed that, under the auspices of the European Atomic Energy Community, the EU would contribute approximately $18 million a year over five years to KEDO, an amount which would go a long way to meeting a US shortfall in financial contributions to cover the cost of the heavy oil being supplied annually to the North (*Korea Herald*, 24 May 1997). In return, the EU would be elevated to become the fourth KEDO executive committee member. The EU cast its decision to contribute financially in terms of the 'high priority' which it attached to the full implementation of the NPT regime and to the desire to be politically engaged in Northeast Asia (*Agence Europe*, 22 November 1995; *Korea Herald*, 1 August 1997). But a subsidiary factor, which was important given the expertise of several European nations in nuclear power technology, was the realization that companies from KEDO member countries would have preference in bidding for the remaining contracts not given out already to the South Koreans (*Korea Herald*, 1 August 1997).

Although at the time when tensions on the Korean peninsula were particularly high, in mid 1994, the debate among Western and Asian governments and opinion leaders about imposing sanctions had occasionally featured voices calling for military action, at least in the form of 'surgical strikes' against the suspect North Korean facilities, the military option had never been seriously considered. There had been little real chance, therefore, that the Europeans would have been called upon to commit troops or logistical support. As the KEDO experience so far has shown, the European role was expected by the Asians – and by the Europeans themselves – to be confined to financial issues. The only argument was over how much and what kind of voice in the subsequent decision-making that financial commitment might buy.

The Taiwan Straits Crisis

The crisis which emerged in the spring of 1996 when China tried to undermine the presidential elections taking place in Taiwan did, however, carry the potential for calls on the Europeans to contribute with a physical presence. China, of course, has never accepted Taiwan's separate existence and has never renounced the use of force to 'reclaim' Taiwan should it embark on a path of 'independence'. This has meant, as discussed in Chapter 6, a consistent Chinese endeavour to prevent Taiwan being recognized by other countries, including the United States and the Western European states. As Taiwan embarked on a new round of moves to try to enlarge its international space from 1993, with a series of 'private' visits by senior politicians, culminating in President Lee Teng-hui's controversial visit to his *alma mater*, Cornell University, in June 1995 to receive an honorary degree, the Chinese became increasingly angry (Lee 1997, pp. 108–117). President Lee's US visit provoked not just strong diplomatic protests but the start of a series of 'war games' by the Chinese PLA (People's Liberation Army) in the Taiwan Straits. Three were held in 1995 and three more in early 1996 in the run-up to the presidential elections (Lee 1997, pp. 117–119).

The exercises were intended not only to show that China felt strongly about Taiwan and would not allow it to become 'independent', but also to influence the outcome of the Taiwanese election so that pro-independence candidates (which included, according to the Chinese, the covert pro-independence figure Lee) would be disadvantaged. While the Chinese did succeed in making it clear to the international community that Taiwan was a serious and sensitive issue for them, they failed to prevent Lee's election victory and, if anything, pushed Taiwanese public opinion away from reunification (Harding 1997, p. 18). They also provoked the United States into its most serious commitment to the defence of Taiwan for nearly three decades. The Americans backed up their rhetoric of denouncing the Chinese actions as 'a deplorable act of intimidation' by dispatching two aircraft carrier groups to the waters adjacent to Taiwan while the exercises continued (Lee 1997, p. 121).

With the notable exception of the Japanese, the Asian states tended to be cautious in public, usually confining themselves to calls for a peaceful resolution of the dispute, although privately they expressed much greater concern about China's belligerency (Harding 1997, p. 18). Among the Europeans the British took a comparatively strong line, issuing three statements calling for restraint on both sides, while Prime Minister Major spoke strongly to Chinese Foreign Minister Qian Qichen when they met in the margins of the ASEM meeting in Bangkok in March 1996 (interview, British Trade and Cultural Office, Taipei, January 1997). The British were also instrumental in pushing the EU to issue a statement urging restraint. The Taiwanese, of course, while appreciative of European support, nonetheless had hoped that the Europeans would do more, possibly even threatening sanctions against China (interview, Taiwan Foreign Ministry, January 1997).

The question remains open, however: should China again threaten this kind of military action against Taiwan, for example in response to subsequent elections (such as the parliamentary ones due at the end of 1998 in which conceivably the ruling Kuomintang might lose power to the opposition which could have a pro-independence predominancy), will the Americans, having shown the way once on their own in March 1996, expect the Europeans to contribute more next time? Almost certainly the Americans would expect a greater European commitment, but beyond the British possibly sending a token back-up force, it is difficult to see the Europeans getting involved directly.

THE ARF

The birth of an intense debate within Europe about the future 'security architecture' for the continent as the Cold War began to wind down was bound to have some echoes in the Asia Pacific region. In 1990–91 both the Canadian and the Australian governments began to float proposals for drawing on the European experience, particularly through the CSCE process, to create some form of Asian-style CSCE organization (Dewitt 1994, pp. 5–8). The response from the region was, in general, unenthusiastic, mainly because of a widely shared feeling that the Asia Pacific region was more complex than the pre-1989 European scene had been, so that European models could not be easily translated to the Asian situation.

But the cool official response masked the beginning of a serious debate among regional policy-makers and advisers. ASEAN's governmental links had long been reinforced by the so-called 'second track' of networks among think-tanks and research institutes within the region. These academic and semi-academic dialogues had often focused on foreign and security policy issues and helped not only to establish a non-governmental group, the Council for Security Cooperation in the Asia Pacific, but also to push the ASEAN member governments themselves towards more formal mechanisms to discuss security issues (Kerr 1994, pp. 397–409).

Although ASEAN played an important political role and acted as a form of security community, at least until the end of the Cold War and the beginning of the solution to the Cambodian problem, it had eschewed a formal security role. However, in 1991 during the annual PMC dialogue meeting with his ASEAN counterparts, Japanese Foreign Minister Nakayama Taro proposed that the annual discussions should include more focused discussions on regional security issues; he talked about a political dialogue aimed at 'enhancing a feeling of reassurance' among the countries of the region, but the implication was clear (Soeya 1993, pp. 26–27). Although the Japanese had been prompted into taking this initiative because of an awareness of discussions going on at the 'second-track' level (interview, Japanese Foreign Ministry official, November 1991), the ASEAN governments were not immediately ready to accept the idea, nor, for that matter, were the Americans (Leifer 1996, p. 24). But by the time of the ASEAN summit in January 1992, the ASEAN leaders were beginning to think about security cooperation through external dialogue (Leifer 1996, p. 21). During the following year the details were slowly fleshed out into a proposal to create the ARF, and a dinner meeting of foreign ministers of interested states in July 1993 agreed to launch it formally the following year.

The ARF held its first formal meeting in July 1994 in Bangkok. It had 17 members: the then six ASEAN countries, the seven formal dialogue partners (the United States, Canada, Australia, New Zealand, Japan, the EU and South Korea) and four observer states (Russia, China, Vietnam and Papua New Guinea). Assessments of this initial meeting have varied. One scholar has described it as 'the most comprehensive discussion of Asian Pacific security issues since World War II' (Nacht 1995, p. 36). Others gave it more modest reviews, noting that the discussion 'lacked focus and was certainly not a dialogue'; Michael Leifer saw it as 'a small but constructive step along a path without clear signposts' (Leifer 1996, pp. 33, 36). Given that the initial meeting lasted only three hours, in reality there had been time for little more than introductory remarks by each of the delegates.

The most important aspect was that such a large number of Asian Pacific countries had actually sat round the same table to talk about security issues. From the European perspective, it was important that Europe was fully represented at such a discussion for the first time too. This is not to deny that some participants felt uncomfortable with European participation, arguing that the Europeans had no credible security commitment to the region and therefore did not deserve a place (Amri 1994, p. 26). Moreover, the European contributions to that initial meeting were criticized as being insufficiently focused on Asia Pacific regional issues. The German Foreign Minister, Klaus Kinkel, one of the two EU representatives present, insisted in speaking in German (a language not widely understood in the Asia Pacific) and in concentrating on the crisis in Bosnia, an issue which held little resonance for any Asian countries except for Malaysia, Indonesia and Brunei, which have majority Muslim populations and have been concerned about the fate of Bosnian Muslims.

Prior to the 1994 meeting there had been considerable argument among the Europeans about who should attend to represent the EU, given the normal European practice of having a '*troika*' system of the three foreign ministers of the member countries which are the immediate past President, current President and next President of the European Council. The ASEAN side, as hosts, insisted on only two delegates for each country/region at the ARF in order to keep the initial meeting to a reasonable size. The Europeans did manage to win a concession from the ASEAN organizers that at the August 1995 ARF meeting in Brunei three EU delegates would be allowed. However, the waters were muddied once again when the French and British governments began to argue that, as UN Security Council members, they should occupy two out of these three slots by right. The ASEAN view was that the exact composition of the three-person EU delegation was up to the Europeans and the direct lobbying by France and Britain was rejected. Finally, at the 1995 meeting and subsequently the usual *troika* system has operated for EU representation, with whichever country holds the EU presidency at the time providing the Foreign Minister to lead the delegation. The massive ill-will generated in the Asia Pacific region by the resumption of French nuclear testing in 1995 ensured that the idea of separate French (and by extension separate British) representation in ARF was effectively dead thereafter. These two states continued to harbour some faint hopes and the British Foreign Secretary, Malcolm Rifkind, visiting Singapore in February 1997, continued to argue publicly that there was still a 'strong case for the UK to be involved on a national basis' (Rifkind 1997). Significantly, his successor in the new Labour government, Cook, when giving a key-note speech on British policy towards Southeast Asia six months later, failed to mention that aspiration (Cook 1997b).

The Brunei meeting of ARF in 1995 did hold more substantive discussions based on a concept paper which advocated 'a gradual, evolutionary approach' to managing security problems in the region (Leifer 1996, pp. 39–41). However, the Chinese reluctance to discuss the South China Sea dispute in a multilateral gathering hampered any steps towards considering possible solutions to the most serious security problem facing Southeast Asia at that time.

With the exception of one issue, European participation was low key, but was generally felt by other participants to have been more relevant than at the previous year's meeting. However, one issue – nuclear testing in the region –

did bring particular tension to the Euro-Asian discussions. ARF's final statement called for an 'immediate end' to such testing. Neither China, which had continued to carry out nuclear testing, with its most recent test prior to the Brunei meeting having been in May 1995, nor France, which had just announced that it would resume nuclear testing in the South Pacific from September 1995, was specifically named but the implication was clear. Bound by the constraints of trying to present a common EU foreign policy stance, the Spanish Foreign Minister, Javier Madriaga, was forced to distance himself from this part of the ARF statement, by arguing that the Comprehensive Test Ban Treaty (CTBT) had not yet become 'legally binding' (*South China Morning Post*, 2 August 1995). Opinion within the EU was actually strongly against the French action to resume testing, and Britain, the only other EU member which possessed nuclear weapons, reiterated its own commitment not to carry out any more tests. But as the lead EU representative, Madriaga had to adopt the unenviable position of supporting France in a manner which did little to endear the Europeans to the Asians.

The July 1996 meeting of ARF, held in Jakarta, was comparatively uneventful, with most of the discussion centred on how to follow up on some recommendations made by working groups established after the Brunei meeting on confidence-building measures, such as publishing defence policy papers, participation in UN peace-keeping operations, and training and personnel exchanges. Although individual participants raised controversial issues, such as the South China Sea dispute and the pace of democratization in Burma (which was formally admitted to the ARF along with India at this meeting), these issues did not become formal items on the agenda and the final communiqué called only for the peaceful resolution of disputes (*The Australian*, 24 and 27 July 1996). While the Europeans had supported efforts by the Australians and Americans to criticize Burma's human rights record (which set them against the Indonesian hosts' desire to avoid discussing sensitive internal political questions), generally the European role was once again a subdued one.

The July 1997 meeting of ARF in Kuala Lumpur was dominated by the issue of Burma again and the *coup d'état* by Hun Sen in Cambodia immediately prior to the meeting. There was considerable agreement within ARF that ASEAN should try to play some kind of mediating role in Cambodia, but this was offset by the more visible differences over Burma, as Japan and the Western members of the ARF, including the EU, criticized the lack of democratic progress in Burma (*Far Eastern Economic Review*, 7 August 1997).

At the outset the European view had been that ARF may 'over time develop into the overall security forum for the Asian region', but that the desire for 'consensus' and for the avoidance of 'conflictual debate' would slow its progress in that direction (Commission 1994). This initial expectation has

been largely justified, judging by the course of ARF's subsequent development. The closing statement by the Malaysian Foreign Minister, Abdullah
Badawi, the Chairman of the 1997 ARF meeting, noted that ARF was pro-
gressing 'at a pace acceptable to all' and emphasized the need to maintain an
'evolutionary approach' and to take decisions by consensus (Badawi 1997).
This implied a lowest common denominator approach.

Whatever reservations some Asian states still have about EU representation, the Asians recognize that the ill-will which might be caused by 'expelling'
the EU is not worth the effort. In the meantime, ARF has slowly expanded its
membership to 21. But, with the exception of the Burmese issue, adding new
members has not been, and is unlikely to be, as controversial as the issue of
the pace and direction of ARF. ASEAN has taken a leading role in setting up
ARF and clearly takes a 'proprietary' or 'pivotal' position in the organization
(Leifer 1996, pp. 45–49). This has resulted in a tendency for ARF to move at
the 'comfortable pace' which ASEAN, including its new members, and often
China, wishes to move rather than the faster pace desired by some other
members, notably Australia and the United States. The EU would normally
fall into the latter group, although it is well aware that its lack of an adequate
political and security dimension and regional presence inhibits how much
leverage the Europeans actually have in practice to push the ARF agenda
along any faster.

CHANGING PRIORITIES AND AGENDAS

The end of the Cold War helped to reinforce a trend already increasingly
evident during the 1980s, namely that international relations were becoming
increasingly complex and that the agenda of issues that needed to be addressed
was lengthening. This has had an impact on the Euro-Asian dialogue too. Apart
from the particular issues discussed above in this chapter, it is possible to
identify a range of other issues which have increasingly impinged on to the
Euro-Asian dialogue and which, taking a very broad rubric given the difficulties
of separating commercial, technological and politico-strategic issues, can con-
veniently be considered under the political and security heading. The concept
of 'security' has indeed taken a very broad definition in recent international
politics discourse and, as has been discussed by Barry Buzan, can now be taken
as covering not just traditional aspects of military, and to a lesser extent
political, security but also the economic, environmental and societal sectors
(Buzan 1991, pp. 432–433). Indeed, in the post-Cold War era, although political–military concerns have not disappeared as quickly or as completely as
some forecasters expected in the immediate post-1989 euphoria of a 'new
world order', it is true that non-military aspects have been pushing their way

closer to the top of the international security agenda. This trend is true for the Euro-Asian dialogue too. The following issues help to encapsulate this 'new' security agenda – and its globalization to include both Europe and Asia.

Conventional and Nuclear Arms Control

Compared with the European experience, where the winding down of the Cold War brought significant breakthroughs in arms control of both conventional and nuclear forces, the overall record in the Asia Pacific region has been much poorer. In the view of Gerald Segal, 'there have been remarkably few formal arms-control agreements in the Pacific since 1945, and even fewer that are still worth the paper they were written on' (Segal 1990, p. 262). Indeed, most of those agreements which did exist, or have come into force during the 1990s, in part or all of the region have been shaped by global rather than regional developments (Findlay 1996, p. 221). The Western Europeans have been keen to see global arms control regimes effectively implemented in the Asia Pacific, although it has to be said that some European countries which rely on arms sales – including to the 'new' markets of the richer Asia Pacific countries – have mixed views over how far the conventional weapons market – and their profits – might be affected. The Asia Pacific countries, especially the medium-sized and smaller ones, have often tended to be 'free riders' on the arms control negotiating efforts of others, including the Europeans (Findlay 1996, p. 221). Apart from one or two examples, there has indeed been little real coordination or cooperation between European and Asia Pacific states in the arms control field.

Clearly the Asia Pacific region has benefited from global agreements in the nuclear weapons field. The importance of the INF Treaty in 1987 has been discussed above. The trend, established by the Reagan–Gorbachev negotiations from the mid 1980s, to reduce also superpower (or ex-superpower) arsenals of strategic nuclear weapons has also been of benefit to both Europe and the Asia Pacific, even though most states have had little option but to sit on the sidelines while these agreements have been negotiated.

There have, however, been two global nuclear weapons agreements which have brought the Europeans and the Asians together in often controversial circumstances. The first is the CTBT, mentioned briefly above in the context of debate within the ARF framework, which was also important to many European and Asian Pacific states as 'a symbol of the nuclear weapon states' willingness to curb their nuclear options' (Findlay 1996, p. 224). Serious negotiations for the CTBT, an idea which had actually been floating around since the 1950s, began in 1994 and were concluded in 1996. The attitude of two of the nuclear weapon states, China and France, however, posed problems for the conclusion and successful implementation of the treaty.

China supported the CTBT as an important step towards the ultimate goal of abolishing nuclear weapons, but argued that it would not cease its nuclear tests until the treaty was signed. Moreover, it argued for a special exemption for peaceful nuclear explosions, an attitude which inevitably invited suspicions from non-nuclear states because of the technical difficulties of differentiating these from military-use explosions (Wu 1996, pp. 583–584). Although the Chinese had conducted fewer nuclear tests since World War II than any of the five nuclear weapon powers, they did not agree to an informally agreed international moratorium instituted in 1992, and carried on testing through until July 1996, when they announced the ending of all their tests.

French policy, however, attracted more international controversy because, after having joined the moratorium for three years, the government of President Chirac resumed testing near Muraroa atoll in the South Pacific territory of French Polynesia in September 1995. The vehemence of the criticism that the French received, both from Europe and the Asia Pacific region, surprised Chirac, who eventually, in January 1996, ended what had been intended to be a series of eight explosions after the sixth. The French had received open criticism from EU partners such as Denmark, Sweden and Spain, as well as from Asian Pacific states such as Japan, the Philippines, and the South Pacific and Australasian states (*Asahi Evening News*, 30 January 1996). One Japanese Cabinet minister publicly described France's actions as 'crazy' and a special governmental envoy was dispatched to Paris to protest (*South China Morning Post*, 13 September 1995). Boycotts of French goods occurred in several places, especially Japan and Hong Kong, and anti-French riots occurred in French territories in the South Pacific. Britain and Germany gave more muted disapproval, but Britain made it clear that it had no intention of resuming testing (*South China Morning Post*, 7 September 1995).

A policy move which had much to do with prestige and pride – demonstrating French status as a major power with an independent nuclear capability – ended up as being totally counter-productive, harming French relations with the Asia Pacific region and ensuring that EU partners were embarrassed.

The second global agreement which has become controversial in recent years is the NPT. This treaty, which entered into force in 1970, can be considered as 'one of the most successful multilateral arms control treaties' in the postwar period (Findlay 1996, p. 224). Almost all European and Asian Pacific states became signatories at an early stage, although China did not join until 1992. Although China had long been critical of the NPT as being unfair in its obligations on nuclear and non-nuclear states (Wu 1996, p. 584), it not only endorsed the extension of the NPT at the international review conference in 1995 but also quietly tried to encourage North Korea to adhere to its commitments under the NPT. As discussed earlier in this chapter, the suspected development of nuclear weapons within North Korea, which had become a signatory of the NPT in 1975 but did not sign the associated safeguard agreement until 1991 and then in 1993 threatened to withdraw completely from the NPT, has been the primary nuclear proliferation concern in the Asia Pacific region in the 1990s. The North Korean issue primarily involved South Korea, Japan and the United States in its resolution, but other Asian states as well as the Europeans publicly voiced their concern for clear verification of what North Korea was doing.

Some observers suggest that other potential nuclear weapon powers in the Asia Pacific region need to be considered. Japan, South Korea and Taiwan all have domestic power nuclear industries as well as the necessary technological expertise to build nuclear armaments should they wish. Indeed, as has subsequently been made public, in the late 1960s–early 1970s (primarily in response to China's acquisition of nuclear weapon capability in 1964), all three 'flirted' with, and then abandoned, the idea of developing such capabilities themselves (Calder 1996b, pp. 72–73). Arguably, if North Korea were to be definitively proved to possess nuclear weapons, then pressure from within those three countries, or at least within South Korea and Japan, to follow suit almost certainly would increase. Political self-restraint among these powers is likely to be continued nonetheless, but the Europeans can play a useful subsidiary role to the Americans in indirectly discouraging any tendency among government leaders in these countries to consider the nuclear option, especially at a time when South Asia has begun to enter a new stage of nuclear competition, with both India and Pakistan testing nuclear devices in May 1998.

Apart from these global arrangements, two regional initiatives need to be mentioned, in that they have impinged on the activities of the two European states with nuclear weapon capability, France and Britain. The first is the Treaty of Raratonga, which came into force in December 1986, establishing a South Pacific Nuclear-Free Zone. Intended to prevent the construction and deployment of nuclear weapons on the territory of the states of the South Pacific, it does not prohibit the transit of nuclear weapons through the sub-region. The treaty had its origins in persistent concern over French nuclear testing in Tahiti and the US–New Zealand dispute over port visits by US nuclear-armed ships (Segal 1990, pp. 263–264). China agreed to abide by the treaty, but both Britain and France refused to become parties. However, with the subsequent removal of non-strategic nuclear weapons from their naval fleets, the issue has 'become academic' (Findlay 1996, p. 231). Indeed, in the autumn of 1997 Britain, under the new Labour government, finally ratified the treaty (*Korea Herald*, 24 September 1997).

The South Pacific is not central to the security of the Asia Pacific region, but the at least partial success of the Treaty of Raratonga did encourage the

ASEAN group to revive the long-standing Zone of Peace, Freedom and Neutrality concept (a Malaysian initiative first adopted as an ASEAN objective in 1971) and to try to add on a nuclear weapon-free zone component. When the idea was first floated in 1987 strong US opposition, and less vocal but similar opposition from France and Britain, stymied the idea (Segal 1990, p. 271). But in 1993–94, as ASEAN began to establish the ARF process, some member countries revived the nuclear weapon-free zone idea. At the December 1995 ASEAN heads of government meeting, a treaty establishing the Southeast Asian Nuclear Weapons-Free Zone was signed. The treaty prohibited the manufacturing, storing and testing of nuclear weapons but not the transit of nuclear-armed ships and aircraft (Leifer 1996, p. 49). The United States objected because it was concerned that the treaty would impede the free movement of naval ships and military aircraft within the region, a view shared by Britain and France. China objected on different grounds, that the geographical limits set out in the treaty would prejudice its sovereign claims to the South China Sea. The ASEAN states have therefore had to try to press these powers to sign up to the treaty, which came into force in March 1997, but so far without success.

By comparison with the modest steps being taken regionally to govern the nuclear weapon issue, the formal arms control and disarmament record in conventional weapons in the Asia Pacific region is virtually non-existent. There have been some policies which can be described as informal and unilateral measures, such as Japan's long-standing self-imposed ban on the export of weapons and China's efforts in recent years to prune down the size of its armed forces. But given that almost all the states in the region depend heavily on conventional weapons for their national security and that several of the Western European states are willing and able to supply them with modern military equipment, and increasingly with associated training programmes and facilities, it is not altogther surprising that the regional states have preferred to keep their options open.

Observers differ about whether an 'arms race' is actually taking place in the Asia Pacific region. Some argue that an 'intense arms competition ... has been continuing for nearly a decade' (Calder 1996b, p. 139). Others say that all the rising figures of defence expenditure in some, but not all, Asia Pacific states suggest is a 'process of force modernisation' and 'there is no concentrated rush to buy in large quantities of weapons' (Cheeseman and Leaver, 1996 p. 215). While, with the exception of the two Koreas and the China–Taiwan interaction, the arms purchases do not fit into the classic highly focused action–reaction spiral model by which an arms race might be defined between two (or more) states, it is undoubtedly true that in the 1990s the region has generally seen rising defence budgets and an increasing emphasis on acquiring the latest military equipment despite the end of the Cold War.

This is in marked contrast to the European situation, where, almost without exception, military budgets have been cut as 'peace dividends' have been sought. However, the economic crises experienced by several Asia Pacific countries in 1997 will undoubtedly impact on defence budgets and weapons-procurement programmes in the coming years (*Far Eastern Economic Review*, 5 February 1998); inevitable cancellations of orders or cutbacks on new acquisitions will dampen arms sales prospects for the European producers.

The one aspect in which one might consider progress to have been made has been in greater transparency of these conventional weapons sales and acquisitions. Japan has played a leading role in this respect in the Asia Pacific region. Although a major importer of US, and to a much more limited extent European, weaponry, Japan has long advocated other countries adopting rather restrictive arms export policies. Here at least, there is a gap in perceptions and policies with some Western European states (Taylor 1995, p. 193). Nonetheless, it was a joint EC–Japanese initiative in 1991 which led to the UN setting up a global surveillance system for international arms sales (Cornish 1994, pp. 24–25). The UN Conventional Arms Transfer Register began operating in 1993 and virtually all of the major arms-exporting nations (excluding North Korea, whose arms exports are not clearly quantifiable) and most of the arms-importing nations are now regularly providing information to this register. Peer pressure within the ARF grouping seems to have played a role in encouraging some hesitant Asian Pacific countries to participate (Chalmers 1997, pp. 108–109) and has even stimulated a debate within ARF about whether a regional version should also be set up.

Human Rights and Democracy

If the nuclear and conventional weapon issues come within the purview of what is normally considered to be military security, the question of human rights and democratization can be considered under the heading of political security. These issues tread into the sensitive area of a country's internal affairs. This has meant that these issues have become the most difficult to handle in the contemporary Euro-Asian political dialogue.

The contemporary debate on human rights tends to depict the so-called 'Asian' view, with its emphasis on the 'community' and socio-economic development and social cohesion as the first priorities, in conflict with the 'West', including both the United States and Western Europe, which focuses on individual rights and liberal democracy. However, it is certainly an over-generalization to talk of one Asian view, since in a continent with such differing socio-economic, cultural and political systems, perceptions of human rights will undoubtedly vary from country to country and between governments and their people (Ghai 1995, pp. 54–55). Even among the members of ASEAN, which have displayed a considerable degree of public unity in contra-distinction to the West, nuances of approach can be seen (Mauzy 1997, pp. 219–224). This is even more the case when the broader Asia Pacific is considered.

The West, arguably, has a more unified set of values than Asia, but again there can be discerned some differences in perception, although these have usually found expression in differences over the utility of human rights in the wider range of foreign policy concerns. The United States has undoubtedly assumed the leadership of the West on human rights issues – and, as such, has been the main focus of Asian Pacific criticism. The Europeans, while sharing similar beliefs, have tended to be 'more pragmatic and less confrontational' than the United States (Mauzy 1997, p. 213). Although some European governments, notably the Dutch and the Scandinavians, have long been vocal on human rights issues, the majority of European states have only begun to highlight these issues since the late 1980s. Encouraged by the positive examples of what German Foreign Minister Genscher called the 'triumph of democracy' in Eastern Europe (*Far Eastern Economic Review*, 20 June 1991) and, within the Asia Pacific, in the Philippines in 1986 and South Korea in 1987, and concerned by the negative regional examples of Burma in 1988 and China in 1989, Western European governments began to raise human rights issues on a more regular basis with their Asian interlocutors.

Gradually, as the tone of the debate became more strident in the early 1990s, individual European governments and the European Commission itself began to link human rights to trade and economic assistance policies. In moving down the path of threatening trade sanctions (over, for example, workers' rights and standards) and applying aid conditionality, the Europeans were working in parallel with, if slightly lagging behind, the Americans. Such attempts were strongly resented and resisted by the Asian Pacific governments, especially by China and key ASEAN members such as Indonesia, Malaysia and Singapore.

Although national reactions in Europe were 'often coordinated, or paralleled, by reactions at the European Parliament or Commission level' (Godemont 1993, p. 98), individual EC governments, and their interested lobby groups, have tended to make the running in response to particular incidents. This has been most clear in the French role on the European reactions to the Tiananmen Square massacre in 1989, the Dutch and Portuguese roles on Indonesian actions in East Timor in 1991, and the British and Danish roles on Burma.

As discussed in Chapter 6, the Tiananmen Square massacre provoked a hostile reaction from all the Western European governments, which responded with a series of diplomatic and commercial sanctions. These were progressively lifted over subsequent years, but a Europe-wide consensus was generally maintained over the pace at which they should be lifted. Where disagreements among the Europeans have come, as discussed in the same chapter, has been since 1996 over how far human rights in China can be usefully promoted by continuing critical resolutions through the UN human rights' organizations.

But in the 1990s the Euro-Asian dialogue over human rights has tended to be dominated by the cases of East Timor and Burma. The killings of peaceful Timorese demonstrators by Indonesian troops in Dili in November 1991 proved to be a focal point of European criticism, but only served to highlight a longer-standing European concern about the methods used by the Indonesians to subdue the Timorese population since the mid 1970s. As discussed in Chapter 5, Dutch 'lecturing' so incensed the Indonesians that they cut off aid ties, but it was the Portuguese who were to prove a particular thorn in the Indonesians' flesh. Portugal, which refused to accept the Indonesian annexation of Timor, turned to its European colleagues for support; similarly, Indonesia appealed to its ASEAN partners.

Even prior to the Dili killings, the EC and the ASEAN sides had clashed at their May 1991 ministerial meeting, over the EC desire to include a human rights clause in any new cooperation agreement. In the first half of 1992, Portugal, which held the rotating presidency of the EC, tried to crank up its campaign against Indonesia. Although a few EC governments did suspend aid programmes, at least until an Indonesian enquiry actually censured the army, Portugal was unsuccessful in getting EC support for a trade embargo on Indonesia. It did get EC support for a resolution to the UNHRC protesting against the situation in Timor, but due to intensive Indonesian lobbying, no formal vote was taken at the UNHRC (MacIntyre 1993, p. 206).

Portugal then blocked EC–ASEAN negotiations for a new cooperation agreement. As discussed in Chapter 5, by the early 1990s both sides felt the need for a broader cooperation agreement, but during two EC–ASEAN meetings in 1992 Portugal refused to allow a decision on negotiations to be taken. While the declarations that came out of the October 1992 Manila EC–ASEAN ministerial meeting did refer in greater detail than ever to respect for UN charters on human rights and to endeavours on social justice, Portugal's proposed specific reference to East Timor was omitted (*Agence Europe*, 26 September; 29 and 31 October 1992). Most EC representatives were encouraged by the ASEAN willingness to make some reference to human rights, but despite efforts by Britain, then holding the EC presidency, Portugal could not be persuaded to relent in its opposition to negotiations.

The net result of these exchanges was that both sides seemed more set than ever in their positions. The EC decided as a matter of general policy that all future economic cooperation agreements with developing countries should include a human rights clause, and this practice has been followed in the agreements concluded subsequently with Vietnam, Laos and Cambodia. The

ASEAN countries, on the other hand, joined in the Asian regional meeting on human rights in Bangkok in April 1993 and subscribed to the Bangkok Declaration which accepted that rights were 'universal in nature' but needed to be considered 'in the context of national and regional peculiarities, and various cultural, historical and religious backgrounds, and with the understanding that norms and values change over time' (Mauzy 1997, p. 221).

Although many EU governments were beginning to lose sympathy with what they saw as excessive Portuguese obduracy over the East Timor issue, the desire to avoid open confrontation within the EU effectively kept them from breaking ranks with Portugal. Neither the 1994 nor the 1997 EU–ASEAN ministerial meeting saw any progress on concluding a new cooperation agreement. Although East Timor was not raised formally during the 1997 meeting (it received only a passing reference in the opening speech by the head of the EU delegation), both sides were aware of its shadow. Agreement was thus reached on sector-specific economic cooperation which would effectively by-pass the Portuguese objections to a new overall agreement (*Agence Europe*, 6 February 1997; *Jakarta Post*, 14 February 1997). The East Timor issue had also figured in the manoeuvrings surrounding the first ASEM Meeting, held in Bangkok in March 1996, but the issue had been defused then by a private meeting between the Portuguese and Indonesian leaders. Bilateral talks have been continuing between Portuguese and Indonesian officials under UN auspices for a number of years, but despite the heightened international interest in the issue, as shown by the award of the Nobel peace prize to two Timorese human rights activists and the offer by South African President Nelson Mandela to mediate, little progress has been made. Britain proposed that an EU delegation visit Timor; Indonesia has agreed, but it is not clear what real impact this visit will have on the situation (*South China Morning Post*, 30 August 1997). Collective EU pressure probably played some role in persuading the Indonesians to be more forthcoming with information about the situation in Timor (Godemont 1993, p. 98), but it has done nothing to induce Indonesia to change its occupation strategy. Ironically, it was the rapidly changing political situation within Indonesia in early 1998, which saw the political demise of Suharto and re-opened the question of the autonomy of East Timor and other regions within the newly emerging but unstable Indonesian polity, rather than European pressure, which offered greater prospects of progress on this issue than at any time in the 1990s.

The issue of Burma has now come to take an equally sensitive role in EU–ASEAN and, indeed, broader EU–Asia discussions. Chapter 5 outlined the critical European responses to the military crackdown in 1988 and the Burmese government's refusal to accept the results of the 1990 elections. The ASEAN side, however, refused to equate human rights with democratization and considered the latter an internal matter of the country concerned. The

ASEAN approach has come to be termed 'constructive engagement', which means not isolating Burma by economic sanctions (such as undertaken by the Europeans), but gentle persuasion and quiet diplomacy to bring about a political liberalization (A. Acharya 1995, pp. 174–175). The Europeans and ASEAN members had agreed to disagree on their approaches to the Burmese problem, until during 1996 the momentum for Burma to join ASEAN began to gather speed at the same time as the Burmese leadership, having made a token gesture by releasing the opposition leader, Ms Aung San, from house arrest, once again reverted to a hard-line approach.

Opinions between the Europeans and ASEAN rapidly became more sharply divided. Over a hard-talking working lunch during the EU–ASEAN meeting in February 1997, the Dutch Foreign Minister, Hans van Mierlo, the head of the EU side, stated that what was happening in Burma was 'absolutely unacceptable' and made it clear that Europe was counting on ASEAN to do more (*Jakarta Post*, 15 February 1997). The ASEAN side replied that once Burma had joined ASEAN it would be influenced by its peers in the way that in Asia 'we marry first and expect the wife to adapt to the marriage' (*South China Morning Post*, 15 February 1997). But with Burmese participation in EU–ASEAN meetings and the ASEM process after the 1998 London summit remaining unsettled, the specific question of human rights and democratization in Burma is set to continue as a controversial issue in the Euro-Asian dialogue.

Although China has also been active in the Asian and Asian–American debates on human rights, and in particular has stressed that these issues fall within the sovereignty of individual countries (Ghai 1995, pp. 56–57), it has been the ASEAN countries that have been at the forefront of the Euro-Asian debate over human rights. Japan has remained silent, almost sitting on the fence between the European and the Asian approaches (it did not sign the 1993 Bangkok Declaration). South Korea and Taiwan have also stayed on the side-lines, although it should be noted that South Korea's experience with democratization prompted one of its leading democratic politicians and now current President, Kim Dae-jung, to publish a treatise turning the Asian values debate on its head by arguing that democracy has actually very deep roots in Asian cultures (Rodan 1996, pp. 334–335). Nonetheless, the divergencies of opinion within the Asia Pacific region and between the region and Western Europe will ensure that the issues of human rights and democratization remain high on the political agenda in the years to come.

Refugees and International Migration

The problem of how to cope with 'societal security', which has been defined by Buzan as 'the threats and vulnerabilities that effect patterns of communal identity and culture' (1991, pp. 247–250), has been growing in importance over the past decade or so. A key component of this has been the concern that inward migration can become a fundamental threat to the social and political stability of individual states. The Europeans have become increasingly concerned about the growing immigration, both legal and illegal, from North Africa and the Middle East into Europe. For Asians, the phenomenon has been associated with increased labour mobility around their region, especially illegal labour movements from relatively poor Asian countries to more advanced economies such as Japan, and the outflow of refugees at various periods from the war-devastated Indochinese area. Although there has been some illegal Chinese emigration into Western Europe, that migratory flow has been a comparatively minor problem, particularly in comparison with such illegal flows into the United States. Undoubtedly the issue which has brought Europeans and Asians most closely together has been the problem of the Vietnamese 'boat people', a generic expression to cover those people who have fled Vietnam (and sometimes Cambodia), either by boat or over land.

Britain and France became the countries most directly involved in the Vietnamese refugee problem: Britain because Hong Kong became a beacon to the Vietnamese boat people and France because of its linguistic, cultural and historical ties to Vietnam. Germany has also been involved but in a variant of the problem: how to deal with the thousands of Vietnamese who had been working in East Germany, many of them illegally, up until reunification of the two Germanies.

1988–89 had seen a sudden influx of Vietnamese 'boat people' into Hong Kong, on levels paralleling those of the earlier 1979–80 inflow. A combination of deteriorating economic conditions inside Vietnam and a firm refusal by the ASEAN countries to accept any more refugees made Hong Kong the favoured destination (Williams 1992, p. 76). Under new regulations introduced in June 1988, the Hong Kong government tried to distinguish by 'screening', genuine refugees from 'economic migrants' and to encourage the latter group to return to Vietnam (Casella 1991, pp. 160–164). Despite harsh and cramped living conditions in the crowded, closed camps, only a miniscule number of the Vietnamese volunteered to be repatriated. In December 1989, therefore, the first group of Vietnamese was 'forcibly' repatriated to Vietnam. The British and Hong Kong governments found themselves hindered by US government and European Parliament opposition, by critical media coverage and by foot-dragging by Vietnam, which was reluctant to do anything to upset the United States at a time when it was angling for better relations (Williams 1992, p. 77), but they could see no alternative.

Eventually, in October 1991 the British, Hong Kong and Vietnamese governments reached an agreement for an orderly repatriation programme for all Vietnamese non-refugees left in Hong Kong. But by 1995 only about 1300

Vietnamese had returned home under this mandatory programme, by contrast with a total by then of 40,000 voluntary repatriations. With arrivals down to a low level after 1991, the Hong Kong government expected that it might have been able to return all the then remaining 21,000 Vietnamese before the July 1997 handover. China had made repeated statements from the early 1990s that it expected Britain to deal with the problem and ensure that no Vietnamese remained on Hong Kong soil by the time of the handover (*Eastern Express*, 16 January 1996). However, the whole repatriation programme almost ground to a halt in the summer of 1995 after a US Congressman's attempts to introduce legislation to allow a further 20,000 refugees into the United States prompted violence in camps in both Hong Kong and Malaysia by inmates who saw new and unexpected hopes of getting to the United States (*Far Eastern Economic Review*, 22 June 1995).

By mid 1997 more than 210,000 Vietnamese had reached Hong Kong in the more than two decades since the fall of Indochina; over 143,000 had been resettled elsewhere as refugees, while Hong Kong itself had accepted less than 1000. Of those who failed to qualify for refugee status, over 51,000 had returned to Vietnam voluntarily and just under 10,000 were forcibly repatriated. Despite the efforts of the Hong Kong government and the UN High Commission for Refugees, around 1300 Vietnamese recognized as refugees remained in Hong Kong, still awaiting third countries willing to accept them (because of their criminal or drugs-related backgrounds they are unlikely to be easily accepted), and about 2500 asylum-seekers were undergoing screening (*Sunday Morning Post*, 17 August 1997). Most of the refugees in Hong Kong have gone to the United States and Canada, but European countries, led by Britain which has accepted 15,000 Vietnamese from Hong Kong, also played a role as recipients. The final step to closing the 'boat people' chapter came with the Hong Kong government's decision, with UN and Vietnamese approval, in January 1998 to end its port of first asylum policy (*South China Morning Post*, 9 January 1998).

The ASEAN countries had borne the brunt of the early refugee flows in the late 1970s but saw a marked decline in the 1980s. By mid 1996 the ASEAN countries had received a total of 620,000 Vietnamese, of which less than 9000 remained in camps (*Far Eastern Economic Review*, 18 July 1996). France did take a much larger role in accepting refugees from ASEAN countries, particularly in the first wave in the late 1970s, so that by 1980 France had taken in 67,000 Vietnamese compared with 15,000 by West Germany and 11,000 by Britain (Harris and Bridges 1983, pp. 54–55). The emergence of the boat people problem did cause tension between the Europeans and the ASEAN countries, over the ASEAN policy of trying to refuse the boat people, on occasions by pushing them back into the sea, and over the perceived failure of the Europeans to resettle refugees quickly enough. For most of the ASEAN countries, but particularly for Malaysia, the boat people influx threatened the delicate balance between the ethnic groups within the country through the apparent racial association of the Vietnamese, some of whom were indeed Chinese-Vietnamese, with the minority Chinese in that country (Newland 1993, p. 87).

Apart from the British role through Hong Kong in repatriating Vietnamese, the Europeans were also involved in trying to aid Vietnam in accepting back these people. In 1991, the EC began an aid programme specifically designed to assist in the reintegration of the 'boat people'. By 1996 a total of $120 million had been given; in March 1996 a further EU–Vietnam agreement provided for an additional $14.5 million in aid (*Eastern Express*, 4 March 1996). The aid has been intended to provide returnees with small business credits, vocational training and health care.

A separate but related problem has been that of the Vietnamese left behind in Germany after the collapse of East Germany. These people went to East Germany in the 1970s and 1980s, mostly as contract labourers. After German reunification about 60,000 returned to Vietnam, but about 95,000 stayed on (this number included those who had entered Germany from other Eastern European countries during the upheavals of 1989–90). Of these, some 55,000 have acquired legal resident permits, but Germany, where anti-foreign sentiment was on the rise in the early 1990s, has been very keen to get rid of the remainder. After tortuous negotiations between Germany and Vietnam over several years, in December 1994 the two countries agreed that Vietnam would take back 20,000 in the first five years and the final remaining 20,000 over a longer unspecified timespan. In return, Germany agreed to provide a package of $65 million in economic aid and $65 million in export credit guarantees to Vietnam (*Financial Times*, 12 January 1995). The agreement has not worked well, however, as Vietnam has been slow to approve the initial groups of repatriates and, indeed, the programme has been running so far behind schedule (only 65 instead of 7500 had returned home by mid 1996) that Germany in 1996 threatened to suspend aid disbursements unless Vietnam's processing worked faster (*Sunday Morning Post*, 26 May 1996).

The German policy on these illegal workers reflects one dilemma of the Europeans in coping with the Vietnamese refugees in a broader context. In Germany in particular there is a paradoxical situation whereby a government committed to social peace and justice and simultaneously determined to combat a revival of neo-Nazi xenophobia actually has to resort to a policy which has strong resonances of the extreme right's 'foreigners go home' pronouncements. At the public level anti-Vietnamese sentiment remains strong in Germany and many of those Vietnamese legally living there complain about racial discrimination in employment, housing and social acceptance. Germans, on the other hand, feel that the Vietnamese are heavily involved in crime, especially the smuggling of cigarettes, and there have been several well-publicized cases of gangland killings among the Vietnamese community in Germany (*South China Morning Post*, 6 January 1997).

Vietnamese 'boat people' settling in other European countries have also experienced problems in adjusting to their new societies, even in France which has had the closest exposure to Vietnam in the past. One study of the Vietnamese community in Britain has noted the problems that the new arrivals faced because of their low level of education and skills, poor English ability, limited previous contact with Western civilization and lack of a pre-existing support community in their new country (Hale 1993, pp. 278–280).

Drugs, Crime, Piracy and AIDS

These are issues which increasingly cross the borderline between domestic and international politics. Indeed, within the EU the newly implemented high degree of freedom of movement 'has blurred the distinction between internal and transnational security' (Politi 1997, p. x). However, the technical and political problems involved often handicap coordinated responses.

Drug-trafficking has become a transnational phenomenon. It has affected not only drug-producing states in the Asia Pacific, such as those involved in the notorious 'Golden Triangle' of Burma, Laos and Cambodia, but also the drug-consuming states, primarily the Western European countries, though some Asian Pacific states such as Malaysia are also suffering. Although most of the heroin produced and smuggled out of the Golden Triangle heads for the US market, some of it certainly finds its way to Europe through the links established by the Hong Kong-based 'triad' gangster groups (Williams 1994, pp. 103–104). The Europeans have identified the drugs problem as one closely related to the socio-economic stability of their own societies.

In addition, increasingly, the drugs trade is having an impact on those states such as China which act as illegal conduits for the drugs. Indeed, since the mid 1990s China has shifted from turning a blind eye to trans-shipments in the past to a heightened concern about the deleterious socio-economic impact of drug abuse and drug-trafficking in the provinces of Yunnan, bordering Burma and the entry point, and Guangdong, bordering Hong Kong and the exit point (Che 1997).

Clearly, international cooperation is needed to break both ends of the supply–demand relationship. The EU has initiated a dialogue on drug-related matters with several Asia Pacific states, including China (Commission 1994, p. 13), and has emphasized that this issue is a topic which should be systematically included in Euro-Asian dialogues. The primary European intentions have been to improve the capacity and willingness of the Asian Pacific governments to fight against drugs and to get them to ratify a number of UN

conventions on narcotic drugs (Commission 1994, p. 13). The EU cooperation agreement with Laos signed in 1997, specifically contains a clause on
EU aid to help reduce opium production by finding alternative crops for small
farmers to grow (European Parliament 1997). A few individual EU member
countries have provided specific assistance to individual Asian Pacific countries to help with drug-related programmes; for example, Britain gave $132
million to China in the 1992–95 period for such activities (British Consulate-
General, Hong Kong, statistics). Some preliminary steps to approach this
issue on a region-to-region basis have also been taken, with a meeting of
European and Asian customs officials, under the ASEM rubric, in Shenzhen
in June 1996 to develop joint procedures for monitoring the trade in chemicals that can be precursors in the production of drugs and for preventing
money-laundering, which is often a by-product of the drug trade (Foreign
Office 1998).

As both Europeans and Asians are highly dependent on shipping their
products to each other and to third markets, another aspect of crime that is of
concern to both is the growth of maritime crime, especially smuggling and
piracy. In 1993 nearly 80 per cent of all piracy cases reported world-wide
occurred in Asian waters (*Nikkei Weekly*, 14 March 1994). The Straits of
Malacca and the South China Sea area bounded by Hong Kong–the Philippines–Vietnam were especially dangerous areas by the early 1990s. Increased
surveillance by the Malaysian and Indonesian navies led to a reduction in
piracy in 1994–95, but the International Maritime Organization warned in
mid 1995 that piracy in the South China Sea was becoming 'quite blatant'
(*South China Morning Post*, 26 July 1995). In 1997, indeed, the waters
around Indonesia became the most dangerous area for piracy in the world,
recording nearly one-quarter of all the cases reported world-wide during that
year (*Sunday Straits Times*, 1 February 1998). With the socio-economic situation inside Indonesia deteriorating in 1997–98, it was expected that attempts
to take up piracy might, if anything, increase during 1998.

Comparative complacency in the Asia Pacific region over AIDS is now
being replaced by very real concern about the medium-term effect of AIDS-
related deaths on economic growth prospects, not least because it is young
people, the most economically active part of the population, who are most at
risk. The World Health Organization estimates that by the year 2000 Asia will
account for nearly 25 per cent of all HIV-infected patients in the world,
probably numbering around 10 million (*South China Morning Post*, 19 September 1995). International cooperation programmes, such as the $2 million
EU project launched in 1994 to train Chinese doctors in the prevention and
treatment of AIDS, can only be part of the answer to the problem.

Environmental Problems

Environmental issues, in a manner that parallels the rise of human rights issues, have rapidly risen up the agenda of Euro-Asian interactions since the late 1980s. This is not to say that these issues have not been explored before, but certainly the growing awareness of the costs of urbanization, industrial development and population growth in Asia Pacific countries other than Japan (which had already started to confront them in the early 1970s), coupled with increased advocacy of environmentalism by European, and other international, NGOs, have given them a heightened degree of importance and, it must be said, tension.

Indeed, the tendency of the late 1980s and early 1990s to pitch discussions over environmental problems in stark confrontational terms did little to help resolve problems. European NGOs openly, and governments more circuitously, criticized Asian Pacific practices, particularly in the natural resource-rich countries of Southeast Asia, while those states responded resentfully and, on occasions, hyper-critically. As individual European countries began to talk about aid conditionality – making future development assistance conditional on environmentally friendly policies by the receiving nations – and about possible environmental trade restrictions, certain Southeast Asian states responded increasingly suspiciously. In the run-up to the Rio Earth Summit in 1992, Malaysian Prime Minister Mahathir criticized the Europeans for double standards over development and the environment, and the following year the Indonesian Foreign Minister, Ali Alatas, spoke of a 'new colonialism in a green guise' (Clad and Siy 1996, p. 69).

Since the mid 1990s, however, some of the stridency has gone out of the debate, as both sides have shown more willingness to think about ways to cooperate to improve environmental conditions without so much carping. In part this is due to the increasing awareness that some environmental problems, such as the phenomenon of 'global warming', are so immense and so impossible for any one country, or even small group of countries, to tackle, that a concerted, synergistic approach by all governments is required (Prins 1990, p. 7).

At the EU level, the most highly developed dialogue on environmental issues has been with Japan. Following the 1991 EC–Japan Joint Declaration, a series of high-level environmental meetings have been held to carry out joint research on three themes in particular: protection of tropical forests, acid rain and global warming. Similar environmental dialogues are expected to be instituted with South Korea and China in the near future. A further example of constructive dialogue has also been the way in which the Europeans, in particular the British, also played a key role with the Japanese in working out a consensus among the industrialized states at the Kyoto climate change conference in 1997 (Satoh 1998, p. 5).

The European Commission, in reviewing its own aid policies towards the developing world in mid 1992, took on board the need to provide more focused aid for specific environmentally related projects, such as protecting the ASEAN rain forests. An informal working group on the environment was set up under the auspices of the EU–ASEAN joint cooperation committee. In 1997 the EU–ASEAN ministerial meeting agreed that the EU would fund the establishment of an ASEAN Regional Centre for Biodiversity Conservation in Manila (ASEAN–EU 1997). As an example of what may well become the norm for the next generation of cooperation agreements with developing Asian nations, the 1997 EU–Laos cooperation agreement specifically included a clause which covered European assistance in the conservation of forest resources in Laos (European Parliament 1997).

Political dialogue has always been the weak part of the Euro-Asian relationship, and the strategic dimension has for long seemed almost non-existent. This chapter has demonstrated some of the ways in which past inhibitions have been overcome since the mid 1980s and in particular since the end of the Cold War. Not only have the Europeans showed more political commitment in solving serious crises such as Cambodia and North Korea, but both Europe and the Asia Pacific have been on a learning curve in terms of how far their own national, or regional, interests in the new international agenda require greater consultation and cooperation with each other. In the years to come, as it becomes increasingly difficult to separate economics from politics, this aspect of the relationship is set to grow in importance.

In any period of flux, policy-makers are confronted with a dilemma: can old structures and mechanisms cope with new substance or do they trap policy-makers into outmoded solutions? The uncertainties of the post-Cold War era undoubtedly concentrated the minds of both Europeans and Asians on whether the embryonic political dialogue and the much more well-established economic discussions might be better extended from the usual country-to-country and EU-to-individual-Asian-country modes into a region-to-region interaction. This was to lead to the birth of ASEM, as discussed in the next chapter.

9. Summits and slumps

Our ASEM baby is no longer a toddler,
but is walking well and is even ready to run
(Shamugan Jayakumar, quoted in *Agence Europe*, 17 February 1997)

The economic turmoil … reduced the tigers to whimpering kittens.
(Dr Mahathir Mohamad, quoted in *Straits Times*, 3 March 1998)

As we approach the end of the 1990s and the start of a new century, three phenomena are set to act as the defining influences on the future course of Euro-Asian relations. The first is the development of a new format for contact at the region-to-region level, the ASEM process. The second is the responses of the Asia Pacific regional states to the setbacks in their economic growth deriving from the financial difficulties which have swept the region from mid 1997. This financial crisis has important social, political and even psychological as well as the more obvious economic consequences for the Euro-Asia relationship. The third is the development of EMU in Europe and the emergence of the new euro currency from 1999. All these phenomena need to be examined in more detail and, as will be seen, they are not unconnected.

THE ORIGINS OF ASEM

The feeling that something has been missing in the Euro-Asia relationship has been around for a long time. But not until recently has the gap been seen as one that could realistically be cured by greater region-to-region interaction. The efforts which have brought about the ASEM process have been aimed at filling this gap.

The political initiative for the ASEM process came from the Singaporeans. Although some businessmen and academics had been playing around for a while with the idea of some kind of Euro-Asia forum, it was Singapore Prime Minister Goh Chok Tong's approach to the French government while on an official visit to Paris in October 1994 that began serious government-level discussion of the feasibility of such a meeting. Although Goh's initiative can be seen as 'an expression of Singaporean activism in international diplomacy' beyond the 'too limited' confines of the Asia Pacific region (Camroux and Lechervy 1996, p. 443), it also reflected wider ASEAN concerns to balance their relationship with the United States by establishing links elsewhere. Singapore therefore had a relatively easy time in persuading the other ASEAN members to come on board for this proposal. France, undoubtedly flattered to be approached first of all among the European states, had to work harder to overcome some European resistance, most notably initially from Germany's Chancellor Kohl (Camroux and Lechervy 1996, p. 443). However, during its term of presidency of the EU France was able to ensure European approval of the principle of such a meeting at the European Council meeting at Cannes in June 1995.

During 1995 the format of the first ASEM was discussed and formalized: Europe would be represented by the 15 member states of the EU and Asia by the existing seven members of ASEAN plus Japan, China and South Korea. The principle that the EU would decide on Europe's representation and ASEAN on Asia's representation was established. Despite lobbying from India, Taiwan and Australia, ASEAN decided to keep the Asian representation limited – and smaller than the European side – for the first meeting. Japan, worried about what signals might be sent to its close ally the United States, and China, fearful that it might turn into yet another forum for criticism of its actions, were initially sceptical, but South Korea was much more open to the concept (Camroux and Lechervy 1996, pp. 443–444). All three, however, finally agreed to participate. On 1 and 2 March 1996, therefore, 25 heads of state or heads of government (three European countries were represented by lesser officials because of domestic political problems) plus the European Commission President, Jacques Santer, met together in Bangkok in what was to be the first ever such meeting between leaders of the two regions.

The ASEM proposal appealed to the Europeans because it coincided with a general review already under way of European policies towards Asia based on a growing realization of the economic importance of the Asia Pacific region and the weakness of European involvement in that region (Camroux and Lechervy 1996, p. 444). This shift in European perceptions was most clearly shown in the European Commission's own policy document drafted in mid 1994 which strongly argued the case for the EU to accord a higher priority to Asia and to adopt proactive and better coordinated strategies towards the region (Commission Communication to the Council of Ministers 1994). The policy document, which was endorsed by the European Council in Essen in December 1994 and by the European Parliament in early 1995, listed four overall objectives: to strengthen the European economic presence in the Asia Pacific; to contribute to stability in the Asia Pacific; to promote the economic development of the less prosperous countries of that region; and to contribute to the development and consolidation of democracy and human rights in that region. Although the Commission's document did not specifically advocate region-to-region discussions, it did argue for greater dialogue with the countries and regional organizations of the Asia Pacific. As such, the Singaporean initiative fitted in well with this European aspiration to do more with the region. During 1995, indeed, the European Commission separately prepared policy documents on relations with China and with Japan, and informal wisemen's groups examined relations with South Korea and with ASEAN.

For the Asian countries, the declared aim of the ASEM process was to reinforce the weak link in the triangle of relations between Asia, Europe and North America. The Asian desire was for Europe to pay greater attention to their region and to have a greater presence in the region, particularly as a means of counter-balancing the role of the United States. Closer links and better understanding could ensure that Europe would not only provide a stronger commercial competitor to the Americans (and enable the Asians to play off commercial rivalry between the two more effectively), but would also offer an alternative and more open market for Asian goods. Politically, too, it would also send a message to the Americans that the Asia Pacific was growing in international stature and had an alternative to the sometimes over-bearing relationship with the United States. There was indeed a certain resonance between the Asians and the Europeans about the United States; both sides saw utility in indirectly reminding the United States of 'the gap between the US rhetoric on free trade and its own behaviour' (Camroux and Lechervy 1996, p. 445). Less clearly articulated in public, but nonetheless an important subsidiary political objective, certainly among some Southeast Asian states, was to provide yet another opportunity – or forum – for China to be drawn out into the international arena and exposed to the norms of interna-tional intercourse (interview, Southeast Asian diplomat, May 1995). Finally, as Malaysian commentators were quick to point out, the composition of the Asian side was almost exactly that advocated by Dr Mahathir in his EAEC proposal for an Asian grouping (see Chapter 7). He was keen to build on this precedent being set.

There was a certain appropriateness in the choice of Bangkok as the site of the first ASEM, because Thailand had been one of the few Asian states to avoid falling under European colonial rule. In the run-up to the summit, both sides were keen to emphasize that it would operate on a new appreciation of their equality as participants; old mind-sets were supposed to be discarded. In addition, the intention was to broaden the agenda away from the usual stuff of Europe–Asia Pacific interactions – economics – to also include political and even security issues. Indeed, as the preparations continued the Asians discovered that the Europeans not only welcomed the chance to discuss issues such as UN reform and disarmament, but they also wanted to bring up questions of human rights and labour standards. The Asians tried to tip the balance back towards trade, investment and cooperation issues and, ultimately, the Europeans drew back from pressing too hard on human rights issues in order to ensure that the atmosphere was not soured on this, the first occasion (*Bangkok Post*, 26 February 1996).

In fact, both sides were prepared to do much to encourage the right atmospherics for the meeting. In order to reduce the possibility of the 'us' and 'them' type of confrontation, the leaders sat around in armchairs, arranged in alphabetical order of the countries participating (the Thai hosts even arranged for the chairs to be flown back to their respective occupants' homes afterwards). The formula appeared to work well; as one Japanese policy adviser noted, one striking aspect was the 'acceptance of an Asian-style discussion', by which was meant a respect for consensus and informality (interview, May 1996). Indeed, it appeared almost as if, in contra-distinction to normally expected negotiating styles, the Europeans seemed content to go for general commitments on continuing trade liberalization through the WTO and on investment promotion, while the Asians were determined to have more concrete proposals endorsed (Camroux and Lechervy 1996, pp. 446–447).

In the end ASEM did agree to a number of initiatives: Singapore would host a new Asia–Europe Foundation for intellectual exchange (founded February 1997); Malaysia would take the coordinating role in developing an Asia–Europe railway network project; and Thailand would be the site of an Asia–Europe Environmental Technology Centre (Chairman's Statement 1996). It was agreed that the next ASEM meeting would be in London in the spring of 1998 and the one after in Seoul in the year 2000. In between meetings, senior officials, foreign ministers and economic ministers would meet and a business forum, for businessmen on both sides, would be developed.

The model of APEC was clearly on the minds of many participants. The Italian Prime Minister, Lamberto Dini, the President of the European Council, hoped that ASEM would 'one day be on a par with the tried and tested links' of APEC, but as the EU Vice-President, Brittan, made clear 'in paralleling the APEC process, we are not aping the APEC process' (*Asian Wall Street Journal*, 4 March 1996). This means that while both sides were prepared to follow APEC in focusing predominantly on economic cooperation issues, there was no intention to mimic APEC either in its specific goals and target dates for trade and investment liberalization or in its slow progress towards institutionalization. Reference instead was made to the WTO and its implementation procedures; the ASEM process should 'complement and reinforce efforts to strengthen the open and rules-based trading system embodied in the WTO' (Chairman's Statement 1996). No ASEM secretariat was suggested; indeed, the Europeans argued that ASEM should not become too bureaucratic or rigid. Summit meetings will be held every two years, not every year as in the case of APEC. There is also one other clear difference between APEC and

ASEM in that, from the very beginning, political dialogue has been an integral part of the ASEM process, whereas despite the efforts of some countries (such as the United States and Australia) political issues have remained largely outside the scope of APEC meetings, even at the annual summit gatherings.

Towards ASEM 2

Both sides were concerned that the momentum of the initial meeting should not be lost. The first ASEM foreign ministers meeting was held in Singapore in February 1997; the focus was more on the method of dialogue than dialogue itself, but the meeting did agree to a South Korean proposal for a 'Vision Group' to be set up to put forward ideas for the development of ASEM (*Agence Europe*, 17 February 1997). The establishment of this group was formalized at the April 1998 ASEM 2 meeting in London. However, two issues remained pending: the content of the political dialogue and the enlargement of ASEM. These two points reflect the dilemma of all the regional groupings under discussion in this book, whether the EU, ASEAN, ARF or APEC, namely, the problems of deepening and/or widening.

Later official-level meetings have built on the preliminary ministerial discussions on these two problems. Given that both sides are committed to discuss political issues in the ASEM process, how far should they go? It has now been agreed that sensitive subjects are not to be avoided in the political dialogue (this actually allowed some discussion of the Burmese issue at the Singapore meeting), but subjects which are in the purview of other fora, which create an uneasy atmosphere and which are strictly bilateral, are likely to be excluded from future ASEM discussions. This makes it difficult, for example, for Portugal to raise the question of East Timor at ASEM meetings (although the Portuguese Prime Minister did manage to get in a passing mention of it during the course of ASEM 2). As the Europeans had tended to hold back in the initial Bangkok meeting, the London ASEM 2 summit did see more forthright discussion of political issues in general, even though the key topic on the agenda was undoubtedly the impact of the Asia Pacific regional financial crisis.

Under the general rubric of deepening, moreover, apart from the inevitable and important discussions on business and financial issues which have resulted in three Asia–Europe Business Forum meetings, ASEM officials also tried in between the two meetings to improve the mechanisms for cooperation on global issues, such as the illicit drug trade and environmental problems, as well as to set up new fora and organizations for promoting cultural and intellectual exchange. Progress was most notable in the latter sphere, with an Asia–Europe Foundation, designed to promote exchanges between think-tanks, peoples and cultural groups, being established in February 1997, and the first Asia–Europe Young Leaders' Symposium being held in Japan the next month (Foreign Office 1998).

The expansion of ASEM participation – or widening – was avoided, and even the debate on the criteria for membership was essentially put on hold until the third ASEM summit in the year 2000. Although there are some potential new members from Europe, such as Switzerland, Russia and the Eastern European states, none of these is pressing so urgently or so controversially as the Asian candidates. Burma, India, Pakistan, Australia, New Zealand and Taiwan head the list of Asian aspirants. China's Foreign Minister, Qian Qichen, has made it clear that China would veto both Australia and New Zealand as 'these are not Asian countries' (*Agence Europe*, 17 February 1997); Malaysia has also made similar sentiments public. This makes Australian and New Zealand participation almost impossible. Since ASEM covers political subjects as well as economic ones, China has also vetoed the admission of Taiwan (both were admitted to APEC on the implicit understanding that economic issues would predominate and, after 1993, that no very senior Taiwanese representative could join the annual APEC summits). However, the ASEAN countries have been split over the question of Indian and Pakistani involvement and further discussion can be expected, although those two countries' decisions to embark on nuclear testing in May 1998 have almost certainly destroyed any chances they might have had of early inclusion in the ASEM process.

The participation of Burma, which joined ASEAN in July 1997, has, however, remained the most controversial issue separating the Europeans and the Asians. Britain, under both the Conservative government and the subsequent Labour government, has made it clear that it does not welcome Burma's participation, even though it is now a fully fledged member of ASEAN (*South China Morning Post*, 12 September 1997). Malaysian Prime Minister Dr Mahathir, who had been a strong advocate of getting Burma inside ASEAN, hinted in September 1997 that he might even consider boycotting the London ASEM if Burma were excluded (*Nihon Keizai Shimbun*, 3 September 1997). But the ASEAN side as a whole seem to have been following a softer line, with the Thais, who are responsible for ASEAN's coordination with the EU, arguing that ASEAN membership does not automatically mean ASEM membership (*Bangkok Post*, 7 October 1997). By the time of the ASEAN summit in Kuala Lumpur in December 1997, even the Malaysians seemed to have accepted that they should not force the issue of Burmese participation at the risk of damaging the ASEM consensus. The ASEAN, Chinese, Japanese and South Korean leaders agreed that no new members would be included at the London ASEM (*Asian Wall Street Journal*, 16 December 1997). However, as South Korean officials admit, it will be difficult to avoid some expansion of

ASEM by the time of the third meeting in Seoul in 2000 (interview, Foreign Ministry, Seoul, November 1997); Burma will surely be pushed by ASEAN to be one of those admitted when the *de facto* membership moratorium is lifted.

The first ASEM economics ministerial meeting was held in Japan in September 1997, by which time the regional economic crisis in Southeast Asia was beginning to impact. Some Asian participants felt that some of the Europeans were a little less enthusiastic about economic cooperation as a result (*Nihon Keizai Shimbun*, 29 September 1997). Japanese Prime Minister Hashimoto Ryutaro, in opening that meeting, warned against excessive pessimism about the Asia Pacific region's economic prospects, arguing that 'it is only natural that growth and stagnation come alternately in capitalist economies' (*Hongkong Standard*, 29 September 1997). The meeting did discuss two plans to be put forward at the London ASEM, for an investment promotion action plan (which will include using the Internet to collate investment possibilities) and a trade facilitation action plan. Despite their rather unexciting names, these plans are intended to boost trade and investment links in the longer term by measures such as simplifying customs procedures and improving IPRs. While these two plans were endorsed at the London summit, their character in implementation terms has been altered by the need to respond to the Asian financial crisis.

The ASEM-related activity since the 1996 Bangkok summit has clearly been designed to ensure that that particular meeting did not end as a one-off jamboree in the sun. The Bangkok meeting has been criticized for adopting a 'laundry list strategy', allowing each country to put forward its favourite project, with no sense of priority (Segal 1997, p. 134). The difficult part, therefore, is to set priorities and to translate all these various initiatives and proposals into practical results. The hosts of ASEM 2, the British, in the months beforehand, certainly tried to emphasize the need for 'good, solid and practical ideas' (*Bangkok Post*, 10 February 1998). The very financial crises which hit the Asia Pacific region certainly acted as a factor in helping to establish priorities since, from the Asian perspective, not everything is as easily achievable as once seemed possible.

Although the ASEM 2 participants were reluctant to commit themselves to a definite expansion of membership and refused to move towards any form of institutionalization, they did agree to meet again in Seoul in the year 2000 and again in Europe in 2002. As such, it is clear that ASEM is going to become a regular item on the international diplomatic circuit, even if the substance is still taking some time to be worked out. For the moment, the political symbolism of meeting, and continuing to meet, is important for both sides. The key to achieving more concrete results will be to get the private sector actively involved in the short term and, in the longer term, to build up the youth and young leader exchanges which will lay the foundations for closer ties between the two regions in the next century.

THE ASIAN FINANCIAL CONTAGION

Since the middle of 1997 a series of financial and economic crises have swept the Asia Pacific region. In the view of Singapore Prime Minister Goh, these constitute the region's 'worst crisis and biggest test since World War II' (*Korea Herald*, 14 January 1998). First Thailand, then Indonesia and finally South Korea had to go to the IMF, other regional and international financial institutions and to key major economic powers, including the European states, for financial assistance to tide them over mounting debt problems. Malaysia and the Philippines have avoided direct appeal to the IMF, but nonetheless have suffered a rocky period and have been forced to introduce their own austerity measures, albeit not as severe as the IMF-imposed ones in Thailand, Indonesia and South Korea. As shown in Table 9.1, by January 1998 the Malaysian ringgit, the Philippine peso, the Thai baht, the Indonesian rupiah and the Korean won had all fallen in value by between 40 and 60 per cent against the US dollar since the beginning of July 1997. Malaysian Prime Minister Mahathir claimed that the currency depreciations had wiped about $200 billion off the wealth of the Southeast Asian nations (*South China Morning Post*, 16 November 1997). Over the July–December 1997 period the stock market indices of those five economies also dropped by around half their value.

Table 9.1   Exchange rate changes of regional currencies (percentage change between 1 July 1997 and 1 January 1998)

	US dollar	UK pound	French franc	German deutschemark
Malaysian ringgit	−44.8	−34.4	−36.0	n.a.
Philippine peso	−41.9	−34.5	−36.5	−36.7
Thai baht	−53.7	−59.4	−49.3	−49.6
Indonesian rupiah	−69.6	−54.7	−56.0	−49.6
Taiwan dollar	−19.2	−12.7	−16.3	−16.9
Singapore dollar	−18.4	−14.4	n.a	n.a.
Korean won	−49.1	−44.0	n.a	−46.2

Sources: *Asian Wall Street Journal*, 8 January 1998, for rates against the US dollar; rate changes against European currencies are the author's own calculations based on currency rates from Bloomberg Financial Services.

Although the early months of 1998 showed some partial but inconsistent recovery in exchange rates and stock markets, the pains of economic restructuring became greater. The Thai and South Korean economies are expected to suffer minus growth or at best zero growth in 1998; Indonesia will be even harder hit, with estimates ranging from the IMF's –10 per cent to some economists' –20 per cent growth (SG Asian Research, 1998).

Just as the earlier economic boom and economic 'miracle' were not universally and consistently in evidence throughout the Asia Pacific region, so it can also be said that the current economic turmoil in certain countries does not mean that the whole region without exception is in deep crisis. Singapore, Hong Kong, China and Taiwan have resisted the financial pressures more successfully, but because they are closely tied into the Asia Pacific economy they have not been unaffected by what has been happening in other parts of the region. The Singapore stock market, for example, continued to shudder in January–February 1998 as the Indonesians debated and argued with the IMF over the merits of setting up a currency board to peg the rupiah to the dollar. The bursting of the property bubble in Hong Kong began to sap confidence and it recorded its first quarterly growth drop for more than a decade in early 1998. With the exception of China, which is expected to achieve around 7 per cent growth (which is below its recent record), all these economies are expected to achieve under 5 per cent growth in 1998. The smaller regional economies, such as the Indochinese states and Burma, have not been so directly affected because of their limited involvement in the regional and global financial markets. However, given that Thailand in particular and other Southeast Asian economies to a lesser extent have been important investors in their economies, they are beginning to suffer some knock-on effects from the regional crisis.

One other regional economy, by far the largest, needs to be included. Japan, as discussed in Chapter 3, had been labouring under its own huge financial problems coupled with a prolonged recession even before the Asian crisis occurred, and, unfortunately, it has not been able to provide the economic leadership and market stimulation for which many other Asia Pacific countries have hoped. A series of stimulus packages released through late 1997–early 1998 proved only to be damp squibs, and even the massive April 1998 package is expected to have only a limited impact. Japan has contributed substantially to IMF and other bailout packages, but has failed to come up with the market stimulation to help other economies export their way out of trouble. Its own growth record is expected to be around zero in 1998.

Views differ as to the underlying and proximate causes of these financial crises, and clearly the situation is not exactly the same in each country. Conspiracy theorists have had a field day; some latching on to the speculative activities of international financiers such as the now notorious George Soros;

others trying to lay the blame on actions by major economic powers such as the Chinese devaluation of the yuan in 1994 or the clear US desire to open Asian markets to US goods and services. But however attractive these theories might seem, they do not provide the real answer. The immediate cause can be put down to foreign over-borrowing by Asian Pacific banks, corporations and individuals on a short-term basis. Banks across the region have found themselves sitting on mountains of non-performing loans. Unlike earlier crises in Latin America, the Asia Pacific is not so worried about government over-spending and sovereign debt; the problem is more with private and short-term debt.

However, there were a number of underlying structural defects which contributed to the severity of the crisis (*Economist*, 7 March 1998; Sharma 1998; Tan 1998): the use of political rather than commercial criteria in the allocation of loans (especially in Thailand and Indonesia), over-expansion of capacity (South Korea), poor supervision of financial institutions (several countries), and a penchant for mega-projects at above-market prices (Malaysia and Indonesia).

The speed and extent to which the turmoil spread were a surprise to almost everyone within and outside the region, including, it has to be said, the IMF itself, which only a few months before had been praising the sound macro-economic policies of countries such as Thailand and South Korea (*International Herald Tribune*, 19 December 1997). In the early weeks of the crisis there was a tendency to underplay the extent of the problem. Even US President Clinton, attending the APEC summit in Vancouver in November 1997, described the problems as just 'a few little glitches in the road' to prosperity (*Asian Wall Street Journal*, 25 November 1997), a view he was soon forced to revise.

The spread of the financial turmoil in the Asia Pacific region is indeed evidence of the extent to which the regional economies are now closely inter-connected, in a way that conceivably even a decade ago was not so clear. But the crisis has also shown how inter-connected the global economy is. This means that Europe too has been affected by the Asian troubles.

The Impact on Europe

In the early stages of the financial crisis the Europeans, like the Clinton administration, tended to underestimate the extent to which it was developing. Most European governments and companies have consistently lagged behind events in appreciating the degree to which the Asian problems might impact on their own economies. There were certainly many Europeans who could not avoid a certain degree of relief and indeed grim satisfaction, given past Asian pronouncements on the superiority of the Asian way of doing things, that all was not well with the Asian 'miracle' and that the Asians appeared human after all (Higgott 1998, p. 4). The South Korean crisis in November 1997 was the one which seemed finally to wake up many Europeans and, in fact, it was the four European members of the G-7 group which were first, ahead of the Japanese and the Americans, in offering help to South Korea (interview, European delegation, Seoul, November 1997). European Commission officials stepped up their surveillance of the Asian financial crisis and even began to consider 'worst-case scenarios' (*Financial Times*, 29 January 1998).

Yet despite the magnitude of the Korean problem and increasing signs of socio-political disorder in Indonesia, even in January 1998 Commission President Santer argued that the direct effect on the European economies of the Asian Pacific economic turmoil would be 'slight', and that he saw no need to revise growth projections for the EU for 1998 downwards as a result (*Nihon Keizai Shimbun*, 12 January 1998). Later the same month, the EU's Monetary Affairs Commissioner, Yves-Thibault de Silguy, also argued that the Asian crisis would have 'only a marginal impact on growth in Europe' (*Financial Times*, 29 January 1998).

Yet this approach has already proved over-optimistic. Indeed, some European leaders, such as Tony Blair, the British Prime Minister, recognized this. When meeting with Japanese Prime Minister Hashimoto Ryutaro in mid January he agreed that the Asian financial crises would have 'a great influence on the global economy' (*Nihon Keizai Shimbun*, 13 January 1998).

In general terms, the global economy has already been pushed into a slowdown which is likely to cut one percentage point off global growth in 1998, although available growth figures have yet to reflect the impact of the Asian troubles fully. Instability in currency markets in early 1998 makes predictions difficult, but there are a number of ways in which the Asian problems will specifically impact on Europe and European business with the Asia Pacific region.

First, European exports to the Asia Pacific will be dampened. The most affected Asian Pacific economies have embarked on austerity measures which include reducing or discouraging imports of 'luxury' or non-essential items, especially consumer goods, and cancelling or re-negotiating some specific government procurement contracts. French exports to the region apart from Japan were 40 per cent down in December 1997 compared with their peak five months earlier (*Nihon Keizai Shimbun*, 25 February 1998). British exports to South Korea in the first two months of 1998 were running at half their 1997 level, and exports to five other major Asian markets had also suffered a sharp decline (*Daily Telegraph*, 27 March 1998).

Although the five most affected Asia Pacific countries have seen their currencies depreciate rapidly against the US dollar, they have also fallen against the major European currencies (though in most cases not quite as drastically; see Table 9.1), so those goods which are still being imported from Europe are becoming more expensive in local currency terms. German exporters are probably in the best position of the major European exporters, as the deutschemark also declined against the dollar during 1997, giving them a competitive price advantage (*International Herald Tribune*, 16 December 1997). However, even in those economies whose currency is either pegged to the dollar or not depreciating so significantly, Asian consumers are likely to be both more cautious purchasers and, in some cases, more interested in rival consumer products coming out of the suffering Asian economies, which are now comparatively cheaper. European exporters will find a decreasing demand for many of their products, especially consumer goods.

Second, imports from these same Asia Pacific countries will increase, as their depreciating currencies have made their products much cheaper and therefore more competitive. For many of these suffering economies, increased exporting seems to be one of the few solutions readily available. Of course, the financial crunch in these exporting countries means that some companies will find it more difficult to get short-term loans or credit from banks, particularly when they need to cover the rising costs of imported raw materials and/or components if they are a key element of their final products. Nonetheless, increased exporting seems certain. One Korean economic research institute forecast that South Korean exports to the EU would rise 17 per cent in 1998, more than double the expected overall growth in Korean exports (*Korea Herald*, 17 January 1998). Also, anecdotal evidence suggests that American, Japanese and European manufacturing companies located in the suffering Asia Pacific countries are turning to export their products to the European and US markets because their local markets have dried up (I am indebted to Heiner Hanggi, of the Modern Asia Research Centre, Geneva, for this information).

The combination of increased exports from these Asian economies and decreasing export opportunities for Europeans will inevitably lead to a deterioration of Europe's bilateral trade imbalances with these Asian countries. For example, according to French statistics, with a drop in its exports and an increase in its imports, in December 1997 France recorded its largest monthly deficit in trade for three years with ten Asia Pacific countries other than Japan (*Nihon Keizai Shimbun*, 25 February 1998). If the past record is repeated – and that is likely to be the case where unemployment remains a serious political problem, especially in France and Germany – then protectionist pressures would again rise within the EU.

Third, the FDI environment is changing, although the picture here is more mixed. Overall, there is likely to be a decline in new European FDI into the Asia Pacific region. Some European companies, especially those operating in the financial sector, are already undergoing consolidation, and even with-drawal in a few cases. In the manufacturing and resource-exploiting sectors, cost-cutting measures are likely to be the order of the day, especially where the products are destined mainly for the local market or for other regional countries with devalued currencies. But exporting from countries with deval-ued currencies to other economies in the region with non-devalued currencies (with China the key target) could be boosted. For example, Swiss–Swedish engineering company ABB is shedding contract workers and cancelling bonuses for its executives at its Thai factories, but is gearing its plants up actually to expand production and develop a new regional export strategy (*Far Eastern Economic Review*, 5 February 1998).

A growing type of investment as a result of the financial crisis, however, is likely to be debt-to-equity conversions and merger and acquisition activity. This may become particularly visible in countries such as South Korea, which under IMF supervision is having dramatically to increase the limits allowed to foreign companies in taking ownership of Korean companies and to liberalize further its regulations on inward FDI. French and Spanish bank-ing groups moved in early 1998 to take over parts of the operations of one of Hong Kong's largest financial groups, Peregrine, when it went bankrupt through over-exposure in Indonesia. British supermarket chain Tesco has bought up Lotus, a leading Thai retailer. German luxury car company Daim-ler-Benz has acquired a controlling share of Japan's Nissan Diesel company. The German Commerz Bank has bought into the Korea Exchange Bank.

Fourth, still looking at FDI, there is likely to be a fall in Asian Pacific FDI into Europe, particularly from South Korea but also from Japan. As noted in Chapter 4, late 1997 and early 1998 saw a number of Korean companies suspend expansion plans or postpone implementing investment projects already agreed. Some of the small and medium-sized companies which have followed the bigger Japanese and Korean companies into Europe as suppliers are likely to withdraw completely. Although provisional figures suggest that Japanese FDI into Europe was still increasing on a yearly basis in 1997, stagnant corporate earnings and the slumping domestic economy suggest that 1998 will see a marked reduction in such flows. Significantly, linked with this slowdown in fresh Japanese FDI have been signs that, in the financial sector at least, there is beginning to be a geographical consolidation as the Japanese institutions close down some of their European operations and concentrate them in Frankfurt and, above all, London, which despite Britain staying out of the first wave of EMU, is still certain to be the leading centre for treasury transactions in Europe (*Look Japan*, December 1997).

Fifth, European banks have found themselves heavily exposed to some of the countries most at risk and have been forced to undertake serious discus-sions with both Asian governments and companies to set up private sector rescue packages to sort out short-term debt repayment problems. On the eve of the crisis in mid 1997, for example, German banks were exposed in South Korea to the tune of $10.6 billion, French banks to $10.1 billion and British banks to $6.1 billion. After crisis talks with the South Korean central bank governor in early 1998, they agreed to work out a roll-over solution which avoided a formal debt rescheduling (*Sunday Morning Post*, 11 January 1998). This picture of heavy European financial exposure is repeated across the region. One German bank alone, Deutsche Bank, is estimated to have about $16 billion in loans outstanding, spread across eight Asia Pacific countries (*Asian Wall Street Journal*, 22 January 1998). Overall, according to figures released by the Bank of International Settlements, as of June 1997 European banks held $365 billion in loans outstanding to Asian banks and companies, more than the total of the American banks ($275 billion) and the Japanese banks ($45 billion) combined (*Far Eastern Economic Review*, 12 February 1998). Indeed, in the second half of 1997, the European banks continued to go in deeper, actually increasing loans to the Asian private sector, while US and Japanese banks drew back. By the end of the year, 47 per cent of all outstanding foreign loans to developing Asia were held by European banks (*Korea Herald*, 26 May 1998).

Worries about Asian Pacific regional financial stability, especially in Indonesia, are certain to continue for the European financial community. While no European banks are likely to be bankrupted by their Asian commitments, their earnings and profits will undoubtedly be hit. Deutsche Bank, for example, suffered a 57 per cent fall in its net profits during 1997, primarily because of its exposure in Asia (*South China Morning Post*, 19 February 1998).

Sixth, flows of people will be reduced. Those European states which benefit from the ubiquitous Japanese, Korean and other Asian tourists will undoubtedly notice a drop-off in visitors. European airlines serving Asia will also suffer in the short run. While the prospect of cheaper holidays in some parts of the Asia Pacific will be attractive for some Europeans, others will shy away from these apparently unstable countries; anyway, European travellers are unlikely to provide sufficient compensation to the airlines for the drop-off in Asian travellers to Europe. British Airways, for example, suspended its flights to Seoul from March 1998 because of the slump in demand. Students and young people, which can be such a fruitful seed for future inter-regional linkages, coming from the worst affected Asian countries to study in Europe may also be reduced in number. The Malaysian government, for example, has already begun to set up new credit-transfer procedures to encourage its students in financial difficulties while studying in Europe to return home to local private universities.

Finally and more positively, if inevitably more nebulously, the European image in Asia will be enhanced if the Europeans continue to act in a responsive manner. Asian Pacific ambivalence about the Americans has increased as a result of the events since mid 1997. The United States was slow to contribute directly to solving the regional crises, tending to limit its early role to endorsing the approach of the IMF, in which admittedly it has an extremely influential voice. Regional initiatives in late 1997 to create some form of Asian regional emergency fund as an alternative to the IMF fell by the wayside, in part because the Americans opposed one particular Japanese initiative, so the Asia Pacific nations fell back on approving the US approach of controlled funding through the IMF. But the result has been a growing resentment of the American role. The Chinese media, for example, denounced US intervention in the financial crises as a cynical plan for 'forcing East Asia into submission [and] promoting the US economic and political model' (*South China Morning Post*, 7 January 1998).

While a few Asian Pacific politicians have been scathing about the West and its financiers in general, thereby including by implication the Europeans, on the whole the Europeans have been subject to less direct criticism. For example, even though cumulatively the European states contribute a larger share financially to the IMF than the Americans, it has been the United States which has been cast in the villainous role as the 'controller' of the IMF. While playing a lower key role than that of the United States, the Europeans have therefore also played a less controversial one. By appearing to be constructive rather than gloating or uninterested, the Europeans can prove that they can be a useful friend for those Asian states in need.

The APEC summit in Vancouver in November 1997, despite coming in the midst of the Asian financial crises and, indeed, as the South Korean collapse was becoming so clear, failed to add anything substantial to the IMF-led measures of relief. It seemed to have little to offer when faced with the first real test since its establishment eight years earlier. ASEM, which had set off with less fanfare and lower expectations than APEC, had a better opportunity, as the dust began to settle slightly on the initial stage of the Asian crises, to consider at the London meeting measures and mechanisms which could help to reduce the damage that might occur from any repetition of these crises. Some practical steps, such as the technical assistance which had already been extended by the Bank of England to the Thai authorities on the management of reserves (*Bangkok Post*, 10 February 1998), could be extended to other countries in the region, although specific programmes should be tailored for individual countries. ASEM 2 did endorse a British proposal for a network of experts to provide technical advice in the financial sector (ASEM 2 Closing Press Conference 1998). The British also floated the idea of an ASEM Trust Fund, which would be designed to ease the impact of social change, poverty and labour market reforms and would be managed by the World Bank's special financial operation unit. Although some countries, notably Japan and

Germany, were reluctant to participate for fear of duplicating other international funding programmes, Britain did manage to get the Fund off the ground, with initial pledges from members totalling $25 million (*Straits Times*, 6 April 1998).

Initiatives such as the ASEM Trust Fund and technical assistance programmes, while small scale by comparison with the totality of the problems faced by the Asia Pacific countries, are both practical and distinctive steps by which the Europeans are demonstrating their commitment to the Asia Pacific. Indeed, the impression received by the Asian leaders at the London summit was a favourable one in the sense that the Europeans made it clear that they were not about to desert Asia. Neither were they about to lord it over the troubled Asians. The Europeans had gone into ASEM 1 on the defensive in the face of Asian economic triumphalism, but at ASEM 2 it was, of course, the Asians who were on the defensive. The Europeans wisely resisted the temptation to crow.

THE EURO

Chapter 7 discussed the origins and aspirations of the single European currency programme. Despite scepticism within Europe and the Asia Pacific, the EU is now well down the road to serious implementation of EMU. May 1998 saw the formal designation of the 11 countries which will participate from the outset (Britain, Denmark and Sweden decided not to join for the moment and Greece failed to meet the criteria). In general, apart from stubbornly high unemployment in some countries, the economic conditions for the euro-11 are favourable (*Economist*, 7 March 1998). Although the EU members quarrelled over who would be the head of the new European Central Bank (and, in the process, no doubt confirmed the views of sceptical Asians that the whole venture would never really get off the ground), the mechanisms are now firmly in place for the introduction of the euro. Not only European citizens but their Asian counterparts will have to get used to this new development.

However, no one really knows how a common currency will work among countries which vary in size and economic structure. The economic implications of EMU are still not clear, in part because the volatility of the euro could significantly affect implementation. There will be further consolidation and efficiency gains among European industry, especially in the banking sector, but these may well have to be balanced against politically sensitive rises in unemployment. Nonetheless, overall, the extra competition should help further to stimulate economic dynamism within Europe (Munchau 1997, p. 4).

Given the recently heightened Asian sensitivity to currency-related issues, the Europeans will have to continue to reassure the Asians that the single currency will not be manipulated to protect European jobs from cheaper Asian imports coming out of the affected countries.

However, the emergence of the euro from January 1999 could have more of an impact on Euro-Asia trade transactions than might have been the case if no financial crisis had occurred. At the moment, although the Germans de-nominate much of their Asian trade in deutschemarks, in general the US dollar is the dominant currency in Euro-Asian trade. It was always likely that that would change after 1999, but the trend for Asians increasingly to trade in the euro instead of the dollar is likely to be accentuated as a result of the financial crisis. As Philip Bowring has argued, a single currency in Europe and continued exchange rate volatility in Asia suggest that a diversification of trading currencies away from the mighty dollar would be 'opportune' for the Asians (Bowring 1998).

A unified capital market should also enlarge Europe's role as a source of long-term bond finance, to which Asians are now likely to be more attracted rather than their previous short-term bank borowings (*South China Morning Post*, 6 April 1998). Regional central banks will increasingly hold the euro as a reserve currency. Currently, on average around 20 per cent of Asian coun-tries' foreign currency reserves are held in European currencies. With a unified euro, once initial scepticism about the Europeans' ability to hold together is dissipated, Asians are likely to increase their share of reserves held in the euro.

For Japan, of course, the emergence of the euro after 1999 has one further implication, in so far as it will challenge the embryonic role of the yen as an international currency. Since the 1980s the Japanese government and Japa-nese financial circles have been talking about making the yen into a major international currency, but even within the Asia Pacific region it has tended to act as a supplementary, not a rival, currency to the US dollar. Speaking in the margins of the 1997 IMF/World Bank conference in Hong Kong, one Japa-nese government official admitted that unless the government took measures to increase the yen's international competitiveness, it would 'sink under the two giant currencies' (*Korea Herald*, 25 September 1997).

The emergence of the euro has also stimulated some debate within the Asia Pacific about a common currency within the region. Embryonic attempts within ASEAN in early 1998 to encourage the Singaporeans to allow their dollar to be used as a unit of currency in intra-ASEAN exchanges failed as the Singaporeans argued that they did not have the strength to maintain such a role. But ASEAN members are continuing to have serious conversations about a group link to a basket of the dollar, yen and euro as a way of stabilizing exchange rates (*Korea Herald*, 8 April 1998).

As demonstrated above, these three factors – the ASEM process, the Asian financial crisis and the birth of the euro – cannot be totally separated. They are certain to act as key variables in the evolution of the Euro-Asian relationship. They will interact not just in the areas of trade, investment and financial flows as well as political interests, but also, and arguably most importantly, in the psychological arena – in terms of how each region perceives the other and desires to interact with it. With the euro likely on balance to enhance Europe's economic attractiveness, commercial competitiveness and political status in the world during a period when the Asia Pacific is still recovering from the battering to its own self-esteem, is licking its wounds and preparing to restore the lost growth momentum, both sides are looking at each other with new eyes. The rhetoric of a balanced and equal relationship, much beloved by leaders at the ASEM meetings, may actually be closer to reality than at any time in the past half-century.

10. Looking back and looking forward

We have an almost unlimited amount now to learn from the cultures
on the other side of the planet, in terms of philosophy and values
as well as techniques and methods.
(British Member of Parliament, David Howell,
Sunday Morning Post, 22 October 1995)

The Europe–Asia relationship has seen a number of changes since the days of
Marco Polo. In broad historical terms, a number of different periods of
interaction can be demarcated, although inevitably dating can only loosely be
applied given the range of countries involved and the differing dynamics in
their individual interactions with the other region. The first period would
cover the initial contacts in ancient times through to the beginning of serious
European colonization in the early/mid 19th century. This was characterized
by intermittent and sometimes accidental cultural cross-fertilization and trade
flows, with on balance more going from Asia to Europe than *vice versa*. The
second period, from the mid 19th century until World War II, was the period
of formal European imperialism and colonization throughout much of the
Asia Pacific region. This was essentially an exploitative and dominant phase
for the Europeans.

The third period began with the Japanese attack on European possessions
in the Asia Pacific region, which first laid bare the European weaknesses, and
covered the subsequent struggles for independence in the 1950s. Military
disaster, loss of prestige and loss of territory by the Europeans meant that
Asians began to look at them in a different and far less submissive light. The
fourth period began in the mid 1960s, as the Europeans effectively disappeared from the Asia Pacific scene and the Asians themselves arrived in
Europe as energetic and competitive traders and later investors. Europe was
on the defensive as they were forced to look at the Asians in a new way, as
effective – sometimes too effective – competitors. The balance of influence
had swung to the Asia Pacific. The fifth period began in the second half of the
1980s as the Europeans began to wake up not only to the need to get their
own act together within Europe, a process which was accelerated by the
collapse of communism in Eastern Europe, but also to the challenges and
potentialities of the booming Asia Pacific economies. The period was one of
re-exploration and even re-invention, particularly for the Europeans, but it

was also one in which the rising interest in regionalism in both areas and the sustained self-confidence of the Asians militated against a really balanced relationship. Now, as argued in Chapter 9, three defining but inter-connected characteristics (ASEM, the Asian financial crises and the euro) are set to combine to create a new sixth and potentially more balanced period in Euro-Asian relations.

Taking the analysis down a level from the broad region-to-region approach, a number of nuances can be seen in the way in which European states and the Commission have approached Asia. In terms of interests and priorities, two generalizations can be made. First, once the colonial era was over and the physical withdrawal completed, Europe's reintroduction to the Asia Pacific was almost exclusively through economics. Commercial competition, markets and money dominated the Euro-Asian relationship from the 1960s to the mid 1980s. Political and security concerns began to grow slowly from then on and, taking a very broad definition of security (as employed in Chapter 8), in the post-Cold War era these elements undoubtedly became more significant, but they failed to displace the role of economics. Too much of the relationship is still devoted to the business of doing business.

Second, there has been a shift in the country focus of European interests. In the colonial era and through to the mid 1960s, Southeast Asia (both modern-day ASEAN and Indochina) ranked high in European concerns. Then the emerging economic power of Japan redirected European attention; Japan remained the primary focus until the mid 1990s, predominantly because of the economic challenge but also because there gradually developed some European hopes of political dialogue. However, the intra-European process of rethinking Asian policy as a whole in 1994–95 inevitably diluted the role of Japan. The net result, paradoxically, has been the emergence of China as the mainspring of Europe's Asia policy; the Hong Kong handover and the Asian financial crisis has only reinforced this tendency.

At a seminar on Euro-Japanese relations one day back in the 1980s, a colleague of mine, wishing to play devil's advocate, asked why both sides, so distant geographically and culturally should bother to be involved with each other. The same question might equally well be asked about Europe and the broader Asia Pacific.

Despite the growth in trade, aid, investment and technology linkages between Europe and the Asia Pacific region noted in Chapters 3, 4, 5, and 6, the relationship has yet to become a fully rounded one. Economic issues – some of them quite contentious – have tended to dominate the agenda of bilateral meetings, whether between individual countries or between the European Commission and Asian countries and organizations. By contrast, the political dialogue has been, and remains, under-developed, despite some of the more positive developments acknowledged in Chapter 8. The cultural, educational and other links are still comparatively insubstantial. Some individual EU member states have, of course, been able to develop strong links with individual Asian Pacific states, but others have almost none. At the Community-wide level, relations between the two regions still leave much to be desired.

The recent Asian financial crises have raised anew the question of whether Europe should bother to be interested in the Asia Pacific and whether Asia–Europe links are important. In fact, the recent Asian economic troubles have actually shown that neither side can afford to ignore the other. European companies, manufacturers and financial corporations are being affected by the currency turmoil, economic slowdown and, in some countries, socio-political instability, but this does not mean that it is time for the Europeans to get cold feet about doing business in and developing ties with the Asia Pacific. Similarly, in these testing times, the Asians find that they not only need the financial support of European institutions but also that there are lessons in corporate governance, macro-economic management and financial reconstruction that can be learnt from Europe.

However, in the increasingly interdependent world of the late 1990s, when the global political and economic orders are in a continuing state of flux, both sides do need to reassess the nature and depth of their relationship.

Long-term partnerships acquire durability in part because of an embedding of common or, at the very least, shared values, which can provide a bedrock to sustain the relationship even when there are tensions on substance. Within Western Europe, this can be seen in a belief in political liberalism, the primacy of market economics, a deep sense of security community, and relatively similar societies and cultures. With only a few modifications, these values extend to the transatlantic relationship too. But how far can common values between Europe and the Asia Pacific be identified? There are some signs of shared, if not exactly common, values emerging and, indeed, converging, although in some dimensions, particularly regarding democracy and market-led economics, positions are still well apart between some Europeans and some Asians.

At the policy level, the degree and pace of convergence will be affected by the extent to which priorities and interests overlap. The starting point for many Europeans and Asians in recent years, even decades, has usually been that a closer relationship is desirable, even very desirable, but not absolutely essential. When they have come together, the core issues of interest to both have been trade, investment and aid links and more general issues of the management of the international economy. While these issues are still important, as the recent financial crises in Asia have confirmed, there are signs of a growing overlap of interests in the political sphere and, as argued in Chapter 8, global issues such as the environment, AIDS, crime and nuclear proliferation which add to the viability of dialogue.

The EU's policy measures towards the Asia Pacific have in general been rather piecemeal and inconsistent. The 1994 Asia strategy paper failed to lay out a comprehensive and coherent policy and, anyway, spread itself too wide by trying to include South Asia as well as the Asia Pacific. The series of separate policy documents and initiatives on European relations with individual countries or sub-regions since then need to be better coordinated. The fact that China became the subject of a second policy paper in March 1998 suggests that it has become the focus of European policy-making at the expense of other regional states. More should be done – and the continuing but slow-moving process now under way to strengthen the EU's mechanisms for foreign policy can help – on the coordination of national policies. The Asians, on the other hand, have to recognize that whatever the attraction of bilateral contacts and the undoubted continuing importance of those contacts, they will also have to take the EU increasingly seriously as the main interlocutor in Europe, not just on economic but also on political and security issues.

Richard Higgott has argued that the net effect of the Asian financial crisis will be to increase interest in East Asian, as opposed to Pacific-wide, regionalism (Higgott 1998, p. 6). Certainly, Asian disillusionment with the Vancouver APEC meeting's results, ambivalence about the American role in the Asian financial crisis, and preliminary intra-regional discussions about reducing dependence on the US dollar as the first step to an 'Asian currency', suggest that the Asians may well be turning in on themselves, or at least trying to redefine themselves in contra-distinction to the Americans. However, it is still early days – and Singaporean reluctance to allow its currency to become a regional one suggests that there are serious limits to such regionalization. On balance, however, East Asian regional identity or consciousness could become strengthened, but probably through an EAEC-type forum without Dr Mahathir's strident anti-Westernism, given ASEAN's own stumblings and APEC's declining credibility. As such, ASEM, which posits, or at least up until now has posited, the EAEC membership as its Asian component will be well suited to accomplishing a region-to-region dialogue with Europe which is consistent with Asian aspirations.

It is difficult to move quickly from a tradition, or at least a practice since the 1960s, of mutual neglect to one of mutual interest, understanding and benefit. Commitment and education are required. This has to involve the EU, member governments, companies and individuals. The boom in information technology means that more information about Europe is available in the Asia Pacific and *vice versa*, but greater information *per se* does not automatically lead to greater understanding. The quality of the information, to which more focused exchanges among media personnel can contribute, and the interpretation of that information are crucial. Inevitably, although inter-regional initiatives such as the ASEM process can undoubtedly help to cast a more favourable and positive overall framework and environment, much will continue to be done – and indeed needs to be done – at the level of bilateralism, whether between individual European and Asia Pacific countries or between their companies and peoples.

The series of financial crises pummelling the Asia Pacific in 1997–98 does not mean that the region should be counted out. European governments and companies should be aware that the resilience of the Asia Pacific economies and their peoples means that most will ultimately be successful in riding the storm, even though it will take several years in some cases. For the Europeans the need to 'think Asian' has by no means disappeared.

Bibliography

Acharya, Amitav (1995), 'Human Rights and Regional Order: ASEAN and Human Rights Management in Post-Cold War Southeast Asia', in James T.H. Tang (ed.), *Human Rights and International Relations in the Asia-Pacific Region*, London: Pinter, pp. 167–82.

Acharya, Rohini (1995), 'The Case for China's Accession to the WTO: Options for the EU', in Richard Grant (ed.), *The European Union and China: A European Strategy for the Twenty-First Century*, London: Royal Institute of International Affairs, pp. 54–74.

Akao, Nobutoshi (ed.) (1983), *Japan's Economic Security*, London: Gower.

Amri, Zain (1994), 'The ASEAN Regional Forum: Hope for Success but Tread with Caution', *Asian Defence Journal*, August, 22–6.

Aoki, Takeshi (1997), 'Malaysia: Laying the Groundwork to Meet the Need for an Industrial Structure', in Kitamura Kayoko and Tsuneo Tanaka (eds), *Examining Asia's Tigers*, Tokyo: Institute of Developing Economies, pp. 38–46.

Araki, Yoshihara (1997), 'Indonesia: Growth Process in the 1990s and Future Adjustment Issues', in Kitamura Kayoko and Tsuneo Tanaka (eds), *Examining Asia's Tigers*, Tokyo: Institute of Developing Economies, pp. 57–86.

ASEAN–EU Ministerial Meeting (1997), 'Joint Declaration', 14 February. Internet: http://europa.eu.int/en/comm/dg01/linkas5.htm.

ASEM 2 Closing Press Conference (1998), 'Edited Transcript', 4 April. Internet: http://www.fco.gov.uk/t...998/apr/04/presscon.txt.

Aung San, Suu Kyi (1995), *Freedom from Fear*, London: Penguin.

Badawi, Dato Seri Abdullah Haji Ahmad (1997), 'Chairman's Statement at Fourth Meeting of the ASEAN Regional Forum', 27 July. Internet: http://www.aseansec.org/politics/pol-arf4.htm.

Bergsten, Fred (1994), 'APEC and World Trade: A Force for Worldwide Liberalization', *Foreign Affairs*, May–June, 20–26.

Boey, Kim Cheng (1992), *Another Place*, Singapore: Times.

Borthwick, Mark (1992), *Pacific Century: The Emergence of Modern Pacific Asia*, Boulder: Westview Press.

Bourke, Thomas (1996), *Japan and the Globalisation of European Integration*, Aldershot: Dartmouth.

Bray, John (1992), 'Burma: Resisting the International Community', *Pacific Review*, **5**, (3), 291–96.

Bray, John (1995), *Burma: The Politics of Constructive Engagement*, London: Royal Institute of International Affairs.

Bridges, Brian (1986), *Korea and the West*, London: Routledge and Kegan Paul.

Bridges, Brian (1990), 'Deepening the EC–Korean Economic Relationship', *Korea & World Affairs*, Spring, 66–85.

Bridges, Brian (1992), 'Japan and Europe: Rebalancing a Relationship', *Asian Survey*, March, 230–45.

Bridges, Brian (1993), *Japan and Korea in the 1990s*, Edward Elgar: Aldershot.

Bowring, Philip (1998), 'It's Time Asia Thought About the Euro and the Yen', *International Herald Tribune*, 1 March.

Brittan, Sir Leon (1996), 'Europe and Hong Kong: Prospects for Cooperation into the Next Century'. Speech in Hong Kong, 31 May.

Brittan, Sir Leon (1997), 'Statement on China', 6 March. Internet: http://europa.eu.int/comm/dg01/ip97189.htm.

Buzan, Barry (1991), 'New Patterns of Global Security', *International Affairs*, July, 431–51.

Cabestan, Jean-Pierre (1990), 'Sino-European Relations', in Gerald Segal (ed.), *Chinese Politics and Foreign Policy Reform*, London: Kegan Paul International.

Cable, Vincent (1994), 'Overview', in Vincent Cable and David Henderson (eds), *Trade Blocs?: The Future of Regional Integration*, London: Royal Institute of International Affairs, pp. 1–16.

Cable, Vincent and David Henderson (eds) (1994), *Trade Blocs?: The Future of Regional Integration*, London: Royal Institute of International Affairs.

Caithness, Lord (1991), 'Interview', *Diplomacy*, No. 1, p. 34.

Calder, Kent (1996a), 'U.S.–Japan Relations: The Bypass Phenomenon', *Look Japan*, October, 28–9.

Calder, Kent (1996b), *Asia's Deadly Triangle: How Arms, Energy and Growth Threaten to Destabilize Asia Pacific*, London: Nicholas Brealey.

Callon, Scott (1995), *Divided Sun: MITI and the Breakdown of Japanese High-Tech Industrial Policy, 1975–1993*, Stanford: Stanford University Press.

Camroux, David and Christian Lechervy (1996), '"Close Encounter of a Third Kind?": The Inaugural Asia–Europe Meeting of March 1996', *Pacific Review*, **9**, (3), 442–53.

Casella, Alexander (1991), 'The Refugees from Vietnam: Rethinking the Issue', *World Today*, August/September.

Census and Statistics Department, Hong Kong (1997), *External Investment in*

Hong Kong's Non-manufacturing Sectors 1995, Hong Kong: Hong Kong Government.

Chairman's Statement of the Asia–Europe Meeting (1996), Bangkok, 2 March.

Chalmers, Malcolm (1997), 'The Debate on a Regional Arms Register in Southeast Asia', *Pacific Review*, **10**, (1), 104–23.

Chan, Steve (1990), *East Asian Dynamism: Growth, Order, and Security in the Pacific Region*, Boulder: Westview Press.

Che, Wai-kin (1997), 'The Drug Problem in Guangdong Province', in Joseph Cheng (ed.), *Guangdong Province*, Hong Kong: Chinese University Press.

Cheeseman, Graeme and Richard Leaver (1996), 'Trends in Arms Spending and Conventional Arms Trade in the Asia-Pacific Region', in Gary Klintworth (ed.), *Asia-Pacific Security: Less Uncertainty, New Opportunities?*, New York: St. Martin's Press, pp. 198–218.

Chen, Edward K.Y. (1989), 'China–EC Economic Relations: Experience and Prospects', in Giuseppe Schiavone (ed.), *Western Europe and South-East Asia: Co-operation or Competition?*, London: Macmillan, pp. 174–96.

Chen, Edward K.Y. and Kui-Wai Li (1994), 'Manufactured Export Expansion in Hong Kong and Asian-Pacific Regional Cooperation', in Shu-Chin Yang (ed.), *Manufactured Exports of East Asian Industrializing Economies: Possible Regional Cooperation*, New York: M.E. Sharpe, pp. 103–34.

Chin Kin Wah (1991), 'The Five Power Defence Arrangements: Twenty Years After', *Pacific Review*, **4**, (3), 193–203.

Chiu Jong-jen (1993), 'From Economic Relations to Political Ties: The ROC and Western Europe in the 1990s', in Bih-Jaw Lin (ed.), *Asia and Europe: A Comparison of Developmental Experiences*, Taipei: Institute of International Relations, National Chengchi University, pp. 193–233.

Clad, James and Aurora Medina Siy (1996), 'The Emergence of Ecological Issues in Southeast Asia', in David Wurfel and Bruce Burton (eds), *Southeast Asia in the New World Order: The Political Economy of a Dynamic Region*, London: Macmillan, pp. 52–73.

Clifford, Mark (1994), *Troubled Tiger: Businessmen, Bureaucrats, and Generals in South Korea*, New York: M.E. Sharpe.

Colchester, Nicholas and David Buchan (1990), *Europe Relaunched*, London: Hutchinson.

Commission Communication to the Council of Ministers (1992), 'A Consistent and Global Approach: A Review of the Community's Relations with Japan', COM(92) 219, Brussels, 6 June.

Commission Communication to the Council of Ministers (1994), 'Towards a New Asia Strategy', Brussels, 6 July.

Commission Communication to the Council of Ministers (1995), 'A Long Term Policy for China–Europe Relations', COM(95) 0279, Brussels, 4 September.

Commission Office in Hong Kong (1997), 'Commission Launches New Policy on Hong Kong', press release, 24 April.

Cook, Robin (1997a), 'Three Priorities in Foreign Policy'. Internet: http://www.fco.gov.uk/special/97may02/cooknamed.html.

Cook, Robin (1997b), 'South-East Asia and Beyond: Britain's Partners for the 21st Century'. Speech at Malaysian Institute of Diplomacy and Foreign Relations, 28 August. Internet: http://www.fco.gov.uk/texts/1997/aug/28/malaysia.txt.

Coox, Alvin (1988), 'The Pacific War', in Peter Duus (ed.), *The Cambridge History of Japan: Vol. 6. The Twentieth Century*, Cambridge: Cambridge University Press, pp. 315–82.

Copland, Ian (1990), *The Burden of Empire: Perspectives on Imperialism and Colonialism*, Melbourne: Oxford University Press.

Cornish, Paul (1994), 'The UN Register of Conventional Arms', *World Today*, February, 24–5.

Cortazzi, Sir Hugh (1992), 'Britain and Japan: A Personal View of Postwar Economic Relations', in T.G. Fraser and P. Lowe (eds), *Conflict and Amity in East Asia*, London: Macmillan.

Council of Ministers Conclusions (1992), 'EC–Japan Relations', Brussels, 15 June 1992.

Curry, Robert Jr (1996), 'AFTA and the European Union' in Joseph Tan (ed.), *AFTA in the Changing International Economy*, Singapore: Institute of Southeast Asian Studies.

Dassu, Marta (1997), 'The Marco Polo Syndrome: Italy's Merchant Approach to China'. Paper presented to conference on EU's relations with China and the two Special Administrative Regions, Macau, May 1997.

Davenport, Michael and Sheila Page (1991), *Europe: 1992 and the Developing World*, London: Overseas Development Institute.

Davis, Michael (1990), *Constitutional Confrontation in Hong Kong*, New York: St. Martin's Press.

De Melo, Jaime and Arvind Panagariya (1993), 'Introduction', in Jaime de Melo and Arvind Panagariya (eds), *New Dimensions in Regional Integration*, Cambridge: Cambridge University Press.

Dent, Christopher (1997), 'Economic Relations between the EU and East Asia: Past, Present and Future', *Intereconomics*, January/February, 7–13.

Dent, Christopher and Claire Randerson (1996), 'Korean Foreign Direct Investment in Europe: the Determining Forces', *Pacific Review*, **9** (4), 531–52.

Dewitt, David (1994), 'Common, Comprehensive and Cooperative Security', *Pacific Review*, **7**, (1), 1–15.

Dieter, Heribert (1997), 'APEC and the WTO: Collision or Co-operation?', *Pacific Review*, **10**, (1), 19–38.

Dimbleby, Jonathan (1997), *The Last Governor: Chris Patten and the Handover of Hong Kong*, London: Little, Brown and Co.

Domenach, Jean-Luc (1990), 'Challenges in Asia: French foreign policy', in Francoise de la Serre, Jacques Leruez and Hellen Wallace (eds), *French and British Foreign Policies in Transition*, London: Berg, pp. 186–203.

Drakakis-Smith, David (1992), *Pacific Asia*, London: Routledge.

Drifte, Reinhard (1996), *Japan's Foreign Policy in the 1990s: From Economic Superpower to What Power?*, New York: St. Martin's Press.

Drysdale, Peter (1988), *International Economic Pluralism*, Sydney: Allen & Unwin.

Duncanson, Dennis (1968), *Government and Revolution in Vietnam*, London: Oxford University Press.

Eberle, James (1998), 'Strong Men at the Ends of the Earth?', *World Today*, May, 37–9.

Economic Planning Board Task Force (1991), *Implications of EC Integration on the Korean Economy*, Seoul: Economic Planning Board.

Edmonds, Richard Louis (1995), 'Macau and Greater China', in David Shambaugh (ed.), *Greater China: The Next Superpower?*, Oxford: Oxford University Press, pp. 226–54.

El-Agraa, Ali M. (1988), 'The Internal Market: Japanese Reaction', *Anglo-Japanese Economic Journal*, Oct.–Dec.

Elgin, Michaela (1997), 'China's Entry into the WTO with a Little Help from the EU', *International Affairs*, **73**, (3; July), 489–508.

Emmott, Bill (1992), *Japan's Global Reach: The Influences, Strategies and Weaknesses of Japan's Multinational Companies*, London: Century.

Esterline, John and Mae Esterline (1990), *How the Dominoes Fell: Southeast Asia in Perspective*, Lanham: University of America Press.

European Parliament (1997), 'Resolution on European–Laos Cooperation Agreement'. Internet: www.europarl.eu.int/dg1/a4/en/a4-97/a4-0216.htm.

Ferdinand, Peter (1995), 'Economic and Diplomatic Interactions between the EU and China', in Richard Grant (ed.), *The European Union and China: A European Strategy for the Twenty-First Century*, London: Royal Institute of International Affairs, pp. 26–40.

Ferdinand, Peter (1996), 'The Taiwanese Economy', in Peter Ferdinand (ed.), *Take-off for Taiwan?*, London: Pinter, pp. 37–65.

Fifield, Russell (1958), *The Diplomacy of South East Asia, 1945–1958*, New York: Harper and Bros.

Findlay, Christopher and Andrew Watson (1997), 'Economic Growth and Trade Dependency in China', in David S.G. Goodman and Gerald Segal (eds), *China Rising: Nationalism and Interdependence*, London: Routledge, pp. 107–33.

Findlay, Trevor (1996), 'Disarmament, Arms Control and the Regional Security Dialogue', in Gary Klintworth (ed.), *Asia-Pacific Security: Less Uncertainty, New Opportunities?*, New York: St. Martin's Press.

Flaesch-Mougin, Catherine (1990), 'Competing Frameworks: The Dialogue and its Legal Basis', in Geoffrey Edwards and Elfrede Regelsberger (eds), *Europe's Global Links: The European Community and Inter-regional Cooperation*, London: Pinter, pp. 27–42.

Foreign Affairs Committee (House of Commons) (1994a), *Public Expenditure; The Pergau Hydro-electric Project, Malaysia, the Aid and Trade Provision and Related Matters*, Vols I and II, London: HMSO, Third Report, Session 1993–94.

Foreign Affairs Committee (House of Commons) (1994b), *Relations between the United Kingdom and China in the Period Up To and Beyond 1997*, Vol. II, London: HMSO.

Foreign Broadcast Information Service (1993), *Daily Report: East Asia*, FBIS-EAS-93-049-A, 16 March, Washington: U.S. Government Printing Office.

Foreign Office, United Kingdom (1998), 'Activity since ASEM 1'. Internet: http://asem2.fco.gov.uk/inter.

Francks, Penelope (1992), *Japanese Economic Development: Theory and Practice*, London: Routledge.

Freudenstein, Roland (1991), 'Japan and the New Europe', *World Today*, January, 11–16.

Fung, K.C. and Lawrence J. Lau (1997), 'Foreign Economic Relations', in Maurice Brosseau, Kuan Hsin-chi and Y.Y. Kueh (eds), *China Review 1997*, Hong Kong: Chinese University Press, pp. 209–34.

Gann, Lewis (1984), 'Western and Japanese Colonialism: Some Preliminary Comparisons', in Ramon Myers and Mark Peattie (eds), *The Japanese Colonial Empire, 1895–1945*, Princeton: Princeton University Press, pp. 497–525.

Ghai, Yash (1995), 'Asian Perspectives on Human Rights', in James T.H. Tang (ed.), *Human Rights and International Relations in the Asia-Pacific Region*, London: Pinter, pp. 54–67.

Godemont, Francois (1993), 'Europe and Asia: The Missing Link', in *Asia's International Role in the Post-Cold War Era: Part II*, London: International Institute for Strategic Studies, pp. 94–103.

Godemont, Francois (1997), *The New Asian Renaissance: From Colonialism to the Post-Cold War*, London: Routledge.

Godemont, Francois and Regine Serra (1997), 'French Policy Towards China: A Redefinition'. Paper presented to conference on EU's relations with China and the two Special Administrative Regions, Macau, May 1997.

Grant, Richard (ed.) 1995, *The European Union and China: A European Strategy for the Twenty-First Century*, London: Royal Institute of International Affairs.

Grilli, Enzo (1993), *The European Community and the Developing Countries*, Cambridge: Cambridge University Press.

Haggard, Stephan (1988), 'The Politics of Industrialization in the Republic of Korea and Taiwan', in Helen Hughes (ed.), *Achieving Industrialization in East Asia*, Cambridge: Cambridge University Press, pp. 260–82.

Hale, Samantha (1993), 'The Reception and Resettlement of Vietnamese Refugees in Britain', in Vaughan Robinson (ed.), *The International Refugee Crisis*, London: Macmillan, pp. 273–92.

Han, Man-Hee (1994), *Japanese Multinationals in the Changing Context of Regional Policy*, Aldershot: Avebury.

Han, Sun-Taik (1992), *European Integration: The Impact on Newly Industrialising Countries*, Paris: OECD.

Hanabusa, Masamichi (1979), *Trade Problems between Japan and Western Europe*, Farnborough: Saxon House.

Hanabusa, Masamichi (1982), 'The Trade Dispute: A Japanese View', in Loukas Tsoukalis and Maureen White (eds), *Japan and Western Europe*, London: Pinter, pp. 119–30.

Harding, Harry (1997), 'US–China Relations, 1995–97: From Crisis to Hope to Uncertainty', in Y.Y. Kueh (ed.), *The Political Economy of Sino-American Relations: A Greater China Perspective*, Hong Kong: Hong Kong University Press, pp. 9–27.

Harris, Stuart (1997), 'China's role in the WTO and APEC', in David S.G. Goodman and Gerald Segal (eds), *China Rising: Nationalism and Interdependence*, London: Routledge, pp. 134–5.

Harris, Stuart and Brian Bridges (1983), *European Interests in ASEAN*, London: Routledge & Kegan Paul.

Higgott, Richard (1998), 'Shared Response to the Market Shocks?', *World Today*, January, 4–6.

Hindley, Brian (1988), 'Dumping and the Far East Trade of the European Community', *World Economy*, December, 445–63.

Hindley, Michael and James Bridges (1996), 'Europe and North Korea', in Hazel Smith, Chris Rhodes, Diana Pritchard and Kevin Magill (eds), *North Korea in the New World Order*, London: Macmillan.

Ho, Y.P. and Y.Y. Kueh (1993), 'Whither Hong Kong in an Open-door, Reforming Chinese Economy?', *Pacific Review*, **6**, (4), 333–51.

Ho, Yin-Ping (1992), *Trade, Industrial Restructuring and Development in Hong Kong*, Honolulu: University of Hawaii Press.

Hoare, James (1997), 'Britain and Korea, 1797–1997', unpublished manuscript.

House of Lords Select Committee on the European Communities (1989), *Relations between the Community and Japan*, London: HMSO.

Houweling, Henk (1997), 'Dutch–Chinese Bilateral Relations: Constant Elements in a Changing World System'. Paper presented to conference on EU policies towards China and the Special Administrative Regions, Macau, May 1997.

Howe, Christopher (1996), *The Origins of Japanese Trade Supremacy*, Hong Kong: Oxford University Press.

Howe, Sir Geoffrey (1992), 'Japan and the United States – a European Perspective', *World Today*, July, 126–9.

Hsieh, Chiao Chiao (1996), 'Pragmatic Diplomacy: Foreign Policy and External Relations', in Peter Ferdinand (ed.), *Take-off for Taiwan?*, London: Pinter, pp. 37–65.

Hughes, Richard (1976), *Borrowed Place, Borrowed Time. Hong Kong and its Many Faces*, London: Andre Deutsch.

Inoguchi, Takashi (1993), *Japan's Foreign Policy in an Era of Global Change*, London: Pinter.

Invest in Britain Bureau (1996), *Electronics UK: You Can Make It In Britain*, London: Department of Trade and Industry.

Ishikawa, Kenjiro (1990), *Japan and the Challenge of Europe 1992*, London: Pinter.

Jackson, Tim (1993), *Turning Japanese: The Fight for Industrial Control of the New Europe*, London: Harper Collins.

Japan Information Centre (1983), *Anglo-Japanese Relations: A Framework for the 1980s*, London.

Japanese Foreign Ministry (1992), 'The Japanese Government's Basic Policy Towards the EC', Tokyo, June, London: The Embassy of Japan.

JETRO (1990), *Current Situation of Business Operations of Japanese Manufacturing Enterprises in Europe*, Tokyo: JETRO.

Johnson, Chalmers (1982), *MITI and the Japanese Miracle*, Stanford: Stanford University Press.

Julius, DeAnne (1990), *Global Companies and Public Policy*, London: Royal Institute of International Affairs.

Kapur, Harish (1986), *China and the European Economic Community: The New Connection*, Dordrecht: Martinus Nijhoff.

Kerr, Pauline (1994), 'The Security Dialogue in the Asia-Pacific', *Pacific Review*, **7**, (4), 397–409.

Khin, Myo Chit (1984), *A Wonderland of Burmese Legends*, Bangkok: Tamarind.

Kimura, Michio (1997), 'Singapore: Regional Development as a Cause of Instability', in Kitamura Kayoko and Tsuneo Tanaka (eds), *Examining Asia's Tigers*, Tokyo: Institute of Developing Economies, pp. 28–37.

Kirby, Stephen (1988), 'Linking European and Pacific Strategies', *Pacific Review*, **1**, (3), 236–47.

Kolko, Gabriel (1997), *Vietnam: Anatomy of a Peace*, London: Routledge.

Korhonen, Pekka (1997), 'Monopolizing Asia: The Politics of a Metaphor', *Pacific Review*, **10**, (3), 347–65.

Kreinin, Mordechai and Michael Plummer (1992), 'Effects of Economic Integration in Industrial Countries on ASEAN and the Asian NIEs', *World Development*, **20**, (9; September), 1345–66.

Kueh, Y.Y. and Thomas Voon (1997), 'The Role of Hong Kong in Sino-American Economic Relations', in Y.Y. Kueh (ed.), *The Political Economy of Sino-American Relations: A Greater China Perspective*, Hong Kong: Hong Kong University Press, pp. 61–92.

Kwarteng, Charles (1992), 'Confronting the European Single Market of 1992: Challenges for the ACP and ASEAN Countries', *Journal of Developing Societies*, July–August, pp. 223–39.

Langhammer, Rolf (1987), 'EEC–ASEAN Relations: Institutional Deepening but Modest Economic Impact', in Christopher Stevens and Joan Valoren van Themsat (eds), *Europe and the International Division of Labour*, London: Hodder and Stoughton, pp. 133–49.

Lao, M.H. (1993), 'Obstacles to Peace in Cambodia', *Pacific Review*, **6**, (4), 389–95.

Larsen, Stanley and James Collins (1975), *Allied Participation in Vietnam*, Washington, DC: Department of the Army.

Lau, Teik Soon (1989), 'Regional Security: Problems and Prospects in South-East Asia', in Giuseppe Schiavone (ed.), *Western Europe and South-East Asia: Co-operation or Competition?*, London: Macmillan, pp. 61–74.

Leake, David (1989), *Brunei: The Modern South-east Asian Islamic Sultanate*, Jefferson, North Carolina: McFarland & Co.

Lee, Chae Woong (1990), 'The EC 1992: Trade Policy Implications for Korea', *Korea & World Affairs*, Spring, 54–65.

Lee, Peter Nan-shong (1997), 'Jiang Zemin versus Lee Teng-hui: Strained Mainland–Taiwan Relationship', in Maurice Brosseau, Kuan Hsin-chi and Y.Y. Kueh (eds), *China Review 1997*, Hong Kong: Chinese University Press, pp. 108–34.

Lehmann, John-Pierre (1992), 'France, Japan, Europe, and Industrial Competition: The Automative Case', *International Affairs*, **68**, (1; January), 37–53.

Leifer, Michael (1989), *ASEAN and the Security of South-East Asia*, London: Routledge.

Leifer, Michael (1996), *The ASEAN Regional Forum*, London: International Institute for Strategic Studies.

Leung, Kit-fun, Beatrice (1997), 'The Implementation of the Sino-British Declaration 1984 and the Sino-Portuguese Declaration 1987', unpublished paper.

Leung Wing-Fai (1995), 'Trade', in Stephen Y.L. Cheung and Stephen M.H.

Sze (eds), *The Other Hong Kong Report 1995*, Hong Kong: Chinese University Press.

Lim, Linda Y.C. (1996), 'ASEAN: New Modes of Economic Cooperation', in David Wurfel and Bruce Burton (eds), *Southeast Asia in the New World Order*, London: Macmillan, pp. 19–35.

Lin, Tzong-Biau and Victor Mok (1980), *Trade Barriers and the Promotion of Hong Kong Exports*, Hong Kong: Chinese University Press.

Lloyd George, Robert (1992), *The East–West Pendulum*, London: Woodhead-Faulkener.

Lowe, Peter (1981), *Britain in the Far East: A Survey from 1819 to the Present*, London: Longman.

Luhulima, C.P.F. (1992), 'ASEAN–European Community Relations: Some Dimensions of Inter-regional Cooperation', *Indonesia Quarterly*, **20**, (3; Third Quarter), 24–30.

MacIntyre, Andrew (1993), 'Indonesia in 1992', *Asian Survey*, **33**, (2; February), 204–10.

Mackerras, Colin (ed.) (1995), *East and Southeast Asia: A Multidisciplinary Survey*, Boulder: Lynne Rienner.

Mackie, J.A.C. (1988), 'Economic Growth in the ASEAN Region: The Political Underpinnings', in Helen Hughes (ed.), *Achieving Industrialization in East Asia*, Cambridge: Cambridge University Press, pp. 283–326.

Maclean, Nicolas (1995), 'Towards the Twenty-First Century: A View from the Private Sector', in Richard Grant (ed.), *The European Union and China: A European Strategy for the Twenty-First Century*, London: Royal Institute of International Affairs, pp. 41–53.

Mathews, John (1996), 'High Technology Industrialisation in East Asia', *Journal of Industry Studies*, **3**, (2), December, 1–77.

Matsunaga, Nobuo (1994), 'The Security of the Asia-Pacific and the Relationship between the Security of the Asia-Pacific Region and the Security of Europe'. Speech, 6 December. Internet: http://www.mofa.go.jp/apecinfo/www/member/member/info1.htm.

Mauzy, Diane (1997), 'The Human Rights and "Asian Values" Debate in Southeast Asia: Trying to Clarify the Issues', *Pacific Review*, **10**, (2), 210–36.

McIntosh, Malcolm (1987), *Arms Across the Pacific*, London: Pinter.

McLaughlin, Andrew (1994), 'ACEA and the EU–Japan Car Dispute', in R.H. Pedler and M.P.C.M. van Schendelen (eds), *Lobbying the European Union*, Aldershot: Dartmouth, pp. 149–65.

Mendl, Wolf (1984), *Western Europe and Japan between the Superpowers*, London: Croom Helm.

Mengin, Francoise (1993), 'The Prospects for France–Taiwan Relations', in Bih-Jaw Lin (ed.), *Asia and Europe: A Comparison of Developmental*

214   *Europe and the challenge of the Asia Pacific*

Experiences, Taipei: Institute of International Relations, National Chengchi University, pp. 101–24.

Meynell, Benedict (1982), 'Relations with Japan: The Problem and the European Community's Response', in Loukas Tsoukalis and Maureen White (eds), *Japan and Western Europe*, London: Pinter, pp. 100–118.

Mishalani, Philip, Annette Robert, Christopher Stevens and Ann Weston (1981), 'The Pyramid of Privilege', in Christopher Stevens (ed.), *EEC and the Third World: A Survey*, London: Hodder and Stoughton.

Mols, Manfred (1990), 'Cooperation with ASEAN: A Success Story', in Geoffrey Edwards and Elfrede Regelsberger (eds), *Europe's Global Links: The European Community and Inter-Regional Cooperation*, London: Pinter, pp. 66–83.

Morris, Warwick (1996), 'UK Policy towards North Korea', in Hazel Smith, Chris Rhodes, Diana Pritchard and Kevin Magill (eds), *North Korea in the New World Order*, London: Macmillan.

Munchau, Wolfgang (1997), *EMU: Political and Economic Implications*, London: Royal Institute of International Affairs, Briefing Paper No. 38.

Murata, Ryohei (1987), 'Political Relations between the United States and Europe: Their Implications for Japan', *International Affairs*, Winter, 1–9.

Mya Maung (1992), *Totalitarianism in Burma: Prospects for Economic Development*, New York: Paragon.

Nacht, Michael (1995), 'Multinational Naval Cooperation in Northeast Asia: Some Plausible Considerations for 2010 Based on What We Know in 1994', *Korean Journal of Defense Analysis*, Summer, 29–47.

National Consumer Council (1990), *Consumer Electronics and the EC's Anti-dumping Policy*, London: National Consumer Council.

Nester, William (1993), *European Power and the Japanese Challenge*, London: Macmillan.

Neves, Miguel Santos (1995), 'Towards a Common China Policy for the EU: A Portuguese Perspective', in Richard Grant (ed.), *The European Union and China: A European Strategy for the Twenty-First Century*, London: Royal Institute of International Affairs, pp. 75–88.

Newall, Sir Paul (1996), *Japan and the City of London*, London: Athlone.

Newland, Kathleen (1993), 'Ethnic Conflict and Refugees', *Survival*, **35**, (11), Spring, 81–101.

Ng, Victor Fook Ai and Shu-Chin Yang (1994), 'Changing Strategies of Manufactured Export Expansion in Singapore', in Shu-Chin Yang (ed.), *Manufactured Exports of East Asian Industrializing Economies: Possible Regional Cooperation*, New York: M.E. Sharpe, pp. 175–88.

Ngai, Gary (1996), 'Small but Splendid: On Macau's Role in Regional Integration and Competition and its Relations with Europe and the Latin World'. Unpublished paper presented to conference on relations between the EU and China in the Twenty-first Century, Arrabida, Portugal, June 1996.

Noland, Marcus (1997), 'China in the World Economy', in Y.Y. Kueh (ed.), *The Political Economy of Sino-American Relations: A Greater China Perspective*, Hong Kong: Hong Kong University Press, pp. 277–89.

Nozawa, Katsumi (1997), 'Philippines: Reforms Reveal Results', in Kitamura Kayoko and Tsuneo Tanaka (eds), *Examining Asia's Tigers*, Tokyo: Institute of Developing Economies, pp. 69–79.

Nuttall, Simon (1996), 'Japan and the European Union: Reluctant Partners', *Survival*, **38**, (2; Summer), 104–20.

Oh, John C.H. and Ruth M. Grubel (1995), 'The North Korean Nuclear Weapons Crisis: The United States and its Policy Options', *Korea Observer*, **26**, (1; Spring), 97–116.

Parry, Thomas (1988), 'The Role of Foreign Capital in East Asian Industrialization, Growth and Development', in Helen Hughes (ed.), *Achieving Industrialization in East Asia*, Cambridge: Cambridge University Press, pp. 95–128.

Pelkmans, Jacques and Alan Winters (1988), *Europe's Domestic Market*, London: Routledge.

Peou, Sorpong (1997), *Conflict Neutralization in the Cambodian War: From Battlefield to Ballot Box*, Oxford: Oxford University Press.

Pilger, John (1996), 'The Betrayal of Burma', *The World Today*, **52**, (11; November), 277–79.

Pilkington, Alan (1996), 'Learning from Joint Venture: The Rover–Honda Relationship', *Business History*, **38**, (1), 90–114.

Politi, Alessandro (1997), *European Security: the New Transnational Risks*, Paris: Western European Union Institute for Security Studies.

Pomfret, Richard (1996), 'Blocs: The Threat to the System, and Asian Reactions', in Bijit Bora and Christopher Findlay (eds), *Regional Integration and the Asia-Pacific*, Melbourne: Oxford University Press, pp. 13–24.

Porter, Jonathan (1996), *Macau: The Imaginary City*, Boulder: Westview Press.

Prins, Gwyn (1990), 'Politics and the Environment', *International Affairs*, **66**, (4; October), 711–30.

Putnam, Robert and Nicholas Bayne (1987), *Hanging Together: Cooperation and Conflict in the Seven-Power Summits*, London: Royal Institute of International Affairs.

Regelsberger, Elfriede (1989), 'The Relations with ASEAN as a "Model" of a European Foreign Policy?', in Giuseppe Schiavone (ed.), *Western Europe and South-East Asia: Co-operation or Competition?*, London: Macmillan, pp. 75–93.

Regnier, Philippe (1993), 'Spreading Singapore's Wings Worldwide: Traditional and New Investment Strategies', *Pacific Review*, **6**, (4), 305–312.

Rhee, Yung Whee (1994), 'Managing Entry into International Markets: Lessons from the East Asian Experience', in Shu-Chin Yang (ed.), *Manufactured Exports of East Asian Industrializing Economies: Possible Regional Cooperation*, New York: M.E. Sharpe, pp. 53–83.

Richardson, Hugh (1989), *EC–Japan Relations: After Adolescence*, Oxford: Nissan Occasional Paper Series, No. 12.

Riedel, James (1988), 'Economic Development in East Asia: Doing What Comes Naturally?', in Helen Hughes (ed.), *Achieving Industrialization in East Asia*, Cambridge: Cambridge University Press, pp. 1–38.

Rifkind, Malcolm (1997), 'Britain and South East Asia – A Lasting Relationship'. Speech at Institute of Policy Studies, Singapore, 12 February. Internet: http//www.fco.gov.uk/current/1997/feb/fssngpr.txt.

Risse-Kappen, Thomas (1995), *Cooperation Among Democracies: The European Influence on U.S. Foreign Policy*, Princeton: Princeton University Press.

Roberti, Mark (1994), *The Fall of Hong Kong: China's Triumph and Britain's Betrayal*, New York: John Wiley & Sons.

Roberts, David (1993), 'Cambodia's Uncertain Future', *Pacific Review*, **6**, (1), 71–6.

Robinson, Geoffrey (1996), 'Human Rights in Southeast Asia: Rhetoric and Reality', in David Wurfel and Bruce Burton (eds), *Southeast Asia in the New World Order: The Political Economy of a Dynamic Region*, London: Macmillan, pp. 74–99.

Rodan, Garry (1996), 'The Internationalization of Ideological Conflict: Asia's New Significance', *Pacific Review*, **9**, (3), 328–51.

Rothacher, Albrecht (1983), *Economic Diplomacy between the European Community and Japan, 1959–1981*, Aldershot: Avebury.

Saito, Shiro (1990), *Japan at the Summit: Japan's Role in the Western Alliance and Asian Pacific Co-operation*, London: Routledge.

Satoh, Haruko (1998), *The UK and Japan: A Special Relationship into the 21st Century*, London: Royal Institute of International Affairs, Briefing Paper No.46.

Schram, Stuart (ed.) (1994), *Mao's Road to Power: Revolutionary Writings 1912–1949*, Vol. II, New York: M.E. Sharpe.

Segal, Gerald (1990), *Rethinking the Pacific*, Oxford: Clarendon Press.

Segal, Gerald (1993), *The Fate of Hong Kong*, London: Simon and Schuster.

Segal, Gerald (1997), 'Thinking Strategically about ASEM: The Subsidiarity Question', *Pacific Review*, **10**, (1), 124–34.

Segal, Gerald and David S.G. Goodman (1997), 'Introduction: Thinking Strategically about China', in David S.G. Goodman and Gerald Segal (eds), *China Rising: Nationalism and Interdependence*, London: Routledge, pp. 1–5.

Sekiguchi, Sueo (1982), 'Japanese Direct Investment in Europe', in Loukas Tsoukalis and Maureen White (eds), *Japan and Western Europe*, London: Pinter, pp. 166–83.

SG Asian Research (1998), *Quarterly Economic Review: Asia*, 24 April, Singapore: SG Asia.

Sharma, Shalendra (1998), 'Asia's Economic Crisis and the IMF', *Survival*, **40**, (2; Summer), pp. 27–52.

Sheridan, Kyoko (1993), *Governing the Japanese Economy*, Cambridge: Polity.

Shibusawa, Masahide (1984), *Japan and the Asian Pacific Region*, London: Croom Helm.

Shibusawa, Masahide, Zakaria Haji Ahmad and Brian Bridges (1992), *Pacific Asia in the 1990s*, London: Routledge.

Shih, Tsuen-Hua (1990) 'Trade Relations between the ROC and the EEC: Reviews and Prospects', unpublished paper to Joint Conference on the Industrial Policies of the Republic of Korea and the Republic of China, Kyongju, Korea, 12–13 April 1990.

Smith, Alasdair (1994), 'The Principle and Practice of Regional Economic Integration', in Vincent Cable and David Henderson (eds), *Trade Blocs?: The Future of Regional Integration*, London: Royal Institute of International Affairs, pp. 17–34.

Soeya, Yoshihide (1993), 'Japanese Attitudes and Policies toward a Security Framework', in Y.Y. Kueh and Brian Bridges (eds), *Asian Pacific Security after the Collapse of the Soviet Union*, Hong Kong: Lingnan College Centre for Asian Pacific Studies, pp. 23–32.

Spence, Jonathan (1996), 'Marco Polo: Fact or Fiction?', *Far Eastern Economic Review*, 22 August, 36–45.

Stryk, Lucien and Takashi Ikemoto (1973), *Zen Poems of China and Japan*, New York: Grove Press.

Subrahmanyam, Sanjay (1993), *The Portuguese Empire in Asia 1500–1700*, London: Longman.

Swann, Dennis (1996), *European Economic Integration: The Common Market, European Union and Beyond*, Cheltenham: Edward Elgar.

Taga, Hidetoshi (1994), 'International Network among Local Cities: The First Step towards Regional Development', in Francois Gipouloux (ed.), *Regional Economic Strategies: A Comparative Perspective*, Tokyo: Maison Franco-Japonaise.

Takahashi, Fumiaki (1993), 'What Role for Europe in Asian Affairs?', in *Asia's International Role in the Post-Cold War Era: Part II*, London: International Institute for Strategic Studies, pp. 104–115.

Takeuchi, Sawako (1991), 'Prime Minister Cresson's Anti-Japanese Rhetoric', *Japan Echo*, Winter, 76–80.

Tan, Augustine H.H. (1998), 'IMF Is Not Geared Adequately to Help', *Straits Times*, 23 January.

Tanaka Toshio (1992), 'EC Integration and Japan: Opportunity for Cooperation'. Paper presented to RIIA–JIIA Symposium on Western Europe and Japan: Partnership in a Changing World, Royal Institute of International Affairs, June 1992.

Tarling, Nicholas (1992), *The Cambridge History of Southeast Asia Vol. 2: The Nineteenth and Twentieth Centuries*, Cambridge: Cambridge University Press.

Taylor, John (1991), *Indonesia's Forgotten War: The Hidden History of East Timor*, London: Zed Books.

Taylor, Robert (1990), *China, Japan and the European Community*, London: Athlone.

Taylor, Trevor (1995), 'Conclusions: The West European and Japanese Security Agendas', in Trevor Taylor and Seizaburo Sato (eds), *Future Sources of Global Conflict*, London: Royal Institute of International Affairs.

Thompson, Roger (1994), *The Pacific Basin since 1945*, London: Longman.

Thorne, Christopher (1978), *Allies of a Kind: The United States, Britain and the War against Japan, 1941–1945*, London: Hamish Hamilton.

Tokinoya, Atsushi (1997), Speech, untitled, at Centre for European Policy Studies, Brussels, 12 February. Internet: http://www.jmission-eu.be/speeches/ceps.htm.

Tseng, Osman (1995), 'A Straitjacket on WTO Membership', *Free China Review*, **45**, (2; February), 52–6.

Tung, Chee-Hwa (1998), Speech (untitled at the International Institute for Strategic Studies, *Financial Times* conference, Hong Kong, 28 May.

Turner, Louis (1982), 'Western Europe and the NICs', in Louis Turner and Neil McMullen (eds), *The Newly Industrialized Countries: Trade and Adjustment*, London: George Allen & Unwin, pp. 135–43.

Turner, Louis (1987), *Industrial Collaboration with Japan*, London: Routledge & Kegan Paul.

Van den Ham, Allert (1993), 'Development Cooperation and Human Rights: Indonesian–Dutch Aid Controversy', *Asian Survey*, **33**, (5; May), 531–9.

Van Wolferen, Karel (1989), *The Enigma of Japanese Power: People and Politics in a Stateless Nation*, London: Macmillan.

Von Kirkbach, Friedrich (1990), 'Recent Trade Patterns between NIEs and Western Europe', in Manfred Kulessa (ed.), *The Newly Industrializing Economies of Asia*, Berlin: Springer-Verlag.

UNCTAD (1996), *Sharing Asia's Dynamism: Asian Direct Investment in the European Union*, Geneva: United Nations.

Wallace, Helen (1989), *Widening and Deepening: The European Community and the New European Agenda*, London: RIIA Discussion Paper No. 23.

Wallace, Helen and Alasdair Young (1996), 'The Single Market: A New Approach to Policy', in Helen Wallace and William Wallace (eds), *Policy-Making in the European Union*, Oxford: Oxford University Press, pp. 125–55.

Wallace, William (1990), *The Transformation of Western Europe*, London: Pinter.

Wanandi, Jusuf (1995), 'ASEAN's Domestic Political Developments and their Impact on Foreign Policy', *Pacific Review*, **8**, (3), 440–58.

Wang, James C.F. (1994), *Comparative Asian Politics: Power, Policy and Change*, Englewood Cliffs, NJ: Prentice Hall.

Wannamethee, Phan (1989), 'The Importance of the EC for South-East Asia: The ASEAN Perspective', in Giuseppe Schiavone (ed.), *Western Europe and South-East Asia: Co-operation or Competition?*, London: Macmillan, pp. 21–38.

Whitehead, Sir John (1992), 'The Multiplication Factor in U.K.–Japan relations', *Japan Times Weekly*, 13–19 April, p. 9.

Whitla, Paul, Brian Bridges and Howard Davies (1995), 'European and American Investment in the Chinese Economic Area', unpublished report, prepared for JETRO, Hong Kong.

Wilkinson, Endymion (1990), *Japan versus the West: Image and Reality*, London: Penguin.

Williams, Michael (1992), *Vietnam at the Crossroads*, London: Pinter.

Williams, Phil (1994), 'Transnational Criminal Organisations and International Security', *Survival*, **36**, (1; Spring), 96–113.

Wong Yiu-chung (1997), *Restructuring the Party – State Relations: China's Political Structural Reform in the 1980s*, Hong Kong: Lingnan College, Centre for Public Policy Studies, Working Paper No. 69 (25/97).

Woolcock, Stephen and Hiroko Yamane (1993), *EC–Japanese Trade Relations: What are the Rules of the Game?*, London: Royal Institute for International Affairs.

Woolcock, Stephen and Michael Hodges (1996), 'EU Policy in the Uruguay Round', in Helen Wallace and William Wallace (eds), *Policy-making in the European Union*, Oxford: Oxford University Press, pp. 301–24.

World Bank (1993), *The East Asian Miracle: Economic Growth and Public Policy*, Oxford: Oxford University Press.

Wright, L.R. (1970), *The Origins of British Borneo*, Hong Kong: Hong Kong University Press.

Wu Yun (1996), 'China's Policies towards Arms Control and Disarmament: From Passive Responding to Active Leading', *Pacific Review*, **9**, (4), 577–606.

Yahuda, Michael (1994), 'China and Europe: The Significance of a Secondary Relationship', in Thomas Robinson and David Shambaugh (eds),
Chinese Foreign Policy: Theory and Practice, Oxford: Clarendon Press,
pp. 266–82.

Yahuda, Michael (1995), 'The Foreign Relations of Greater China', in David
Shambaugh (ed.), *Greater China: The Next Superpower?*, Oxford: Oxford
University Press, pp. 35–58.

Yahuda, Michael (1996), *Hong Kong: China's Challenge*, London: Routledge.

Yang Shu-Chin (1994), 'Open Industrialization in East Asia and the Quest for
Regional Cooperation: An Overview', in Shu-Chin Yang (ed.), *Manufac-
tured Exports of East Asian Industrializing Economies: Possible Regional
Cooperation*, New York: M.E. Sharpe.

Yeung, Yue-man (1995), *Growth Triangles in Pacific Asia: A Comparative
Perspective*, Hong Kong: Hong Kong Institute of Asia Pacific Studies.

Yoshida, Mikimasa (1997), 'Thailand: The Ability to Move to Stable Growth
in Question', in Kitamura Kayoko and Tsuneo Tanaka (eds), *Examining
Asia's Tigers*, Tokyo: Institute of Developing Economies, pp. 47–56.

Zasloff, Joseph (1991), 'Political Constraints on Development in Laos', in
Joseph Zasloff and Leonard Unger (eds), *Laos: Beyond the Revolution*,
New York: St. Martin's Press, pp. 3–15.

Index

222   *Europe and the challenge of the Asia Pacific*

Britain
    colonization in Asia Pacific 8–11
    decolonization 14
    FDI in 31–2, 34, 35–6, 68–9
    financial support of KEDO 157–8
    marginalization in Europe 135, 136–7
    political relationship with Japan 45–6
    Vietnamese 'boat people', response to
        174–5, 177
    see also Hong Kong
Brittan, Sir L. 63, 80, 82, 99, 104, 110,
    119, 184
Brunei 14, 151–2
bubble economy, Japan 28, 30, 32
Burma
    admission to ASEAN and economic
        growth in 82
    application to join ASEM 186, 187
    colonization of 10
    decolonization of 14
    divisiveness of in EC–ASEAN
        relationships 87–90
    human rights record 88–9, 150, 163,
        170–73
    impact of Japanese occupation 13

Cambodian crisis 84–6, 140, 148, 150,
    154–6, 163
campaigns to secure access to Japanese
    market 29–30
car manufacturing 23–4, 36, 61, 62,
    127–9
CFSP (common foreign and security
    policy), Europe–Japan 44
chaebols, South Korea 52–3, 67
China
    application for membership of WTO
        102–5
    colonization of, limited 6–7, 8–9, 11
    development aid to 100–102
    economic modernization 91–2, 93
    European policy towards 97, 111–12,
        118–20, 133
    FDI in 97–100
    Hong Kong, reversion to 6, 15–16
    human rights issues 106–9, 112, 151,
        170
    see also Tiananmen Square massacre
    Macau, reversion to 15–16, 113–14
    market access in 93–7

nuclear testing in Asia Pacific 163,
    166
political relationship with Europe
    105–8
response to Asian financial crisis 48
Taiwan, relations with 114–18, 159,
    160
China–Europe Business Forum 99
China–Europe International Business
    School 99, 101
Chirac, J. 99, 108, 118, 166
Cold War 146–9, 153
colonialism in Asia
    arrival of 6–12
    decolonization 12–17
    legacies of 17–18
Commercial and Cooperation Agree-
    ment (EC–Macau) 114
commercial opportunities in Taiwan
    115–16
commercialization of aid 81–2, 101–2
common European policy towards Asia
    Pacific, factors inhibiting 122–3
common foreign and security policy
    (CFSP), Europe–Japan 44
common market *see* European Commu-
    nity
communism, impact of collapse of on
    moves towards EMU 124–5
competition, role in Euro-Asian
    relations 200
Comprehensive Test Ban Treaty (CTBT)
    163
Conference for Security and Coopera-
    tion in Europe (CSCE) 44–5
conventional arms control 165, 168–9
Council for Security Cooperation in the
    Asia Pacific 160
crime, international dialogue concerning
    177–8
CSCE (Conference for Security and
    Cooperation in Europe) 44–5, 160
CTBT (Comprehensive Test Ban Treaty)
    163, 165–6
cultural and religious diversity in Asia
    Pacific 3
Cultural Revolution, China 91, 93, 94,
    105, 119
currency depreciation in Asia, impact on
    European exports to 191–2